Making Realism Work

How relevant is social research? For ⸜ ⸝rned with influencing the direction of social policy today, social rese⸜ ⸝seems either too theoretical and remote from the problems of the everyday world, or too concerned with number-crunching and unintelligible 'facts'. The contributors to this volume seek to show how realist social research allows us to make genuine discoveries, of relevance to social policy, which recognise the complexity of the real world.

In this innovative book, theorists and researchers from various social science disciplines explore the potential of realist social theory for empirical research. The examples are drawn from a wide range of fields – health and medicine, crime, housing, sociolinguistics, development theory – and deal with issues such as causality, probability and reflexivity in social science. Varied and lively contributions relate central methodological issues to detailed accounts of research projects which adopt a realist framework.

Making Realism Work provides an accessible discussion of a significant current in contemporary social science and will be of interest to social theorists and social researchers alike.

Bob Carter is a Senior Lecturer in Sociology at the University of Warwick. He is the author of *Realism and Racism: Concepts of Race in Sociological Research*, and the co-author (with Alison Sealey) of *Applied Linguistics as Social Science*.

Caroline New teaches Sociology in Bath Spa University College. She is the author of *Agency, Health and Social Survival: The Eco-Politics of Rival Psychologies* and various journal articles applying realism to feminism and gender.

Critical Realism: Interventions

Edited by Margaret Archer, Roy Bhaskar, Andrew Collier, Nick Hostettler, Tony Lawson and Alan Norrie

Critical realism is one of the most influential new developments in the philosophy of science and in the social sciences, providing a powerful alternative to positivism and post modernism. This series will explore the critical realist position in philosophy and across the social sciences.

Critical Realism
Essential readings
Edited by Margaret Archer, Rhoy Bhaskar, Andrew Collier, Tony Lawson and Alan Norrie

The Possibility of Naturalism, 3rd edition
A philosophical critique of the contemporary human sciences
Roy Bhaskar

Being and Worth
Andrew Collier

Quantum Theory and the Flight from Realism
Philosophical responses to quantum mechanics
Christopher Norris

From East to West
Odyssey of a soul
Roy Bhaskar

Realism and Racism
Concepts of race in sociological research
Bob Carter

Rational Choice Theory
Resisting colonisation
Edited by Margaret Archer and Jonathan Q. Tritter

Explaining Society
Critical realism in the social sciences
Berth Danermark, Mats Ekström, Jan Ch. Karlsson and
Liselotte Jakobsen

Critical Realism and Marxism
Edited by Andrew Brown, Steve Fleetwood and John Michael Roberts

Critical Realism in Economics
Edited by Steve Fleetwood

Realist Perspectives on Management and Organisations
Edited by Stephen Ackroyd and Steve Fleetwood

After International Relations
Critical realism and the (re)construction of world politics
Heikki Patomaki

Capitalism and Citizenship
The impossible partnership
Kathryn Dean

Philosophy of Language and the Challenge to Scientific Realism
Christopher Norris

Transcendence
Critical realism and God
Margaret S. Archer, Andrew Collier and Douglas V. Porpora

**Critical Realist Applications in Organisation and
Management Studies**
Edited by Steve Fleetwood and Stephen Ackroyd

Making Realism Work
Realist social theory and empirical research
Edited by Bob Carter and Caroline New

Also published by Routledge

Routledge Studies in Critical Realism
Edited by Margaret Archer, Roy Bhaskar, Andrew Collier,
Nick Hostettler, Tony Lawson and Alan Norrie

Making Realism Work

Realist social theory and
empirical research

Edited by Bob Carter and
Caroline New

Routledge
Taylor & Francis Group

LONDON AND NEW YORK

First published 2004
by Routledge
2 Park Square, Milton Park, Abingdon, Oxfordshire, OX14 4RN

Simultaneously published in the USA and Canada
by Routledge
29 West 35th Street, New York, NY 10001

Routledge is an imprint of the Taylor & Francis Group

© 2004 Bob Carter and Caroline New for editorial matter and selection;
contributors for their own contributions

Typeset in Garamond by
Rosemount Typing Services, Auldgirth, Dumfriesshire
Printed and bound in Great Britain by
The Cromwell Press, Trowbridge, Wiltshire

British Library Cataloguing in Publication Data
A catalogue record for this book is available from the
British Library

Library of Congress Cataloging in Publication Data
A catalog record for this book has been requested.

ISBN 0–415–30061–4 (hbk)
ISBN 0–415–34771–8 (pbk)

Contents

List of figures and tables

Figures

Tables

Contributors

Dave Byrne is Professor of Sociology and Social Policy at the University of Durham. He has worked as an academic and in community research. His interests include urban issues, participatory research and the quantitative programme in social sciences. Publications include *Complexity Theory and the Social Sciences* (Routledge 1998) and *Interpreting Quantitative Data* (Sage 2002).

Bob Carter is Senior Lecturer in Sociology at the University of Warwick. He is the author of *Realism and Racism: Concepts of Race in Sociological Research* (Routledge 2000) and, with Alison Sealey, *Applied Linguistics as Social Science* (Continuum forthcoming).

Wendy Dyer is currently a Research Associate with the Centre for Public Mental Health, University of Durham. She completed a PhD in Sociology at the University of Durham in 2002. During her research she constructed a framework from complexity theory and realistic evaluation and, along with the technique cluster analysis, used this to map the different institutional careers experienced by people referred to a custody diversion team for mentally disordered offenders.

Marni Freeman was a Senior Research Fellow at the Centre for Nursing, Midwifery and Health Visiting Research, University of Brighton until January 2004, having had a background in both acute and community health care. She gained her DPhil in Organisational Psychology at Sussex University, her thesis exploring the lack of congruence between theory and practice in the field of learning disabilities and its outcomes in terms of carer stress. Her research has encompassed both quantitative and qualitative research approaches, the latter within the framework of illuminative evaluation and case study. During the past four years she has combined her academic work with part-time practice as a health visitor.

Angie Hart is a principal lecturer in the Centre for Nursing and Midwifery Research, University of Brighton. She has a background in applied medical sociology and social anthropology with particular expertise in psychosocial aspects of health inequalities in child and maternal health.

She has a long history of carrying out empirical research projects and has published widely on them. Her most recent books include *Adoption, Support and Therapy: New Approaches To Practice Development*, with Barry Luckcock, (Jessica Kingsley 2004). Recent articles include (with Val Hall and Flis Henwood), 'Helping health and social care professionals develop an "inequalities imagination": a model for use in education and practice', *Journal of Advanced Nursing* (2003) and (with Flis Henwood) 'Articulating gender in the context of ICTs in health care: the case of electronic patient records in the maternity services', *Critical Social Policy* (2003). Dr Hart is also a practising child and family therapist in the NHS.

Paul Higgs is a Senior Lecturer in Sociology at University College London, where he teaches medical sociology in the medical school. He is joint editor of the journal *Social Theory and Health* and is co-author of *Cultures of Ageing: Self, Citizen and the Body* (2000). His research interests include the study of class, cohort and generation.

Tim May is Professor of Sociology and Director of the Centre for Sustainable Urban and Regional Futures, University of Salford. He previously worked at Durham (1995–99) and Plymouth (1989–95). In addition to articles, he has authored and co-edited books on organisational change, social research, ethnography and philosophy, methodology and social theory. His recent writings include *Social Research: Issues, Methods and Process* (Open University Press 2001); with Zygmunt Bauman, *Thinking Sociologically* (Blackwell 2001); *Qualitative Research in Action* (as editor, Sage 2002) and, with Malcolm Williams, a special edited edition of *International Journal of Methodology* (2002) and a symposium on the work of Rom Harré in the *European Journal of Social Theory* (2002). He is also editor of the book series *Issues in Society* (Open University Press).

Caroline New has published work about gender and social theory, including *Agency, Health and Social Survival: The Eco-Politics of Rival Psychologies* (Taylor and Francis 1996). Articles on gender include 'Realism, deconstruction and the feminist standpoint ', *Journal for the Theory of Social Behaviour* (1998); 'Oppressed and oppressors? The systematic mistreatment of men', *Sociology* (2001); and 'Feminism, critical realism and the linguistic turn', in J. Cruickshank (ed.) *Critical Realism: The Difference It Makes* (Routledge 2003). Caroline teaches Sociology at Bath Spa University College.

Wendy Olsen is a Lecturer in Socio-economic Research in the Cathie Marsh Centre for Census and Survey Research at the University of Manchester. She also teaches development studies for the Open University. Her current research projects include globalisation and women's employment; time use of men and women; part-time employment strategies; debt-bonded labouring; and inter-disciplinary socio-economic analyses of social exclusion.

Ray Pawson is a Senior Lecturer in the School of Sociology and Social Policy at Leeds University. He is the author of *A Measure for Measures: A Manifesto for Empirical Sociology* (Routledge 1989) and, with Nick Tilley, *Realistic Evaluation* (Sage 1997).

Ian Rees Jones is Professor of Sociology of Health and Illness at St George's Hospital Medical School, London. His research interests include historical sociology and health, the relationship between life events and illness and the sociology of lay and professional relations. He is author of *Professional Power and the Need for Health Care* (Ashgate 1999).

Graham Scambler is Professor of Medical Sociology at University College London. His interests include philosophy and social theory as well as issues of health and illness. He has published widely in academic journals and recent books are *Health and Social Change: A Critical Theory* (OUP 2002) and *Sport and Society: History, Power and Culture* (OUP forthcoming).

Alison Sealey is a Senior Lecturer in Applied Linguistics at the University of Reading. She has explored the applications of social theory to the study of language in various publications, and is the author of *Childly Language: Children, Language and the Social World* (Longman 2000) as well as, with Bob Carter, *Applied Linguistics as Social Science* (Continuum forthcoming).

Malcolm Williams is a Principal Lecturer in Sociology at the University of Plymouth. He has authored/co-authored four books in the area of social research methodology/method. His latest book, *Making Sense of Social Research* (2003), is published by Sage. He has also published extensively in the area of migration and housing need.

Acknowledgements

The contributions to this volume were based on papers presented to the seminar series 'Realising the Potential: Realist Social Theory and Empirical Research', funded by the Economic and Social Research Council (ESRC). The editors acknowledge with thanks this award, and the administrative support and hospitality provided by Bath Spa University College. Many thanks go to those who regularly attended and contributed to the seminars (in addition to those whose work is included in this volume), as well as to those who have commented on drafts of the papers. These include Margaret Archer, Jim Collolly, Ian Crinson, Norman Crowther, Berth Danermark, Ruth Kowalsky, Tony Lawson, Andrew Sayer and Jan Wuisman.

Introduction

Realist social theory and empirical research

Of all the philosophies of social science, social realism is probably the most optimistic about the possibility – and the necessity – of reaching significant knowledge of the social world as a result of systematic, principled investigation. Inevitably, its critics ask what there is to show for such optimism. This book takes the position that what knowledge we do have can best be understood in realist terms, even if the method used to acquire it was not self-consciously realist. Contributors will further argue that empirical social research is more effective in yielding good descriptions and explanation of the social world when its design deliberately follows realist principles.

In this chapter we shall introduce some of the key terms and concepts employed in realist social theory. As one of the chief purposes of our Introduction is to indicate to the uncommitted that realism has a good deal to offer, the following account will assume no prior knowledge of realist vocabulary. Nevertheless, we hope that those familiar with realism in the social sciences will still find something of interest here, if only to disagree with our approach.

Naturalism

One of the most basic realist principles is naturalism, the view that *in some central respects* society can be studied in the same way as nature. In *The Possibility of Naturalism* Bhaskar (1989) argues that those who are sceptical about naturalism are making the mistake of believing what positivists say about natural science, that is, that it aims to discover universal laws governing the phenomena we observe. If natural science really did discover invariant causal laws explaining why things happen, there would be no hope of a similar project for the social world. The complexities of human ambition, desire, interests and relationships are such that social relations could never be reduced to a set of unchanging generalisations. This does not mean that human behaviour is inexplicable or chaotic, but that the many interwoven dimensions of social life are roughly patterned rather than law-determined. However, the contrast with the natural world has been overdrawn. Many causal 'laws' in the natural sciences are not invariant successions of events but express *tendencies*, the likelihood of certain things occurring, given certain sorts of conditions (Bhaskar 1989: 1–21). (Even water does not invariably boil at 100°C, but only does so when the air pressure is at a certain level.) The gap between the study of the natural and the social worlds is not unbridgeable.

Weber has been one of the most influential figures in the debate between naturalists and those who believe that the study of nature and the study of society are radically different projects. His solution was to combine the search for causal explanation (naturalism) with explanatory principles that were specific to the social sciences (*Verstehen*, or the search for meaning). Social explanations had to explain how a social phenomenon had been *caused* (for example, the transition from feudalism to capitalism did depend in part on the expansion of the forces of production) but equally they had to demonstrate how the phenomenon resulted from meaningful human action – hence the crucial role of the Protestant ethic in generating capitalistic modes of behaviour, such as accumulation and thrift (Weber 2001). Outhwaite describes Weber as 'heroically' attempting to hold together two positions frequently seen as irreconcilable. Weber held that our knowledge of the social world is necessarily perspectival and value-laden, yet also believed it could be objective, in the sense of having validity and scope beyond its original context (Outhwaite 1998: 24). The traditions Weber inspired have renounced the aim of 'objective' knowledge as they have embraced and developed the method of *Verstehen*.

Social realism allows us to approach this apparent problem in a different way, by distinguishing clearly between *our knowledge about the world* (which Bhaskar and other realists have termed the 'transitive' realm), and *the world which is the object of that knowledge* (known as the 'intransitive' realm). As our knowledge is part of the transitive realm, the realm of concepts and theories, it is thus historical, value-laden and 'situated'.   However, in contrast to Weber, realists regard this not as an obstacle but as an opportunity. We could paraphrase Archimedes – 'Give me a place to stand and I will see the world'. There is no view from nowhere, so while our perspectives are necessarily partial and relative, and so is the knowledge these afford, without somewhere to stand no knowledge is possible (Nagel 1986). The 'somewhere' here represents both the social positions of knowers and the theories and concepts on which they draw.

The world to which our concepts and theories more or less adequately refer, the intransitive realm, is neither a product of, nor constituted by, our theories about it. It is fashionable to attribute the properties of knowledge (its partial, provisional nature) to the objects of knowledge, a mistake which Bhaskar terms the 'epistemic fallacy' (Bhaskar 1989: 133). Social phenomena may well be affected by our knowledge of them *once it has been formulated* (e.g. knowledge of the increased numbers of cohabitees in proportion to married couples may make cohabitation a more appealing option; and knowledge of the vulnerability of planes to hijack makes staying at home an appealing option). Nevertheless, the phenomena are existentially distinct from the processes through which we come to know them. Social relations are part of the intransitive realm, as are natural structures. Where positivism underestimated the concept-dependence of social phenomena, the more fashionable hermeneutic approach overestimates it to the extent that the social world is sometimes reduced to our knowledge of it (Bhaskar 1989).

While social realism is naturalist, realists differ about whether and how the differences between the natural and social worlds limit that naturalism (Collier 1994). They agree about the need for interpretive or hermeneutic methods to investigate the social world in terms of its meanings for people. 'Meaning has to be understood, it cannot be measured or counted, and hence there is always an interpretive or hermeneutic element in social science' (Sayer 2000: 17). For realists, such methods are not in conflict with causal explanations. Once we understand the material setting and the cultural meaning of a social practice, we can hope to understand people's options in relation to it and thus their reasons for acting in the ways they do. For example, Marsh, Rosser and Harré's study of football hooliganism shows that there is a material setting for this social practice – it involves predominantly young working-class men. Contrary to popular commonsense assumptions, football hooliganism has an identifiable moral order and career structure, which make it an attractive option to some people for whom it carries identifiable benefits (Marsh, Rosser and Harré 1980). Marsh and colleagues' study is simultaneously an investigation into meaning and into cause. In showing why football hooliganism is an intelligible choice for some people in certain contexts, they also offer an explanation for *why* it occurs. Humans are structured beings, in whom reasons, beliefs and intentions bring about actions, and, as we discuss below, to 'bring about' is to cause.

Structure and agency

The social contexts which people inhabit – the housing and occupational situation for Marsh *et al.*'s respondents, football as a rule-governed spectator sport and as big business – provide people with 'directional guidance' in terms of appropriate beliefs and courses of action (Archer 1995: 213). People as agents and actors are influenced, though not determined, by their structural situations. People choose what they do, but they make their choices from a structurally and culturally generated range of options – which they do *not* choose.

The 'structure–agency debate' is, as one recent commentator has put it, 'widely acknowledged to lie at the heart of sociological theorising' (Archer 2000: 1). It occupies this salient position because of the fundamental nature of the relationship it seeks to examine, namely that between human beings (the source of agency in the social world) and the social relations (structures) that are generated on the basis of their interaction. There are a number of possible ways in which the relations between structure and agency may be interpreted.

Firstly, one may view human beings as determined by the social relations they encounter: as effects, outcomes and/or transmitters of such social relations. In these 'structuralist' accounts, causal primacy in explaining the social world goes to the role played by social structures, whether these be in the form of, for example, cultural codes (as in the work of Levi-Strauss), relations of production (as in deterministic forms of Marxism), discourses (as in many forms of postmodernism) or system needs and socialisation processes (as in the work of Parsons). A diminished view of agency, in which human beings scarcely figure as movers and shakers of the social world, necessarily accompanies this emphasis on the role of structures. A recent example is Goldberg's description of the 'racial state' which:

> (invisibly) defines almost every relation, contours virtually all intercourse. It fashions not just the said and the sayable, the done and doable, possibilities and impermissibilities, but penetrates equally the scope and quality, content and character of social silences and presumptions. The state in its racial reach and expression is thus at once super-visible, in form and force and thoroughly invisible in its osmotic infusion into the everyday, its penetration into common sense, its pervasion (not to mention perversion) of the warp and weave of the social fabric.
>
> (Goldberg 2001: 98)

Here the state has become an agent of protean omniscience, penetrating in profound ways every aspect of social life, leaving little scope for the possibility even of social action to challenge or modify the 'racial state' (since this would presumably require forms of human agency not contoured by the 'racial state').

Directly opposed to structuralism is a 'voluntarist' account that reverses the direction of the explanatory flow, so that social structures are explained solely in terms of the actions of individuals. Causal primacy in explaining the social world goes to human beings and social structures are seen as being derived from people's thoughts (idealism, various forms of interpretivism), or from their habits and conversations (social constructionism, ethnomethodology). For example, Hird draws on the work of Mead, Foucault and Butler to argue that a proper sociological understanding of transsexualism shows both sex and gender to be 'effects' of 'performativity', produced through 'the interactive narration of the self' (Hird 2002: 587). In such accounts, the emphasis on the role of agency is accompanied by an impoverished view of structures, in which social relations are plastic and only flimsily resistant to human reworking.

More recently, a third view of the structure–agency relation has been developed by Giddens: the 'structuration' view (Giddens 1984: 292; Giddens

1987: 645). According to this perspective, social structures only possess a virtual existence until they are 'instantiated' by people, that is, until people take them into account in social action and thereby either reproduce or modify them. Social relations are thus dependent on the knowledgeable activities of human beings and cannot be separated from them. Here neither side of the dyad is awarded explanatory primacy, since they are held to be mutually constitutive. The properties of structure and of agency are only real in conjunction with each other, and cannot be examined or identified separately since not even an analytic separation is possible.

A fourth, realist, view of the agency–structure relation is also possible. It has been developed by theorists such as Archer, Layder, Pawson and Sayer, and starts from the ontological claim that structure and agency each possess distinct properties and powers in their own right (often referred to as *sui generis* properties and powers). Amongst the properties of social structures, for instance, is their *anteriority*, the fact that, for example, property relations, linguistic systems and legal systems precede us. Social structures thus are pre-existing features of the world into which we are born. This points to another distinguishing property of social structures: they are *relatively enduring*. Amongst the powers possessed by social structures are those of *enablement* and *constraint*: structures of discrimination will constrain the discriminated and enable the discriminators; inegalitarian distributions of wealth and income will constrain the poor and enable the rich.

Amongst the *sui generis* properties of people which are relevant to agency are self-consciousness, reflexivity, intentionality, cognition, emotionality and so on. (Some of these properties, such as intentionality and consciousness, we share with other biological organisms.) As reflexive beings capable of highly sophisticated symbolic communication, human beings are able to formulate projects, develop plans, have ambitions, and pursue interests. This ontological endowment means that it is people who make history. People are the only inhabitants of the social world able to reflect upon, and so seek (individually and collectively) to alter or reinforce, the fitness of the social arrangements they encounter for the realisation of their own interests.

This prime power of agency – the power to maintain or modify the world – is not only dependent on the property of self-consciousness. People collectively can exert an influence simply by virtue of their numbers, a property that we might call demographic agency. Thus the unemployed or the homeless, if their numbers reach a threshold of political or social visibility, can prompt changes in economic or housing policy (or, of course, changes in policing policy). The point is that such effects do not rely on the homeless or the unemployed discursively reflecting upon their condition and formally organising as *the* homeless or *the* unemployed. (Although, of course, they may arrive sooner at the threshold of political visibility if they do so.)

The distinct properties and powers of structure and agency thus entail their irreducibility to each other. This undermines the mutually constitutive 'structuration' view of the relationship between structure and agency. It also entails a rejection of the 'structuralist' view, since without an active notion of agency, that is without being able to inquire about who is doing what to whom and why, we cannot arrive at a convincing explanation for structures at all. Once we recognise the *sui generis* powers and properties of agency, it becomes difficult to see people as passive puppets, cultural dopes or discursive effects.

However, a corresponding recognition of the enduring and anterior properties of social structures, and the consequent patterns of constraint and enablement that they generate, undermines the voluntarist view of structure and agency above. If social structures are ineffectual in themselves because they are at any given moment no more than the product of people's conversations or interpretive strategies, then the social theorist is hard pressed to explain the structuring of agency. Such conversations and interpretive strategies are recognisably patterned in ways intelligibly related to the constraints imposed by the structural context and the options which it makes available. For example, Merton pointed out back in the 1960s that if people are denied socially sanctioned access to culturally defined goals, they will seek illegitimate ones (Merton 1968).

The realist view that we are advocating is committed to an explanatory model in which the interplay between pre-existent structures, possessing causal powers and properties, and people, possessing distinctive causal powers and properties of their own, results in contingent yet explicable outcomes.

This model has a number of epistemological implications. The first of these is that realists are able to develop a plausible defence of objectivity. This follows both from our account above of the anteriority of social structures, and also from realism as a more general philosophical position. It is central to realist accounts that the world is in an important sense mind-independent. As particular individuals we confront a world most of which is not directly produced or constructed by us, but is rather the complex outcome of earlier interactions between people and their structural contexts. For example, someone born into a Turkish family living in Germany is not able to acquire German citizenship, a constraint which will shape their life and development in many profound ways. The temporal priority of structures, which renders them intransitive objects of knowledge, means that they exist and have effects independently of our knowledge of them. Thus, for realists, how things are in reality is a different question from how people take them to be. The information afforded us by our participation in social structures can be deceptive. The disgruntled voter who notes the decline of local industry and accounts for it by pointing to the number of 'immigrants' now living in her neighbourhood has an inaccurate understanding of the causal processes bringing about the decline of manufacturing industry (and there are many vested interests encouraging such inaccuracies). As Danermark *et al.* put it: 'A false conception of a phenomenon may be just as important information to the researcher as correct information; it may be an essential aspect of the phenomenon itself that it can be understood in this wrong way' (2002: 36).

Finally, the core realist notion of emergence, with its insistence on the irreducibility of an emergent property to its constituent elements, also presumes the mind-independent nature of the world.

Emergence and stratification

'Emergence' refers to the way in which particular combinations of things, processes and practices in social life frequently give rise to new emergent properties. The defining characteristic of emergent properties is their irreducibility. They are more than the sum of their constituents, since they are a product of their combination, and as such are able to modify these constituents.

For example, language can be seen as an emergent outcome of the practical engagement of the cognitive and reflexive powers of human beings with the powers and properties of the world. Once established in the form of grammars, collocations and so forth and embodied in text or textual analogues, language develops a relative autonomy and properties and powers of its own. These, in turn, constrain and facilitate speakers in various ways by encouraging certain collocations, for instance, and discouraging others (Carter and Sealey 2000: 593). Similarly, Bowker and Star have drawn attention to the ways in which classification systems, such as the World Health Organisation's International Classification of Diseases, are always the emergent products of social interaction. Yet once in place they develop powers and properties of their own, amongst which is their liability to enforce a certain understanding of context, place and time. This 'makes a certain set of discoveries, which validate its [the classification system's (eds)] own framework, much more likely than an alternative set outside of the framework, since the economic cost of producing a study outside of the framework of normal data collection is necessarily much higher' (Bowker and Star 1999: 82).

This ability of emergent properties to modify the powers of their constituents in fundamental ways is an important feature of realist notions of causal explanation. What differentiates an emergent property from, say, an aggregate or a combination of factors X, Y, Z is that the relations between its components are internal and necessary ones, rather than merely regular co-occurrences of diverse features. Families have emergent properties irreducible to those of their constituents, who are not just any collection of individuals but related as sons, daughters, parents, and siblings and so on. Of course, whether a particular person currently belongs to a family is itself contingent, but nevertheless the existence of such relations, as Archer has it, 'is the litmus test which differentiates between emergence on the one hand and aggregation and combination on the other' (Archer 1995: 174).

An ontology of persons and relational structures, each with their respective emergent properties and powers, contingently combining to produce second and third-order emergent properties, implies that the world is not merely differentiated, but also stratified. That is to say, that the different strata are characterised by different sorts of properties. Layder (1997), for example, suggests that it is useful to view social reality as comprising four analytically separable social 'domains': psychobiography and situated activity (which, broadly speaking, refer to different aspects of agency), and social settings and contextual resources (which refer to structures). Layder's model attempts to capture the social and temporal distancing of social relations from lived experience, while recognising that, at the same time, every lived experience is embedded within the other domains. This stratified social ontology raises a series of methodological issues for social research and it is these that the contributors to the book explore in detail.

Explaining the social world

What has been said so far allows us to identify some characteristics of realist explanation. Since realism is naturalist, explanation has similar tasks in both the natural and the social sciences. Since both the social and the natural worlds are stratified, explanation needs to move from the level of the happenings and phenomena to be explained to that of the mechanisms and structures which generate them. Bhaskar (1989) distinguishes between three ontological domains. The 'actual' comprises events, happenings, phenomena, whether or not these are observed. The 'empirical' is a subset of the actual. The 'real' includes both the actual and the empirical, as well as structures and mechanisms which may not be observed or indeed be observable, but which are known by their effects. This is just the beginning of the stratification of the enormously complex social world. Beyond this simple beginning, hierarchical metaphors are misleading. The social world is better imagined as comprising sets of nested structures, and its effect on actors as 'a plurality of interpenetrating constraints deriving from many recognisable "levels" looping back and around each other' (Dyke 1988: 64).

Explanation in the social sciences is not like everyday explanation, in which we are often content to explain one event, such as 'George hit Mary', in terms of another ('she pushed him too far' or 'his medication had worn off') or by reference to past events ('he has a record of violence'). Even in these cases, though, there are implicit generalisations and unstated assumptions about generative mechanisms, giving the misleading appearance of an explanation which works by linking singular concrete events. In trying to explain the social world we usually begin with generalisations; a singular concrete event is only a suitable subject for explanation once we have established what sort of event it is by relating it to structure. Are George and Mary husband and wife? Mental patient and nurse? As in these cases, are there relationships of internal necessity between the social positions held by George and Mary, or is George a passer-by, merely contingently related to Mary? Thus to set up the problem even in everyday explanation we move from the concrete to the abstract, placing George and Mary in social relations.

Before we can explain an event, it must already be conceptualised as part of a pattern.

In the more technical language of the social sciences we may begin with a more organised description of experienced, measured events – statistical partial regularities, or 'demi-regs'. From a realist point of view this first step is often flawed. The variables being measured in the demi-regs are often 'bad abstractions', in which disparate phenomena – language, culture, religion and place of origin, for example – are bundled together in a 'chaotic conception', such as 'ethnicity' (Sayer 1992: 139, and see Sealey and Carter 2001). If dissimilar events are grouped together, partial statistical regularities may obtain, but satisfactory explanation will require disaggregation and reconceptualising. The aim in doing this, though, is not to choose concepts which produce stronger regularities, but to develop abstractions focusing on causally significant common properties (Sayer 1992).

As Danemark *et al.* (2002) point out, abstraction is a crucial part of social research. There is something of a catch-22 here, because while good abstractions at the stage of setting up the problem make satisfactory explanation more likely, it may not be possible to develop good abstractions until models of causal processes and internal relations have been developed. However, social realism makes this more likely by actively looking for the causal powers and liabilities of things and relationships in the social world. Whenever we reach a better understanding of the causal properties of something, we modify our concept of it – this is implied by the realist causal criterion for reality, namely, that something can be known through its effects. In realist explanation, social scientists will move back and forth between theoretical description of things and their interrelationships at various levels, and discovery and explanation of their properties.

The 'statistical mode of explanation' which charts a statistical relationship between variables such as unemployment and school-retention rates is not an explanation at all in realist terms (Nash 1999: 453). To say that two indicators tend to rise or fall together could provide at most an example of what Byrne calls 'traces of reality' (Byrne 1998), the beginning of the explanatory process rather than its conclusion. Some realists have no use for such statistical techniques as multiple regression, where the analyst attempts to pin down whether an association persists in various conditions. However, we believe this can be a valid way of further elaborating the patterns to be explained, so that the 'traces of reality' which are the starting point of our explanatory journey are *better* starting points. It is not, though, a way of 'accounting for' or 'explaining' proportions of the variance.

The task of explanation is twofold. When the starting point is a pattern of events, the task is 'to explain the occurrence of particular events in terms of conjunctures of the causal properties of various interacting mechanisms – i.e. to *retroduce* the effective mechanisms' (Porpora 1998: 343). Retroduction is a mode of inference characterised 'by the move from knowledge of some phenomenon existing at any one level of reality, to a knowledge of mechanisms, at a deeper level or stratum of reality, which contributed to the generation of the original phenomenon of interest' (Lawson 1997: 26).

When the starting point is an already identified causal property of some structured element of the social world, for example an organisation, a social practice or a set of rules for diagnosis, the task is to explain these powers in terms of the internal structure of the thing in question (Porpora, op. cit.). For instance, we might set out to explain the over-representation of women in the UK with diagnoses of depression, based on 'demi-regs' from hospital admissions data and from GPs' prescriptions of anti-depressants. Biomedical psychiatry offers us one straightforward explanation which, whatever its faults, is realist enough. By virtue of their reproductive nature, women are subject to enormous hormonal changes which can affect their mental health at certain points in the life cycle (Dalton 1994). According to biopsychiatry, when women at these vulnerable points become distressed or unable to cope, knowledgeable professionals can recognise those cases in which a pathological process is present, that is, a state of the brain with emergent properties of its own. On this basis, they diagnose and treat. Environmental triggers may enter into the model, but the crucial mechanisms are biological.

Sociologists have not been satisfied with this explanation, suspecting that the diagnostic labels are 'chaotic conceptions' of the sort discussed above, and that the key mechanisms producing the 'demi-regs' are at the social and psychological levels rather than the chemical or neurological. Busfield (1996), among others, has identified a number of co-acting mechanisms which together may produce women's over-representation. Cultural assumptions about gender difference make both men and women more likely to see women as emotional, passive and irrational, and to define them as 'mentally ill'. The gendered division of labour, which gives women primary responsibility for the care of young children, may produce a specific vulnerability. The Diagnostic and Statistical Manual (DSM), which plays a key part both in psychiatric training and in the diagnostic process, uses 'typical cases' that are themselves constructed around gendered assumptions, encouraging psychiatrists to allocate women and men to particular diagnostic categories (Busfield 1996). If we take the DSM as a text with emergent properties, a further task is to explain how its use could contribute to this over-representation of women as depressed.

One empiricist response to such puzzling demi-regs is to produce further demi-regs. One example of this was the over-representation of African-Caribbeans as 'schizophrenic' based on hospitals admissions data. This was challenged by the Policy Studies Institute (PSI) community survey, which suggested that African-Caribbeans are no more likely than white English to 'be schizophrenic' (although more likely to receive treatment), but are more likely to be depressed (and untreated for depression) (Nazroo 1997). Here, one set of putative constant conjunctions is displaced by another, without any challenge to the diagnostic categories themselves. In contrast, Brown and Harris (1978) offer a complex model which has been highly influential in the discussion of gender and depression, although they devised it without studying any men. It is a model of 'situationally generated' emergent capacities and liabilities, which seeks to explain *which* women are likely to become depressed and which are likely to cope when faced with inescapable situations of loss and difficulty. At the sociostructural level, class affects the distribution of 'vulnerability factors': three or more children under 14 at home, presence or absence of an intimate relationship, loss of own mother before the age of 11, and work outside the home. More obviously, class makes 'provoking agents' (stressful life events such as job loss) more or less likely. When 'provoking agents' are present, 'vulnerability factors' are supposed to affect whether current difficulties result in depression, while further 'symptom formation factors' are associated with its severity. Brown and Harris do not use the language of social realism, but they have produced a stratified model of co-acting mechanisms (some spelt out, some implicit) which together bring about the events to be explained (Pilgrim and Rogers 1999). We suggest the model's explanatory power derives from its internal stratification, but it is limited by a failure to be sufficiently stratified. For example, 'loss of own mother before the age of 11' is not really a mechanism, but an indicator at the level of events. The mechanism involved – the real 'vulnerability factor' – remains to be identified. Loss of some sort probably has developmental implications, but the precise familial relationship and the exact chronological age are probably contingent features.

A realist social explanation, then, will not only identify co-acting mechanisms, but will also recognise that mechanisms are stratified. In practice it will never be possible to identify all the co-acting mechanisms: some, perhaps the most constant, become 'context', the stuff of '*in ceteris paribus*' clauses. For sociology, psychological structures are often taken for granted and treated as either wholly predictable and banal or as 'noise'. Yet social explanation always involves the meeting point of structure and agency, and the co-acting of psychological, cultural and social structures that people encounter, use and embody; structures which position them, motivate them, circumscribe their options and their capacity to respond.

Causality and causal mechanisms

Realist explanations go beyond or behind associations, to the social structures and practices that generate them. Valera and Harré have recently taken issue with social realists over the question of whether social structures have causal powers. Harré wants to reduce structures to rules, which 'do not use people, that is they have no causal efficacy, it is people who use rules and ... who are the powerful particulars' (Valera and Harré 1996: 318). As we have seen, social realists have a stronger idea of social structures, and emphasise their pre-existence (as rules, but also as networks of positions, allowing differential access to various cultural and material resources). But Valera and Harré are right to distinguish between the way in which *people* cause things to happen

– by doing things – and the way in which *structures* cause things to happen – by motivating or discouraging, constraining and enabling certain sorts of human action (Carter 2002). They want to restrict the notion of causal powers to entities which by their nature *do* things, i.e. to efficient rather than material causality (Lewis 2000). But although the causal powers of structures require the actions of people to work, nevertheless they bring things about which, if they were different, would not occur in the same way. Therefore, for realists, social and cultural structures are causally efficacious.

There are not two sorts of explanations, which refer to causes and meanings respectively, as Weber suggested. Hermeneutics, or verstehende explanations, are often offered as appropriate to social science in place of causal explanations of events. For realists the former are both a precondition and an aspect of the latter. As Bhaskar points out, hermeneutics are necessary for us to understand the meaning of an action, such as shaking the head or saying 'hello', in a particular social context, language and culture (1989). But correctly to identify the *type* of act, making it intelligible to the researcher/reader, is not to *explain* what actually brought about a particular such act or set of such acts. We are dealing here with beliefs, but also with intentions and motivations, with psychological structures as well as cultural structures of meaning.

On a social realist account, the mental states that mediate between the situational precursors of action and the action itself are among the causes of the action. This is often expressed in terms of the old philosophical question 'Can reasons be causes?' Bhaskar argues most powerfully at some length that reasons, beliefs and other mental states and dispositions can, and must, be causes, otherwise they are condemned to an epiphenomenal limbo where they float in parallel to the real (physical?) causes (Bhaskar 1989: 88). Further:

> unless a reason could function as a cause there would be no sense in a person evaluating (or appraising) different beliefs in order to decide how to act. For either a reason will make a difference to his/her behaviour or it will not. In the former case, it counts as a cause. In the latter case, it is logically redundant, and deliberation, ratiocination (and indeed thought generally) become practically otiose.
>
> (1989: 92)

We prefer to substitute for the formulation 'reasons can be causes', the more accurate formulation 'psychological mechanisms (which include states of mind, beliefs, obsessions and so on) cause actions'. This avoids the inbuilt ambiguity which has bedevilled the 'reasons can be causes' debate. 'Reasons' can refer to what a person, for example Ann, *should* do, given her social positioning, aspirations, vulnerabilities and capacities, in order to meet her goals. We might judge Ann's *actual* actions in instrumental terms, and find the action unreasonable (Ann might or might not agree). Alternatively, Ann's reasons for acting can refer to the mental states which resulted in her action, in contradistinction to the reasons, or rationalisations, she offers in justification. Of course, mental states which bring about action can be complex, stratified, conflict-ridden, and more or less conscious and available to reflection. They are not reducible to the structures and events which bring them about, for mind is not epiphenomenal but has its own structures and causal powers. Mental states are analytically independent of discursive justifications for action, although they may sometimes involve the sort of perception and reasoning that is used to justify action. It is only 'reasons' in the sense of 'mental states' that can be 'causes'. The confusion with justifications has arisen because people frequently do make judgements on the likely effects of their actions in relation to their aspirations, and reflect on how others will judge them. Such judgements and reflections, and the perceptions on which they are based, are part (but only part) of the complex mental processes that bring about action.

If mental states can cause action, then the distinction between interpretive and causal investigations and explanations is not so clear cut. Take the example of an 'interpretive' study of class differences in parent participation in two secondary schools (Crozier 1997). Crozier finds that 'parents' social class location continues to have a direct impact upon their ability to intervene in their child's schooling'. The writer sees this as a hermeneutic investigation, in which she is trying to establish the meaning of, for example, going to the school's parents' evening, for working-class and for middle-class parents. 'The research employed an interpretive paradigm based on the premise of seeking an understanding of the actors' meanings whilst recognising that these are located within a socio-political context' (1997: 189). The interviews with parents are used to establish their class position and their (self-reported) actions in relation to the school – in other words, patterns in events. The possible mechanisms Crozier discusses (though she does not use this term) include:

M1 – Formal structure of relations between school staff, governors and
     parents
M2 – Instantiation in these particular schools
M3 – Parents' understandings of 1 and of relationship between 1 and 2
M4 – Parents' own positions: resources, constraints, opportunities
M5 – Parents' differential cultural capital

Using the interpretive data, and also making inferences about M4, Crozier outlines a model which links these emergent properties, and shows how they might relate to bring about the class differentials in outcome. There is no conflict between this 'interpretive' research and social realism.

Just as the idea that mental states bring about action can get bogged down in the old philosophical problems of 'Can reasons be causes?', so the term 'mechanism' can lead us into the swamps of free will versus determinism. The mechanism metaphor strongly suggests the very Humean notion of causality which social realists reject. We can say categorically that mechanisms in social life *never* work mechanically. Structures are described as generative mechanisms, because when their causal powers are realised they work to make something happen. But the effects of structures are mediated by agency: in social life, nothing happens without the activation of the causal powers of people. Crucial among these is the power to decide. Nevertheless, the liabilities of people as human beings are such that their choices are often constrained in readily intelligible ways which make their options fairly narrow. The price mechanisms of economics work because human beings are pretty similar in terms of needs. Not as similar as we might think, however. When we focus on an economic mechanism, a structure which tends to work in ways which bring about a certain outcome, we often ignore co-acting mechanisms and contexts which are so common as to seem inevitable. In the twenty-first century it can seem obvious that people will work longer to get more pay. Tweaking pay structures will tend to bring about certain behaviour among employees – piece rates will increase productivity, for instance. However, both Marx and Weber describe how in the eighteenth and early nineteenth century the new industrial working class had to be taught new desires, so that they would work longer than was necessary to meet their traditional needs (Marx 1966; Weber 2001).

The contributors to this book use the term 'mechanism' in slightly different ways. For Pawson, who emphasises that the causal powers of people are the source of agency, researchers should search for generative mechanisms in the choices people make and in the capacities they derive from group membership. However, since the operation and effects of generative mechanisms are mediated by social context, the researcher has not only to identify them but also to describe the balance of circumstances 'which enable, modify, or nullify' their action. Pawson's schematic formula is thus $M + C = O$ (this volume, p. 31). But when is Context context, and when is it Mechanism? Do we allocate class structure to context, or is context the set of contingencies which affect the saliency of the class-based motivations, together with other mechanisms acting at the same time, maybe in a different direction? For Scambler, Higgs and Jones, class is most certainly a mechanism, since it distributes various resources and capacities which they call 'capitals'. Together with the causal powers and liabilities of people as humans, these give rise to reasons for acting in certain ways. What the contributors have in common is that they are identifying structures whose combined states result in the exercise of agential powers, which bring about the outcomes which need explaining.

Sociological realism and empirical research

We have so far examined the shared theoretical vocabulary of realist social science and the common ontological assumptions that characterise the realist view of social reality. Chief amongst these are: the crucial role of casual explanation; the centrality of emergent properties and the stratified social ontology that results from the interplay of these; and the methodological emphasis on analysing the relations between structure and agency. These are broad assumptions that do not in themselves supply a programme for empirical social research. Realism's open-endedness on the matter of methodology and method has given rise to some sharp debates about what realist empirical research might look like, indeed whether such a creature is possible or even necessary. Unquestionably, it is the case that much writing about realism and social science has been directed more towards general philosophical concerns unlikely to appeal to the jobbing researcher trying to put together an Economic and Social Research Council (ESRC) bid.

To some extent this is a reflection of the fact that realist approaches to social science are a comparatively recent development. Perhaps the key figures in the advent of a specifically sociological realism were Roy Bhaskar and Rom Harré. Bhaskar's *The Possibility of Naturalism* and Harré's *Varieties of Realism* sought, in different ways, to explore the relevance of realist philosophising to the concerns of social science. These initial efforts were followed up by a number of other contributions (Keat and Urry 1982; Sayer 1984; Layder 1985; Manicas 1987, amongst others). By the end of the 1980s a considerable body of work had accumulated, establishing a compelling case for viewing social reality as an object of knowledge independent of the individual's cognising experience.

For those with an interest in empirical social research, this case left some important, and difficult, questions to be answered. For instance, if reality is independent of us as individuals, how can we ever have knowledge of it and what sort of knowledge would this be? Further questions concern the ontological status of social phenomena. Whilst many would be prepared to go along with the notion of a physical and natural world independent of people's cognising experience – the law of gravity is real in the sense of being unaffected by how we choose to think about it or interpret it – phenomena in the social world seem more dependent on human meaning. Surely, to take an example of Layder's, whether I choose to see a pile of stones as a source of ammunition, a place of worship or as evidence of past architectural endeavour is crucial in determining the nature of my reality. Perhaps more crucially, it determines what I am likely to do – pick them up, drop to my knees or consult the guidebook (Layder 1990: 60).

Sayer has made a similar case, pointing out that social phenomena such as actions, texts and institutions are concept-dependent. Before we can explain how these social phenomena are produced and identify their material effects, we have to understand, read or interpret what they mean. Furthermore, for Sayer (and other realists) science or the production of any other kind of knowledge is a social practice. This means that the conditions and the social relations of production of knowledge will influence its content (Sayer 2000).

Thus we seem to have arrived at some fundamental issues with regard to a realist view of social as opposed to natural reality. First, there is the issue of how we can come to know a reality that is independent of us. This is an epistemological question about what sorts of knowledge we can have. Second, there is the central importance of an interpretive element in the definition of social reality, that is, what is to count as social reality will critically depend on who is doing the counting and what they are doing it for. Together these issues appear to pose some difficult questions for those wishing to do realist social research.

For example, a central claim of realist social science is that societies are 'open' systems. This suggests that the sorts of experimental controls that are possible in laboratory conditions (although the extent of such controls is often exaggerated) cannot be applied to the analysis of social reality. This is not simply because people are reflexive beings, or because social reality has a limitless number of 'variables' interacting upon and influencing each other. It is also because of the emergent properties and powers of people, positions, groups and of the various sorts of social relations from fleeting interactions to enduring institutions. Such emergent properties, it will be recalled, arise from particular combinations of elements and have a causal influence on those elements as well as a reciprocal influence on other emergent properties and powers. Social reality, in other words, tends to resemble a 'structured mess' and 'structured messes' prove notoriously recalcitrant to dissection into variables (see, for example, Bowker and Star 1999; Byrne 1998).

Furthermore, identifying the ontological features of the social world is an activity that must be fully explicit about its relationship to the phenomena of experience; after all, the empirical, phenomenal world is part of the social world, and is the only part to which we have direct access. However, for realists, argues Layder, observation is not an independent appropriation of the ontological and real features of the social world. 'Operationally and existentially independent of our cognising experience they may be,' notes Layder, 'but the elementary structures of the world never escape the net of language and knowledge, as *our* knowledge' (Layder 1990: 53). The aspiration to know the world in its pristine or pure state is doomed because it would imply some notion of a pre-linguistic, intuitive 'knowledge'.

How, then, is empirical research possible in social sciences? Realists have provided a number of answers to this question. One that has attracted recent attention is Pawson's notion of a generative model. A generative model utilises a social ontology of generative mechanisms and emergent powers to examine how the system under investigation is constituted. Only after the model is developed are research hypotheses advanced 'explicit enough to have direct consequences for empirical research and measurement practice' (Pawson 1989: 171). Empirical data (though *not* empirical reality), according to this view, is constructed from theory or, as Pawson elsewhere puts it, 'all measurement is primarily an act of translation' (Pawson 1989: 287). So models tell us what we need to know and how to go about measuring it. In order to do this our models, because they are concerned to grasp generative relations and emergent properties, must draw upon the formal networks of theory within the social sciences since these attempt to encompass all levels of the social world.

Empiricist sociology (whether phenomenological, experiential or material) deals with variables as discrete. This has been a 'recipe for arbitrary and contested operationalisation since measures are based erratically on everyday connotations of the concept in question' (Pawson 1989: 186). Without theory, variables are treated as indicators of given social attributes, such as 'age' or 'social class', and their 'validity' is supposed to consist in their fidelity to commonsense assumptions. Thus, for example, people are seen as having a social class, measured through newspapers read or car ownership. Once found, class can be linked with some other measure. Social class is seen as a simple variable, rather than an emergent relational property. Social scientific concepts are by contrast developed as part of a generative model in which key measurement parameters are known independently of any operation devised to measure them. They allow us to ask what must be the case for class relations to produce the outcomes that they do, and how we can find ways of developing empirical evidence that would enable us to make judgements between different theories.

A further advantage of this strategy of developing concepts within generative models is the possibility it affords for adjudication between theories. In a formal system the meanings of terms and concepts are established by their place in a network of postulates, themselves derived from the structural and technical languages of social science. Pawson again: 'Ordinary language reasoning cannot sustain the development of a logically consistent network of concepts' (Pawson 1989: 243). This view has some profound implications for realist views of the relations between social theory and language (see, for example, Carter and Sealey 2000; Devitt and Sterelny 1999), and once more raises important epistemological questions that thus far have been relatively underdeveloped within realist research.

Probably the major development in realist qualitative empirical research has been Archer's morphogenetic model (Archer 1979; 1989; 1995; 2000). This draws on the realist social ontology outlined earlier and seeks to give concrete methodological form to the analysis of the interplay between structure and agency, or what we have termed, following Archer, analytical dualism.

Analytical dualism for Archer 'accords time a central place in social theory' (Archer 1995: 89), and allows a purchase on the *structuring* of social systems over time. Morphogenesis 'refers to the complex interchanges that produce change in a System's given form, structure or state ("morphostasis" is the reverse)' (Archer 1989: xxii).

The morphogenetic analysis works in terms of three part cycles:

(a) *structural conditioning*, which refers to pre-existing structures that condition but do not determine

(b) *social interaction*, which arises from actions oriented towards the realisation of interests and needs emanating from current agents and leads to

(c) *structural elaboration or modification*, that is, a change in the relations between the parts of the social system.

> What is crucial, then, is that the morphogenetic perspective maintains that structure and agency operate over different time periods – an assertion which is based on its two simple propositions: that structure necessarily predates the actions which transform it; and that structural elaboration necessarily post-dates those actions.
>
> (Archer 1995: 90)

To use Pawson's phrase, morphogenesis is a matter of 'differently resourced subjects making constrained choices amongst the range of opportunities provided' (Pawson and Tilley 1997: 46). Empirical research can then be directed towards discovering in greater and greater detail what Pawson and Tilley helpfully summarise as the three Ws – *what* works for *whom* in *what* circumstances (Pawson and Tilley 1997: 210). There have been some recent attempts to use a morphogenetic approach in qualitative research (see, for example, Carter 2000; Pretorius 1993), but again, at present, its potential for empirical research has yet to be realised.

This is an appropriate point to introduce the present volume. The ESRC funded seminar series on which it is based arose from a growing feeling amongst a number of researchers working within a broadly realist framework that the status of empirical research within the social sciences is under challenge. The challenge has come from two directions. Firstly, the rise of relativist themes, sometimes associated with postmodernism or versions of social constructionism, has placed in jeopardy the notions of objectivity and objective knowledge central to empirical research. Secondly, and partly in response to this first challenge, there has arisen a more technocratic view of empirical research, which tends to sever it from social theory by favouring narrowly defined, policy-oriented projects judged mainly on their usefulness to 'end-users'. In both cases the rich interweaving of empirical work and social theory has become increasingly threadbare. This was one of the central themes discussed in the seminar series, as it set out to explore the resources offered to social research by a realist social science.

Realism as a current within social science is not, of course, a clearly defined set of prescriptions for doing 'realist work', and this is reflected in the broad range of topics covered by the papers presented to the series and rewritten for this book. There is no 'party line' and, as the reader will discover, the application of realist approaches to areas of social research such as health, notions of probability, chaos theory, racism, socio-linguistics and so on, has dissolved some questions, provided provisional answers to others, and thrown up a host of new ones. And since social realism lays no claim to final answers, this is as it should be.

References

Archer, M. S. (1979) *Social Origins of Educational Systems*, London: Sage.

Archer, M. S. (1989) *Culture and Agency: The Place of Culture in Social Theory*, Cambridge: Cambridge University Press.

Archer, M. S. (1995) *Realist Social Theory: A Morphogenetic Approach*, Cambridge: Cambridge University Press.

Archer, M. S. (2000) *Being Human: The Problem of Agency*, Cambridge: Cambridge University Press.

Bhaskar, R. (1989) *The Possibility of Naturalism*, Brighton: Harvester Wheatsheaf.

Bowker, G. C. and Star, S. L. (1999) *Sorting Things Out: Classification and Its Consequences*, Cambridge, MA: MIT Press.

Brown, G. W. and Harris, T. O. (1978) *The Social Origins of Depression*, London: Tavistock.

Busfield, J. (1996) *Men, Women and Madness: Understanding Gender and Mental Disorder*, New York: New York University Press.

Byrne, D. (1998) *Complexity Theory and the Social Sciences*, London: Routledge.

Carter, B. (2000) *Realism and Racism: Concepts of Race in Sociological Research*, London: Routledge.

Carter, B. (2002) 'People power: Rom Harré and the myth of social structure', *European Journal of Social Theory*, 5, 1: 134–42.

Carter, B. and Sealey, A. (2000) 'Language, structure and agency: what can realist social theory offer to sociolinguistics?', *Journal of Sociolinguistics*, 4, 1: 3–20.

Collier, A. (1994) *Critical Realism: An Introduction to Roy Bhaskar's Philosophy*, London: Verso.

Crozier, G. (1997) 'Empowering the powerful: a discussion of the interrelation of government policies and consumerism with social class factors and the impact of this upon parent interventions in their children's schooling', *British Journal of the Sociology of Education*, 18, 2: 187–200.

Dalton, K. (1994) *Once a Month: the Original Pre-Menstrual Syndrome Handbook*, Alameda, CA: Hunter House.

Danermark, B., Ekström, M., Jakobsen, L. and Karlsson J. C. (2002) *Explaining Society: Critical Realism in the Social Science*, London: Routledge.

Devitt, M. and Sterelny, K. (1999) *Language and Reality: An Introduction to the Philosophy of Language*, 2nd edn, Oxford: Blackwell.

Dyke, C. J. (1988) *The Complex Dynamics of Evolutionary Systems*, Oxford: Oxford University Press.

Giddens, A. (1984) *The Constitution of Society*, Cambridge: Polity Press.

Giddens, A. (1987) *Social Theory and Modern Sociology*, Stanford, CA: Stanford University Press.

Goldberg, D. T. (2001) *The Racial State*, Oxford: Blackwell.

Hird, M. J. (2002) 'For a sociology of transsexualism', *Sociology*, 36, 3: 577–95.

Keat, R. and Urry, J. (1982) *Social Theory as Science*, 2nd edn, London: Routledge.

Layder, D. (1985) 'Beyond empiricism: the promise of realism', *Philosophy of the Social Sciences* 15: 255–74.

Layder, D. (1990) *The Realist Image in Social Science*, London: Macmillan.

Layder, D. (1993) *New Strategies in Social Research*, Cambridge: Polity.

Layder, D. (1994) *Understanding Social Theory*, London: Sage.

Layder, D. (1997) *Modern Social Theory* London: UCL Press

Lawson, T. (1997) *Economics and Reality*, London: Routledge.

Lewis, P. (2000) 'Realism, causality and the problem of social structure', *Journal for the Theory of Social Behaviour*, 30, 3: 250–68.

Manicas, P. T. (1987) *A History and Philosophy of the Social Sciences*, Oxford: Blackwell.

Marsh, P., Rosser, E. and Harré, R. (1980) *Rules of Disorder*, London: Taylor and Francis.

Marx, K. (1966) *Capital, Volume III*, Moscow: Progress Publishers.

Merton, R. (1968) *Social Theory and Social Structure*, 3rd edn, New York: Free Press.

Nagel, T. (1986) *The View from Nowhere*, Oxford: Oxford University Press.

Nash, R. (1999) 'What is real and what is realism in sociology?' *Journal for the Theory of Social Behaviour*, 29, 4: 445–65.

Nazroo, J. (1997) *Ethnicity and Mental Health*, London: Policy Studies Institute.

Outhwaite, W. (1998) 'Naturalisms and anti-naturalisms', in T. May and M. Williams (eds) *Knowing the Social World*, Buckingham: Open University Press.

Pawson, R. (1989) *A Measure for Measures: A Manifesto for Empirical Sociology*, London: Routledge.

Pawson, R. and Tilley, N. (1997) *Realistic Evaluation*, London: Sage.

Pilgrim, D. and Rogers, A. (1999) *A Sociology of Mental Health and Illness*, Buckingham: Open University Press.

Porpora, D. (1998) 'Four concepts of social structure', in M. Archer, R. Bhaskar, A. Collier, T. Lawson and A. Norrie (eds) *Critical Realism: Essential Readings*, London: Routledge.

Pretorius, D. (1993) 'The Social Origins of Failure – Morphogenesis of Educational Agency in the Cape Colony', PhD Thesis, University of Warwick.

Sayer, A. (1984) *Method in Social Science: A Realist Approach*, London: Routledge

Sayer, A. (1992) *Method in Social Science: A Realist Approach*, 2nd edn, London: Routledge.

Sayer, A. (2000) *Realism and Social Science*, London: Sage.

Sealey, A. and Carter, B. (2001) 'Social categories and sociolinguistics: applying a realist approach', *International Journal of the Sociology of Language*, 152: 1–19.

Valera, C. and Harré, R. (1996) 'Conflicting varieties of realism: causal powers and the problems of social structure', *Journal for the Theory of Social Behaviour*, 26, 3: 313–25.

Weber, M. (2001) *The Protestant Ethic and the Spirit of Capitalism*, Los Angeles: Roxbury.

Part I

Methodology and measurement

In their different ways the three chapters in this section address the issue of measurement in social research.

Current approaches to policy evaluation advocate conducting systematic reviews of the evidence from smaller scale studies, in which their results are aggregated. Ray Pawson argues that such a move invalidates the entire process of systematic review by confounding the various mechanisms at work, and obscuring the contexts through which such mechanisms operate to produce a range of outcomes. Elsewhere, Pawson has developed the formula: mechanism + context = outcome (M+C=O), which for him are the basis of 'bread and butter' realism (Pawson 2000: 293). If the aim of realist research is to explain the patterns of outcomes that are revealed in empirical work, it needs to do so by identifying generative mechanisms that, for certain subjects *in certain contexts*, give rise to these observed outcomes. For Pawson, the term mechanism 'describes the resources and reasoning that actually constitute the outcomes under research' (ibid. 296). In this conception, mechanisms are recognisable points at which structure mediates agency by constraining, enabling and generally motivating people's actions in ways that give rise to certain tendencies. '[I]t is not programmes that work but the resources they offer to enable their subjects to make them work' (Chapter 1, p. 31) A key question for Pawson in evaluating policy research is therefore: what works, for whom, in what context? (Pawson and Tilley 1997).

The review of evidence based policy, Pawson argues, must proceed not by spurious aggregation but by 'programme theory' that identifies which mechanisms are at work in particular interventions and in which contexts they are likely to produce the desired outcomes. Pawson proposes a 'middle-range' theory, drawing on the work of Robert Merton (1968). Although Merton's 'middle-range' theory has been criticised as 'heavily dependent upon empiricist criteria for the evaluation and production of legitimate theory' (Layder, 1998: 138), Pawson sees Merton as having offered an incomplete but invaluable framework for the empirical researcher. Realism provides the missing elements, including 'an ontological skeleton on which to build explanations' (Pawson 2000: 291).

Like other contributors to this volume, Pawson rejects successionist views of causation, in which the goal is to establish those independent variables responsible for a dependent variable. The elaboration of alternative generative views of causality is the focus of the chapters by Dave Byrne and by Malcolm Williams and Wendy Dyer.

Contrasting the concerns of epidemiology and the individual clinician, Byrne introduces the problem of the relationship between distinct levels of reality – the health of populations and of individuals, and the causal processes relevant to each. He shows that two approaches with very different understandings of causality (a biomechanical model on the one hand and a version of social constructionism on the other) cannot deal with emergent phenomena and with non-linear causal processes that cross levels. Yet since any scientific practice must be able to model reality using quantitative methods, researchers need methods which can incorporate 'the micro, meso and macro levels of social structure and social interaction'. While multi-level modelling remains 'trapped in the linear probabilistic approaches of frequentist statistics', it will not be adequate to this explanatory task (Chapter 2, p. 64).

Byrne's approach to modelling multi-level complexity rejects variables in favour of cases. He argues that retrodiction[1] of individual trajectories from current health status – i.e. tracing *backwards* from known outcomes – will allow the identification of mechanisms which affected those trajectories, without suppressing the real causal complexity involved. Where Pawson advocates reviewing cases in order to establish the contexts in which mechanisms work, Byrne is suggesting the logically prior movement from cases to mechanisms (to solve a different explanatory problem).

The third chapter in this section, by Williams and Dyer, explores the implications of the single case for realist notions of causality. Drawing attention to the relatively minor impact that realist methodological positions have had on quantitative research, they argue that a plausible explanation for this lack of influence lies in the realist insistence on a notion of natural necessity. Sayer, for example, expounds this notion by linking the internal relations of a thing to its causal powers. He writes:

> this conception of causality as a *necessary* way of acting of an object does not, as some have supposed, boil down to the virtual tautology that an object can do something because it has the power to do so ... Scientists often do postulate the existence of such powers, but avoid the tautology by establishing empirically what it is about the substance which gives it this power, which can be identified independently of the exercise of that power. It is surely not a tautology to explain my ability to walk and my inability to fly by reference to my anatomy, musculature, density and shape.
>
> (Sayer, 1992: 105–6)

But for Williams and Dyer, the idea of causal powers which *necessarily tend* to produce certain outcomes is incoherent. They understand it in terms of 'nomic necessity', that is, the relationship between a law of nature and its instances. Accordingly, they seek 'to recast realism in a weaker, contingent form' (Chapter 3, p. 67) by reintroducing the notion of probability as the basis for causal accounts of the social world.

The co-acting of many mechanisms, the functioning of which is context-dependent, means that causal analysis in realist research is invariably tendential. So why do Williams and Dyer insist so forcefully on a Popperian notion of propensity? For empiricists, probability was simply an epistemological problem. For critical realists, probability (to the extent that it is mentioned at all) is second best knowledge, resulting from our incapacity to grasp the complex array of generative and counteracting mechanisms which produce patterns of outcomes. Williams and Dyer argue that this, too, is an empiricist view. For Popper, by contrast, propensity is an ontological feature of the world; we are able to calculate probabilities because the world is structured probabilistically. For Williams and Dyer, the realist notion of powers and properties is an implicit propensity view. Their conclusion, not unlike Byrne's, is that research should be case-based, 'because the probabilities are the ontological characteristics of the situation and not an epistemological tool to stand in for lack of knowledge' (Chapter 3, p. 78).

Note

1   Whereas retroduction is the inference of generative mechanisms from patterns of outcomes, retrodiction is 'the determination of possible antecedent conditions' (Lawson 1997: 221). Retrodiction, then, is the obverse of prediction and can apply to events as well as to mechanisms.

References

Lawson, T. (1997) *Economics and Reality*, London: Routledge.

Layder, D. (1998) *Sociological Practice: Linking Theory and Social Research*, London: Sage.

Merton, R. (1968) *Social Theory and Social Structure*, 3rd edn, New York: Free Press.

Pawson, R. D. (2000) *Archives Européenes de Sociologie*, XLI, 2, 283–325.

Pawson, R. D. and Tilley, N. (1997) *Realistic Evaluation*, London: Sage.

Sayer, A. (1992) *Method in Social Science: A Realist Approach*, 2nd edn, London: Routledge.

1   Evidence-based policy

A realist perspective

Ray Pawson

Introduction: 'what counts is what works'

The British Prime Minister, Tony Blair, is rather well known for his *bon mots* and this little sound-bite about the pragmatist turn in policy-making is amongst his best known. The jury is still out on whether the ideological grip on decision-making has actually relaxed. But one change, for sure, has come to pass. There has been an enormous increase in the apparatus of evidence-based policy-making in recent years.

Nor is this a peculiarly British affair, since this 'utilitarian shift' has been noted as a feature of modern polities across Europe, Australasia and North America (e.g. European Commission 2001).

My concern here is with the methodology of evidence-based policy. Few major public initiatives are mounted these days without a sustained attempt to evaluate them. Rival policy ideas are thus run through endless trials with plenty of error and it is often difficult to know which of them has stood the test of time. Rather than relying on one-off studies, it is wiser to look to the 'weight of evidence', using reviews of all the existing research in a particular policy domain. (See Figure 1.1.)

Systematic reviews, then, are the order of the day in policy analysis. This paper argues for an approach to reviewing the evidence that I will call 'realist synthesis'. The first section offers a realist critique of the orthodox model of systematic review, namely 'meta-analysis'. The second section attempts a miniature demonstration review using 'realist synthesis' on the topic of 'public disclosure' policies, interventions that are often better known by another sound-bite, 'naming and shaming'.

Meta-analysis: a realist critique

Meta-analysis is the original and still the dominant mode of systematic review. Its roots are in evidence-based medicine and the desire to base medical practice on robust demonstrations of clinical excellence. The raw materials typically available to the reviewer in the field are the dozens, sometimes

1 Evaluation research

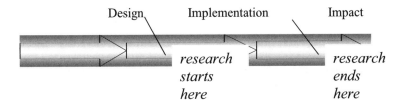

Research power: ♦ ♦ ♦ (individual/research unit)

2 Systematic review

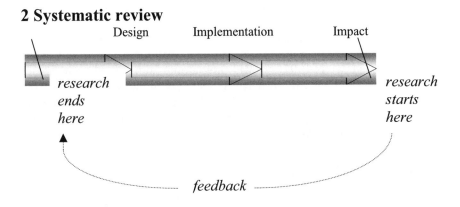

Research power

♦ ♦ ♦ ♦ ♦ ♦ 🐕 (research community)

Figure 1.1 The potential benefits of systematic review

hundreds of trials (usually randomised control trials) required in the development of new treatments. Each will give a clear measure of the impact of the treatment, namely the 'effect size', i.e. the difference between the experimental and the control group in terms of the desired outcome of the intervention.

The detailed practice of evidence-based medicine is, of course, rather more complex than this. But the underlying logic of meta-analysis is that:

1 Treatments are tangible, singular and highly reproducible.
2 Subjects are passive and interventions work independently of human judgement.
3 Randomised controlled trials provide the gold standard evidence.
4 Evidence is brought together by a process of 'pooling' or 'aggregation'.
5 Systematic review is the search for the enduring empirical generalisation.

The first two of these assumptions have been challenged extensively in the realist literature (Pawson and Tilley 1997). Rather than raking over these old coals, I want to examine the case for propositions four and five here by looking briefly at a meta-analysis of some complex social and psychological interventions.

One typical meta-analysis brings together 177 Primary Prevention Mental Health (PPMH) programmes for children and adolescents carried out in the US (Durlak and Wells 1997). PPMH programmes aim 'to reduce incidence of adjustment problems in currently normal populations' and to promote mental health. The interventions included person-centred programmes (which use counselling, social learning and instructional approaches), environment-centred schemes (modifying school or home conditions), and

Table 1.1 Meta-analysis of primary prevention mental health programmes

Type of programme	n	Mean effect
Environment-centred		
School-based	15	0.35
Parent-training	10	0.16
Transition programmes		
Divorce	7	0.36
School-entry/change	8	0.39
First-time mothers	5	0.87
Medical/dental procedure	26	0.46
Person-centred programmes		
Affective education		
Children 2–7	8	0.70
Children 7–11	28	0.24
Children over 11	10	0.33
Interpersonal problem solving		
Children 2–7	6	0.93
Children 7–11	12	0.36
Children over 11	0	–
Other person-centred programmes		
Behavioural approach	26	0.49
Non-behavioural approach	16	0.25

Source: Derived from Durlak and Wells (1997: 129)

specific interventions targeted at 'milestones' (such as the transitions involved
in parental divorce or teenage pregnancy).

A standard search procedure (Durlak and Wells 1997) was then carried out
to find research on cases falling under these categories, resulting in the tally
of initiatives in column two of the table. For each study the various outcomes
assessing the change in the child/adolescent subjects were unearthed and 'the
effect sizes (ESs) were computed using the pooled standard deviation of the
intervention and control group' (Durlak and Wells 1997: 121). After
applying corrections for the small sample sizes in play in some of the
initiatives, the mean effect of each class of programmes was calculated. This
brings us finally to the objective of meta-analysis: a hierarchy of effectiveness
– as in column three.

Let us now move to a realist critique of this strategy. The basic problem
concerns the nature and number of the simplifications that are necessary to
achieve the column of net effects. Each individual intervention is boiled down
to a single measure of effectiveness, which is then drawn together in an
aggregate measure for that sub-class of programmes, which is then compared
with mean effect for other intervention categories. The problem is that this
squeezes out vital explanatory content about the programmes in action. For
the realist, one cannot know how a social programme works without
understanding its multiple mechanisms, outcomes and context. And guess
what are the points of compression in meta-analysis.

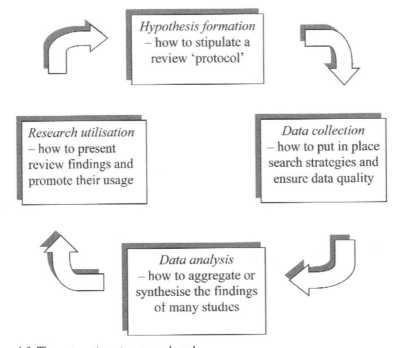

Figure 1.2 The systematic review research cycle

   i   the melding of programme mechanisms;
   ii the oversimplification of programme outcomes;
  iii the concealment of programme contexts.

i Melded mechanisms

Can such an assemblage of policy alternatives constitute a comparison of 'like-with-like', or are they incommensurable interventions that should be judged in their own terms?

To take one example: parenting initiatives may see their pay-off in transformations in daily domestic regimes and in long-term development in children's behaviour. Their evaluation would ideally involve long-term monitoring of both family and child. Yet all Durlak and Wells' studies had to face the single, standard test of success via measures monitoring pre-intervention – post-intervention changes in the child's behaviour.

In short, the categories of meta-analysis have the potential to hide, within and between themselves, significant capacities for generating personal and social change. We need to be terribly careful, therefore, about making any causal imputations to any particular 'category'.

ii Oversimplified outcomes

When we move from cause to effect, the crucial point to recall as we cast our eyes down the outputs of meta-analysis, such as column three in Table 1.1, is that the figures contained therein are means of means of means of means! Outcome measurement is a tourniquet of compression. It begins life by observing how each individual changes on a particular variable and then brings these together as the mean effect for the programme subjects as a whole. Initiatives normally have multiple effects and so their various outcomes, variously measured, are also averaged as the 'pooled effect' for that particular intervention. This, in turn, is melded together with the mean effect from 'study y' from the same subset, which may have used different indicators of change. The conflation process continues until we gather in all the studies within the sub-type, even though by then the aggregation process may have fetched in an even wider permutation of outcome measures. Only then do comparisons begin as we eyeball the mean, mean, mean effects from other sub-categories of programmes. Meta-analysis will always generate its two-decimal-place mean effects but, since it squeezes out much ground-level variation in the outcomes, it remains open to the charge of spurious precision.

iii Concealed contexts

No individual-level intervention works for everyone. No institution-level intervention works everywhere. The net effect of any particular programme is thus made up of the balance of successes and failures of individual subjects and locations. What this points to is the need for a careful look at subject and contextual differences in terms of who succeeds and who fails within any programme. And the point, of course, is that this is denied to a meta-analysis, which needs unequivocal and uniform base-line indicators for each case. At the extreme, we can still learn from a negative net effect of a single evaluation study, since the application of an initiative to the wrong subjects and in the wrong circumstances can leave behind vital clues about what might be the right combination. No such subtlety is available in an approach that simply extracts the net effect from one study and combines it together with other programmes from the same stable to generate an average effect for that sub-class of programmes.

Let me now try to draw together the lessons of the three criticisms of meta-analysis. Arithmetically speaking, the method always 'works' in that it will produce mechanically a spread of net effects of the sort we see in Table 1.1. The all-important question is whether the league table of efficacy produced in this manner should act as an effective guide to future policy making. Should the PPMH meta-analyst advise, for instance, on cutting parenting programmes and increasing affective education and interpersonal problem-solving schemes, especially for the under-7s? My answer would be an indubitable 'no'. The net effects we see in column three do not follow passively from application of that sub-class of programmes but are generated by a range of underlying programme mechanisms (the differences between which are unmonitored), the range of contexts in which the programme is applied, and the variety of measures which are used to tap the outcome data.

Realist synthesis

The realist interpretation of programme efficacy may be expressed as follows (Pawson and Tilley 1997). The causal power of an initiative lies in its underlying mechanism (M), namely the resources (material, cognitive or emotional) it provides that are expected to influence the subject's actions. Whether this mechanism is actually triggered depends on context (C), the characteristics of both the subjects and the programme locality. Programmes, especially over the course of a number of trials, will therefore have diverse impacts over a range of effects, a feature known as the outcome pattern (O) (see Figure 1.3). Following this logic gives us a different focus on the review process. The entry point is perhaps the most significant point of departure. Realism adopts a 'generative' understanding of causation. What this tries to break is the lazy linguistic habit of basing evaluation on the question of whether 'programmes work'. In fact, it is not programmes that work but the resources they offer to enable their subjects to make them work. This process of what subjects do with the intervention stratagem is known as the programme 'mechanism' and it is the pivot around which realist evaluation

Initial programme

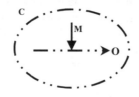

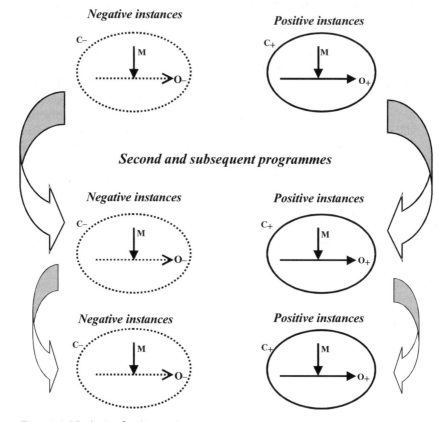

Figure 1.3 The logic of realist synthesis

revolves. There is no expectation, however, that mechanisms work uniformly, for their causal powers are always contingent on context.

Such reasoning allows us to pinpoint the juncture when meta-analysis becomes ensnared and supplies a way of untying the tangle. The fundamental flaw in work such as the above is that outcomes are being compared by 'programme', a level of aggregation which prevents any analysis of the mechanisms and context that actually constitute these interventions. The solution comes in two parts, the first of which is to change the unit of analysis in systematic review. Since it is 'programme mechanisms' that trigger change rather than 'programmes' as such, it is much more sensible to base any systematic review on 'families of mechanisms' rather than on 'families of programmes'. Mechanisms are the active ingredients of social interventions and it is imperative that they are identified and conceptualised in order to become the locus of comparison for the whole exercise.

The second tidal change in logic is to consider what is happening when, in meta-analysis, studies are 'pooled'. The language of aggregation and the statistics of the weighted-average dominate the exercise. The image is of the same programme being played out on a larger and larger canvas. Realists place no faith in universal remedies; the same mechanism will fire, misfire or go completely unnoticed according to circumstances. The way of 'pulling this together' is to try to account for such variation and this means that the essential point of review is not aggregation but 'comparison'.

This feature of programme building provides a great opportunity for the study of what realists call 'contrastives' (Lawson 1997). In common sense terms, this amounts to saying that more consequential lessons are to be learned if we try to test out the same policy idea by seeing how it turns out in diverse settings. The basic strategy is depicted in the main body of Figure 1.3 and it is based upon following the fortunes of the 'dominant mechanism' (M), through which it is assumed that a programme works. Realism assumes that each time a programme mechanism is brought into operation, it will meet with both success and failure. Programme A is then reviewed with the aim of trying to distinguish for which subjects and in which circumstances it has been successful and unsuccessful. 'Success' is depicted throughout the figure by a solid line and 'failure', appropriately enough, is signalled by a dashed line. The reviewer's basic task is to sift through the mixed fortunes of the programme (both solid and dashed lines), attempting to discover those contexts (C+) that have produced solid and successful outcomes (O+) from those contexts (C-) that induce failure (O-).

The review process is then repeated across other initiatives featuring the same underlying mechanism with the aim of gathering together the various permutations of success and failure. In realist jargon, the aim is to differentiate and accumulate evidence on positive and negative CMO configurations. If all goes to plan, the ensuing policy advice will be to seek out the latter and avoid the former.

I close this sketch of principles of realist synthesis by considering its end-product. The contrast may be drawn pointedly:

i meta-analysis performs calculations to reveal 'best buys';
ii realist synthesis delves into inconsistencies to build 'programme theories'.

The basic idea of systematic review is to draw transferable lessons from existing programmes and initiatives. Realist synthesis assumes that the transmission of lessons occurs through a process of theory-building rather than assembling empirical generalisations. There is an obvious affinity here with the 'theory-driven' approaches to evaluation (Bickman 1987; Chen and Rossi 1992; Connell *et al.* 1995; Pawson and Tilley 1997). Each of these begins with the notion that programmes are conjectures taking the form: 'if we apply programme X this unleashes process Y, which will result in Z'. The task of evaluation by these lights is to gather evidence to see if the programme theory occurs as planned and, if it should not, then to amend it to account for the divergent outcomes.

Realist synthesis accelerates this process around many, many cycles with a systematic review of an ensemble of different programmes purporting to use the same underlying mechanism. Knowledge resolutions occur as follows. The process starts with programme A, which we discover works in certain expected ways for certain subjects. We accept these findings not only because we are able to show the appropriate correlation but also because we are able to produce a theory of how it works. We then take this explanation to a second programme B, which works ostensibly using the same programme theory. If B performs exactly as predicted, then we have achieved an extension of the scope of the theory. If B has mixed results (as it will) we will need to enlarge, amend and re-specify the theory. The process goes on through an examination of programmes C, D, E, etc. This process of *theory-contingent transfer* (Shadish *et al.*, 1991) is depicted in Figure 1.3 by the curved left and right arrows linking the different initiatives.

Social interventions are so complex that there is little hope of reproducing them lock, stock and barrel and, even if one could, they are so context sensitive that the 'same' assemblage may then go on to misfire. However, what one can do by way of planning in open systems is to gather vast experience of the options and possibilities and to figure out what kinds-of-things work for what kinds-of-subjects in what kinds-of-situations. One can multiply that experience by looking beyond the administrative category and into the essential policy ideas. Such a process may allow the policy-maker a better chance of steering clear of past mistakes – whilst not, of course, avoiding new ones. Cumulative knowledge about the whos, whys and wherefores of programme success is not tied to the paraphernalia of each initiative but occurs through a process of abstraction. Realist synthesis thus ends up with theory.

Public disclosure policy

I now turn to a miniature demonstration project that will attempt to put into practice the rationale for realist synthesis described above. The policy intervention under scrutiny here is the idea of using 'public disclosure' to overcome recalcitrant behaviour – a strategy often better known as 'naming and shaming'. Policies are often borrowed from one domain to the other, as the following brief catalogue suggests:

- Sex offender registration ('Megan's Law')
- Naming prostitutes' clients ('outing johns')
- School 'league tables' (on exam performance, absence rates, etc.)
- Identification of and special measures for 'failing schools'
- Hospital 'star ratings' (UK) and mortality and surgeon 'report cards' (US)
- EU beach cleanliness standards and 'kite marking'
- Local press adverts for poll tax non-payment and council rent arrears
- Car crime indices and car safety reports
- Mandatory (public) arrest for domestic violence
- Roadside hoardings naming speeding drivers.

Whilst the 'targets' involved here are very different, all of the above involve some 'misdemeanour' being drawn to the attention of a wider public with the idea that 'sunlight is the best of disinfectants: electric light the most efficient policeman' (Louis Brandeis's 'dictum', quoted in Fisse and Braithwaite 1983: vii).

Disclosure policies are characterised by a sequence of mechanisms rather than a 'master mechanism'. No epistemological alarm bells ring here, however, for all the schools of theory-driven evaluation anticipate that a programme will contain multiple mechanisms, and in an earlier work it has been shown that even a simple mechanical initiative like CCTV surveillance generates its effect in multiple ways (Pawson and Tilley 1997). The first step in the review of public disclosure policies is thus to extract the sequence of mechanisms to be put to scrutiny and this is summarised as Figure 1.4. 'Public disclosure' is not a singular measure, nor even a pair (naming and shaming), but in fact has four identifiable stages.

Step 1: problem identification

The first step in all initiatives listed above is to gather data to throw fresh light on the problems to be tackled. At first sight this is a mechanical process, classifying and enumerating items such as: exams passed, waiting-list lengths, or sex offences committed. But these 'classifications', 'registrations', 'league tables' are not neutral facts; they always carry a purpose. They are precepts. They contain, in the very way they are put together, an implicit explanation of the behaviour that is measured. For instance, one might enumerate exam passes by pupil, by teacher, by school or by district; the choice of 'unit of analysis' is clearly not a 'neutral' or a 'natural' one. A breakdown by pupil will tend to assign responsibility for educational achievement to the individual, whereas a breakdown by school suggests that exam success and failure lies at the institutional level. Hence the key mechanism involved in stage one of the process depends on the extent to which this official explanation of the problem draws widespread support.

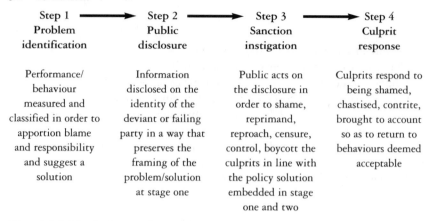

Step 1 ➝	Step 2 ➝	Step 3 ➝	Step 4
Problem identification	Public disclosure	Sanction instigation	Culprit response
Performance/ behaviour measured and classified in order to apportion blame and responsibility and suggest a solution	Information disclosed on the identity of the deviant or failing party in a way that preserves the framing of the problem/solution at stage one	Public acts on the disclosure in order to shame, reprimand, reproach, censure, control, boycott the culprits in line with the policy solution embedded in stage one and two	Culprits respond to being shamed, chastised, contrite, brought to account so as to return to behaviours deemed acceptable

Figure 1.4 Public disclosure policies (policy architect's theory)

Blame and responsibility are already allocated in the drawing up of this official data. The public gaze is directed at certain wrongdoers and for this mechanism to fire depends on widespread public, civic and legal support for the initial framing of the problem.

The programme theory emerging here is that public notification programmes should quantify the issue to be addressed in a way that allocates responsibility for the problem. Here, I will draw the contrast between the UK Home Office's Car Theft Index, the registration of high-risk sex offenders in the US's Megan's Law, and the publication of school performance tables by the Department for Education in the UK.

The Car Theft Index (Houghton 1992) itemises risk of theft into three categories: *red* (more than 21 cars in every 1000 on the road stolen); *amber* (between 4 and 21 per K); *green* (less than 4 per K). Actuarial tables are then supplied in a particularly user-friendly way in booklets and on the Web. Manufacturers are distinguished and colour-coded tables are supplied for every model and year of each car on the road (providing there are sufficient numbers for statistically reliable results).

Sex offenders who prey on the young range from homicidal psychopathic sadists to nuisance offenders inappropriately attached to children. The variation in the likelihood of individuals re-offending and in the danger they pose is acknowledged in the US registers via a rating system that is applied in the majority of jurisdictions. Sex offenders are classified Tier I (low risk), Tier II (moderate risk) and Tier III (high risk). These risk calculations then anchor the rest of the system, with the detail of information monitored and the extent of public notification depending on the tier to which the offender is assigned.

The data published in the school performance tables are much more compendious. The first major public examinations (GCSE) occur in the fifth year of secondary education and the Department for Education published the following information in respect of them:

- Number of 15-year-old pupils
- Percentage achieving 5 or more GCSE passes at grades A*–C
- Percentage achieving 5 or more GCSE passes at grades A*–G
- Percentage achieving 1 or more GCSE passes at grades A*–G
- Numbers and percentage passes of those taking other (vocational) qualifications
- Average points score per 15-year-old
- School progress measure
- Number of pupils in year 11 regardless of age
- Percentage of these achieving 5 or more GCSE passes at grades A*–C
- Number of pupils aged 15 with special education needs
- Plus a range of other 'background indicators' for each school.

Let us first contrast the integrity of the data collected in each case. Without valid and reliable information at step one, the remainder of the sequence is palpably less predictable. The Car Theft Index is produced by the Home Office, using data from the Police National Computer and information from the Driver and Vehicle Licensing Authority. There are some problems due to mistakes in recording registration numbers and with cars being reported stolen erroneously, but these errors are not considered biased against model range and the base-line information has never been seriously challenged. The education data come either from routine administrative records or the public examination system with in-built and fastidious quality control systems. Although interpretation of the school performance data is (as we shall see) hotly contested, its reliability is rarely questioned.

Sex offender registration, by contrast, operates with a huge array of operational practices and definitions. Presser and Gunnison (1999: 301) describe the range of methods in play at the time of submission of their paper as follows: 'Some states (e.g. California) rely solely on criminal history. Some states defer to the determination of one law enforcement official, such as the county prosecutor. Some (e.g. Georgia) automatically subject certain sex offenders, such as paedophiles, to notification requirements. Finally, some states use actuarial risk instruments.' Lonborn (1998) quotes an Assistant Bureau Chief in the Illinois State Police as follows: 'We have some great stories. We registered an 86-year-old man in a nursing home, a quadriplegic and an individual in the Federal Witness Protection program. We even registered a man currently in a coma, so I think the program has been pretty aggressive.'

A rather pragmatic programme theory emerges from these comparisons, which is that public notification programmes should only be attempted in respect of activities for which it is possible to extract valid and reliable information. Even across the small number of cases considered here, we can see that it doesn't work like this at all. The reason is that actual programme theory in place at step one is not about recording actions and events passively, rather its purpose is actively to apportion blame and responsibility for major issues of public concern.

A closer comparison of Megan's Law and the school league tables reveals some interesting contextual differences in this respect. The former has been challenged repeatedly in the courts on the grounds that harassment and vigilantism often follow public disclosure and that the inaccuracies and inconsistencies associated with the assessment into tier III mean that risk classifications have no constitutional basis. More to the point, however, is its survival in the face of almost all such challenges and adjudications. The end result is that, imperfect as they are, the definitions and classifications that make up the registration process have rolled forth into the public domain. Empirical evidence on this point comes from many sources (Levi 2000; Earl-Hubbard 1996; National Centre for Missing and Exploited Children 1997).

It is possible to give a flavour of some of the judgements as follows: 'The Registration and Notification Laws are not in themselves retributive laws, but laws designed to give people a chance to protect themselves and their children. They do not represent the slightest departure from our State's or our county's fundamental belief that criminals, convicted and punished, have paid their debt to society and are not to be punished further. They represent only the conclusion that society has the right to know of their presence not to punish them, but in order to protect itself ... The characteristics of some of [these offenders], and the statistical information concerning them, make it clear that ... reoffense is a realistic risk, and knowledge of their presence a realistic protection against it.' (Levi 2000: 580 quoting Doe v. Poritz.)

The framing of the school league tables has taken a much more tortuous path. Its beginnings were in a body of academic work known as 'school effectiveness research'. This sought to show that, even when social and other factors were taken into account, there remained differences amongst schools which could be ascribed to the quality of schooling itself (Rutter et al. 1979: Coleman et al. 1996). Such a notion appealed to successive governments in the UK because it carried the implication that by changing schools standards could be driven up. One way in which this was contemplated was the 'informed choices' mechanism (DfE 1992) in which information on the examination results of all schools was published. Parents upon studying the information would be able to discriminate between schools. Under the introduction of a quasi-market regime, the best would therefore be supported and the rest would have to pull up their socks.

When the idea was first introduced, the results were published in 'raw' form without any adjustment for intake and a major furore followed about the failure to compare 'like with like' (Thomas 1998; Goldstone and Myers 1996). Schools with high achieving intakes do well on the tables for that reason alone. In this case, the resulting challenge was successful (up to a point) in that by 1998 'value added' measures, taking into account the effects of differential inputs, were incorporated in the performance tables (Saunders

1999). It appears as the 'school progress measure' in the growing mound of information provided as listed above.

How does one account for the vast difference in the mode, magnitude and reliability of information passed to the public in theses two cases? It is not too difficult to put a finger on the likely contextual differences. Megan's Law swept on to the statutes following the enormous public outcry at the brutal death of Megan Kanka at the hands of released sex offender Jesse Timmendequas. The courts responded to the wave of sentiment that 'something must be done' and were thus able to brush aside the constitutional challenges forwarded by minor lobbies (released sex offenders and some civil rights bodies). Blame is thus squarely and conveniently apportioned to the pathological individual rather than the system that releases him. School league tables, by contrast, emerged as a process of negotiation between educational research foundations, government agencies, unions and politicians. The initial push was an academic idea grabbed by politicians, and there are interesting accounts of how gamekeepers turned poachers during the course of the development of the tables (Goldstein and Woodhouse 2000). The school effectiveness research that spawned the idea that 'schools make a difference' actually assumed that pupils, teachers, schools and governments could all make a difference. And this multi-level account of educational success gradually crept into the published information

The nature and integrity of the published information obviously colour all that follows in these initiatives. In these three instances we see information that is constitutionally authoritative but capricious, that is consensual but complex, and that is relatively unchallenged and uncomplicated. No doubt there are several other permutations. Part of the explanation is to do with the complexity of the behaviour under scrutiny. But we also have the beginning of a theory to explain the content of notifications in respect of the stakeholder alliances and the power differentials that bring them into play.

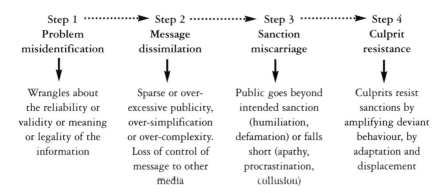

Figure 1.5 Public disclosure policies (unintended consequences)

Step 2: public disclosure

The whole point of public disclosure is that, on hearing the 'news', it becomes the public's responsibility to deliver the remedy. It is the success or failure of the exchange of ideas that is the key mechanism at the second stage of the process. The preferred solution to the problem is also usually seeded at stage two. The body of information is usually published alongside advice on how to act upon it. The favoured motif here is 'an informed public' being able to safeguard its children against sex attack, being able choose the better schools, being able to opt for the shorter waiting-list, etc. The mechanism under test in the second part of the review is thus about the integrity of the official framing of the problem and whether it holds in the passage to the public. A 'simulation' exercise by Petrosino and Petrosino (1999) takes on the difficult task of trying to estimate the difference Megan's Law makes to the capacity of the public to defend itself against predatory attacks. Registers were created largely in response to stranger-predatory crimes, which are relatively rare and obviously difficult to predict. This research attempts to answer the question: 'In what percentage of sex attacks will notification give the victim (or their family or community) a prior chance to observe the threat and thus to avoid or avert it?'

Evaluating 'preventative measures' provides research with one of its toughest tasks, for it amounts to trying to put a figure on what-might-have-happened-but-did-not. Petrosino and Petrosino (1999) confronted the task ingeniously by working backwards from actual offences, seeking to discover retrospectively how many current offenders *would have been* under surveillance given the newly prevailing arrangements. Their estimate is as follows:

> Using secondary data on 136 criminal sexual psychopaths, the authors found that 27 percent of the sample had a prior conviction that met the requirement of the Massachusetts Registry Law before their most recent sex crime. Of these 36 offenders who would have been eligible for the registry, 12 committed a stranger-predatory offence: 24 offended against family, friends or co-workers. It is assumed here that those without a record are untouched by the notification process. It is also supposed that notification has little protective effect on the victim's 'associates', who will in all likelihood already know of the previous convictions.
>
> (Petrosino and Petrosino 1999: 149)

Petrosino and Petrosino's next step was to examine the *modus operandi* of the twelve stranger-predatory offenders (who would in future become registrants) in order to estimate the likelihood of aggressive, proactive warnings getting to potential victims and the victims being able to defend themselves. In half a dozen of these cases, it was thought unlikely that the victim could have been forewarned or forearmed by notification because these six offenders were from out of state, and a couple of them just ignored outright the community's capacity to respond (kidnap from a public place). The simulated notification chain thus ends with six victims who may have had any realistic chance of responding to warnings (Figure 1.6).

A study carried out in London aimed to test out parents' use and understanding of the school league tables (West *et al.* 1998). Some 100 mothers of children about to transfer to secondary schools on which the performance information had recently been published were interviewed. Only 8 per cent reported that they had not seen the information. The remaining sample were asked whether they 'understood the tables'. The performance data cover a lot of ground and are published in several forms and, as the reader can imagine, they are somewhat brutal in terms of volume alone. A slight majority of parents (55 per cent) who had seen the performance tables claimed to have understood them. Unsurprisingly, this result varied significantly with parents' education.

In terms of theory development, this pair of examples does not prompt any general theories about contextual variation in interpretation of the published materials. The interesting contrastives are in fact within cases – families and relatives versus strangers in the former, and relatively well and lesser educated parents in the latter. The main reason for the illustrations is in fact to show how the effects of the different mechanisms of public disclosure interact and compound as they pass down the implementation chain.

We have seen complexity build at stage one and we have seen comprehension slide at stage two – precisely for those parents who are likely to find themselves on the receiving end of poor schooling.

136 serious sex offences (offenders considered criminal sexual psychopaths)

100 no previous criminal record

36 had a previous offence that would have been eligible for the registry

24 victims within family or known to offender

12 committed stranger-predatory offence

6 offenders from out of state

6 cases remain with the potential to respond to community notification

Figure 1.6 The diminishing target of Megan's Law in Massachusetts

Step 3: sanction instigation

At stage three, we come to the policy-maker's expectations about the safeguards and sanctions that are envisaged as a result of public notification. An informed public is supposed to rethink its choices – but no single line of defence is foreseen. Clearly, the people are meant to respond in a manner that befits the problem.

By getting transgression out into the open, the public is supposed to sweep it away. So goes the theory at work in the third stage of these initiatives, though there is no uniform expectation of the nature of public sanction.

Schram and Milloy (1995) have conducted the only study on Megan's Law to approximate to the so-called gold standard of the controlled comparison. They compared the recidivism rates of members of the first group of sex offenders released to Washington's notification regime (1990–1993) to a 'matched' sample selected from offenders released prior to the enactment of the new law. Matching was performed by ensuring both groups had the same overall spread of offences, as well as the same array of victim types. Recidivism rates were calculated by tracking each offender from release, the key comparison being performed in terms of the percentage re-arrested from each group for a sexual offence within four-and-a-half years of release. The headline results from the study are as follows:

- At the end of the 54 months at risk in the community, the notification group had a slightly lower estimate rate of sexual recidivism (19 per cent) than the comparison group (22 per cent). This difference was not found to be statistically significant.
- Although there were no significant differences in overall levels of general recidivism, the timing of re-arrest was significantly different for the notification and comparison groups. Offenders subjected to community notification were arrested for new crimes much more quickly than comparable offenders who were released without notification (Schram and Milloy 1995: 3).

To be sure, this is a single, small-scale, state-specific study. Great disappointment followed the publication of these re-offence figures. This together with other evidence indicates that public surveillance might have a rather small role in the containment of sex offenders. There is, however, a stunning clue within Schram and Milloy's results that may be a pointer to the nature of the sanctions that follow disclosure. Re-offence remained unchanged but the speed of arrest quickened in the post-1990 group. This is tantamount to saying that the regime change favoured detection rather than prevention. Law enforcement has a much-enhanced weapon to record the whereabouts and *modus operandi* of active offenders and this may be the active mechanism induced by Megan's Law (Pawson 2002).

The Car Theft Index (CTI) was introduced into the UK in 1992 and has been an annual production ever since. From 1993 there has been a steady decline in car theft, following the introduction by manufacturers of a range of security features. In the early period of the index, new and recent model cars were stolen more often, the pickings being obviously much greater. The position is currently reversed, with cars lacking the now standard, manufacturer-installed, high-tech immobilisers becoming the favoured target. None of these overall shifts, however, demonstrats a shaming causal nexus.

Motor manufacturers compete with each other. They tend to spend on items they suppose will increase the allure of a model to the public and to make savings on matters not estimated to be widespread priorities. Hence, once upon a time, it could be said: 'the notion that they might compete in developing a more secure vehicle for the better good of the British public was quite foreign to them' (Laycock and Tilley 1995). This suggests that the 'shaming action' of the CTI could not have had sufficient clout to be entirely responsible for the widespread upgrading of vehicle security. Such a speculation is deepened given that the public was for a time also shielded from concerns about security by the insurance system. But this context, too, was about to change.

The index was introduced in response to rapidly increasing thefts. At the same time, the UK car insurance industry was on the end of its first serious losses and beginning to move from a tactic of spreading risks to the point where it would refuse to insure vehicles of high-risk design. For a time it became impossible to insure particular makes and models except at exorbitant prices and, through its pocket, the public became aware, perhaps for the first time, of the real costs of poor vehicle security. The link from theft rates to market concerns really became consolidated, however, with a leap in rigour of the 'group rating system'. This resulted in much more steeply graduated insurance premiums (Roberts 1997). A 'vehicle security assessment' administered by *Thatcham UK* became formally part of the grouping process and this had the effect of pitching information on car security directly into the cost of car ownership. Realism always questions 'what it is about a policy that makes it work', and in this case the mechanism may well have been double-headed, with shaming sanctions giving way to consumer forces. It is likely that only the first CTI had the shock-troop's function, which was then consolidated by the insurance infantry. There is little reason to believe that on its sixth and seventh outings the CTI contains fresh information capable of high levels of shaming and this transformation of causal powers may be entirely typical of the successful disclosure initiative.

Hospital 'report cards' or 'star ratings' have been introduced in both the US and the UK. These public data bases are particularly well advanced in some US states, which disclose performance data right down to the level of the individual surgeon. Marshall *et al.*'s (2000) review of the response to health care performance data in the US examines the applicability of the 'public accountability', 'market orientation' and 'professional orientation' models of public disclosure. Much of the political rhetoric and published programme theory on 'report cards' in the US anticipated that disclosure would bring discipline to health provision by better informing *purchasing decisions*. The reviewers conclude, however, that 'currently available performance data has little impact on consumer choice' (Marshall *et al.* 2000: 9).

There is a prima facie case for considering that publicity will shape medical markets in the US, where there is quite a robust health market because of the substantial purchasing power of employer-managed care plans. However, Marshall's review reveals that these users seem to prefer 'process to outcome data' (patient satisfaction scores over performance data) and even 'utilisation rates over clinical measures' (turnstile turnaround to mortality measures). Market-inspired changes seem to be restricted to the provision of entirely new services rather than adjustments to clinical practices (Longo *et al.* 1997). In other words, a hospital only responded economically when report cards revealed complete inactivity in a particular health pursuit – to which the response was to fill the 'gap in the market'.

Is there a pattern to these three instances? Although popularly known as 'naming and shaming', public disclosure outcomes in these cases do not seem to depend, in the long-term anyway, on the dishonour of the culprits. Shaming is a 'self-conscious emotion' or a 'reputational mechanism' (Braithwaite 1989) and may, therefore, only be expected to act as a trigger to longer-term response. Certainly, sex offenders have to live with registration, car manufacturers cannot abandon production in the light of security classification, and hospitals (and schools) have to get on with the daily grind despite their place in the league tables.

So what are the prime mechanisms? Well, Megan's Law seems to work through practical policing; vehicle security improvements may have arrived mainly as a response to the insurance premium market; and hospital report cards seem to have been absorbed principally by the bureaucracy. Public disclosure is meant to change behaviour – but seems effective only in relation to what organises that behaviour in the first place. What is more, in each of the above cases it is the information providers rather than the public who are the key agents of change.

Step 4: culprit response (outcomes)

In the final phase of these initiatives, we reach the policy-maker's expectations about how the various recalcitrants will respond. The glare of publicity together with increased public involvement is supposed to induce the shamed to mend their ways. Again, no single pathway of response is envisaged on the part of those being 'labelled'.

Are transgressors returned to the fold in the harsh light of publicity or do they twist and resist? A frequent target of disclosure initiatives is the class of debtors, defaulters and non-payers. One such group were the poll-tax protesters in the UK in 1991.

The 'naming' in this instance took the form of a whole series of warnings, followed by listing the names and addresses of defaulters in the local newspapers. It is the political context of the measure that is of interest here. The 'community charge' was a new form of local taxation, levied with a flat rate per head and thus (un)popularly know as the 'poll tax'. It had an exceedingly difficult legislative passage, was subject to much protest (Burns 1992) and was indeed withdrawn and amended subsequently – being deemed 'uncollectable'. In the midst of this action, local qualitative accounts (Reynolds 1992) reveal that many defaulters were overjoyed and indeed celebrated en masse when their names appeared in the local papers. Here we arrive at the key atom of evidence. Being subject to disclosure in these circumstances became a badge of honour.

A more complex response to public disclosure has emerged from schools, itself a function of their league table position. Several tactics, which fall somewhat short of the intended pedagogic changes, are open to the school wanting to up its league table position. One method is to remove from the school roll children who were persistently late or absent, especially if they also had poor achievement records. Although it is mere correlational evidence, the number of exclusions in secondary schools rose from 3,000 to over 10,000 in the first three years of the tables (Gillborn 1996).

The key indicator that first reached the public eye was the school's percentage of 'good passes' (considered historically as grades A* to C) at GCSE. This encouraged schools to concentrate on getting the C–D borderline cohort up to scratch. Klienman *et al.* (1998) report how some schools introduced teacher mentoring, volunteer helpers, after-school coaching and holiday revision courses aimed, quite unusually, at this marginal, low-to-middle ranking group. Interestingly, the government became sufficiently aware of this targeting and responded themselves in 1997 with the addition of a better-rounded indicator, the 'average points score' per pupil. Using this indicator to map changes over the initial period of the league tables provides some unwelcome news about 'driving up standards' (West and Pennel 2000). From 1993 to 1997, the top decile of students improved grades by 4.4 per cent, whilst the bottom decile's performance actually fell by 0.1 per cent (excluding exclusions!).

The most obvious non-educational route to higher performance is to 'cream skim'. If those responsible for admission are able to select certain pupils and select-out others, this itself will drive up standards. Gerwitz *et al.* (1993) recorded some of the actions taken to attract high attaining/middle-class pupils, which included the re-introduction of streaming, de-integration of special needs pupils, informal selection at interview and reputation building by increasing exclusions. The more sophisticated 'school progress' indicators show that schools making most progress on the raw grades do so on the back of changes in intake (West and Pennel 2000).

The reaction of sex offenders to Megan's Law, perhaps not surprisingly, is overwhelmingly negative. But this is not the bravura opposition mounted by the poll-tax protesters. Sex offenders operate by stealth and secrecy and their main reaction to community surveillance is anguish and the desire to return to anonymity. This quiet resistance operates at every point in the process. Indeed, even at pre-release, it appears that the wiliest of inmates may attempt to circumvent the law. English *et al.* (1996) note that in Oregon, after notification was first enacted, 'there was a huge scramble among offenders to admit to their crime' (English *et al.* 1996: 7). The inmates' ploy, it seemed, was to attempt to demonstrate that they were sufficiently on the road to recovery that they did not need to be subject to the highest levels of public notification.

Released offenders are responsible for maintaining and updating their own initial registration. Here then is another rather sinister opportunity for sliding into obscurity, with Bedarf (1995) reporting that in Tennessee 28 per cent of offenders move without registering again.

Finally, in this section I want to consider the reactions of Ford Motor Company officials to the Car Theft Index. I have suggested above that long-term changes in car security in the UK are probably due to a market mechanism and the influence of the insurance industry. The index, however, may have operated as something like a shaming sanction – if only in the first wave of adverse publicity. In the first outing of the index, one manufacturer in particular was caught in the spotlight. The presentation of the data in the first report (Houghton 1992) highlighted the 'worst of the worst'. Seven ranges of cars were identified as 'high risk' in the 1992 report and Ford made six of them. Ford's annual reports show that, shortly after this disclosure, the company made the decision to transform vehicle security (the introduction of an entirely new key system) and from 1992 to 1994 the index data reveal a 60 per cent improvement in the rate of theft across the Ford range.

This section reveals some marked contrasts in the responses of different groups upon their actions being thrown open to public scrutiny. The whole purpose of this paper has been to show that evidence-based policy must in fact take the form of evidence-refined theory. And the key weapon in that quest is to examine the fortunes of the same policy in different contexts. So what has been discovered in this final section? Poll tax protesters revelled in the glory of publicity. Schools followed the first law of performance indicators – attend to the indicators rather than the performance. Sex offenders tried their all to slink from the community gaze. And board room wisdom was that in adversity corporations should look to protect their reputation.

Is there a theory to be developed to explain this outcome pattern? In this instance there is no need for the intrepid reviewer to scratch his head in search of fresh conjectures. All this is the stuff of a venerable old theory and a middle-range theory to boot. Table 1.2 plots the basic framework of Merton's 'reference group theory' (Merton 1968). The core idea, put very simply, is that most social activities will establish an in-group and an out-group. In trying to understand the behaviour of these parties it is necessary to understand their precise reference group affiliation. In particular, the theory contrasts the different behaviours of out-group members in terms of whether they have the capacity for membership of the mainstream and whether they have the desire to so belong.

The core aim of all policies under consideration here, put very, very simply, is for the in-group to apply public pressure on the out-group to conform to the highest or, at least, acceptable standards. The response, for Merton, will be shaped by the group's basic motivations and capabilities. Poll-tax protesters are the paradigmatic antagonistic ineligibles and unlikely to be pulled or shoved, shamed or enticed into conforming. Sex offenders are detached non-members, and whether on the road to reform or re-offence are wary of close scrutiny by in-group members. Schools that are poor performers normally aspire to improve their league positions, whilst not often possessing the capacity to do so. Such marginals, according to Merton, will often attempt to take short cuts into membership, gaining some of the trappings of membership without the proper rights of passage. Finally, we have the case of Ford. They are, of course, full in-group members and, strictly speaking, not on the conceptual matrix on display in Table 1.2. If, however, we consider the fall from grace represented by slipshod production as a wobble in their membership, then Merton's theory tells us that eligible candidates for the in-group will do all in their power to promote (or in this case to recover) their reputation. For them, it is a priceless asset.

The policy community has latched on to the idea of using systematic review in order to go back and revisit all the accumulated evidence about particular initiatives. The aim of this paper has been to show that such a strategy can be quite fruitless without the guiding hand of theory. Learning from the past is also a matter of also retaining the hard-won lessons of the old theories.

Table 1.2   Merton's typology of aspirations to group membership of eligibles and non-eligibles

Attitude toward membership	*Eligible for membership*	*Ineligible for membership*
Aspire to belong	Candidate for membership	Marginal Man
Indifferent to affiliation	Potential member	Detached non-member
Motivated not to belong	Autonomous non-member	Antagonistic non-member

Source: Merton (1968: p. 344)

References

Bedarf, A. (1995) 'Examining sex offender community notification laws', *California Law Review*, 83, 3: 885–939.

Bickman, L. (ed.) (1987) 'Using program theory in evaluation', in *New Directions for Program Evaluation*, No 33. San Francisco: Jossey Bass.

Braithwaite, J. (1989) *Crime, Shame and Reintegration*, Cambridge: Cambridge University Press.

Burns, D. (1992) *Poll Tax Rebellion*, Stirling: AK Press

Chen, H. and Rossi, P. (1992) *Using Theory to Improve Policy and Programme Evaluations*, Westport: Greenwood Press.

Coleman J., Campbell, E., Hobson, C. and MacPartland, J. (1996) *Equality of Educational Opportunity*, Washington, DC, Government Printing Office.

Connell, J., Kubish, A., Schorr, L. and Weiss, C. (1995) *New Approaches to Evaluating Community Initiatives*, New York: Aspen Institute.

Department for Education (1992) *School Performance Tables: Public Examination Results 1992*, London: HMSO.

Durlak, J. and Wells, A. (1997) 'Primary prevention mental health programs for children and adolescents: a meta-analytic review', *American Journal of Community Psychology*, 25, 2: 115–52.

Earl-Hubbard, M. (1996) 'The child sex offender registration laws', *Northwestern Law Review*, 90: 788–862.

English, K., Pullen, S. and Jones, L. (eds) (1996) *Managing Adult Sex Offenders: A Containment Approach*, US Dept. of Justice, Lexington, Kentucky: American Probation and Parole Association.

European Commission (2001) *Governance in the EU: A White Paper*, European Commission: Brussels. COM (2001) 428 final.

Fisse, B. and Braithwaite, J. (1983) *The Impact of Publicity on Corporate Offenders*, Albany: State University of New York Press.

Gerwitz, S., Ball, S. and Boew, R. (1995) *Markets, Choices and Equity in Education*, Buckingham: Open University Press.

Gillborn, D. (1996) 'Exclusions from school', *Viewpoint*, No. 5, Institute of Education: London.

Goldstein, H. and Woodhouse, G. (2000) 'School effectiveness research and educational policy', *Oxford Review of Education*, 26: 353–63.

Goldstone, H. and Myers, K. (1996) 'Freedom of information: towards a code for performance indicators', *Research Intelligence*, 57: 12–16.

Houghton, G. (1992) *Car Theft in England and Wales: The Home Office Car Theft Index*, Crime Prevention Unit Paper No. 33, London: HMSO.

Klienman, M., West, A. and Sparkes, J. (1998) *Investing in Employability*, London: LSE.

Lawson, T. (1997) *Economics and Reality*, London: Routledge.

Laycock, G. and Tilley, N. (1995) 'Implementing crime prevention' in M. Tonray and D. Farrington *Building a Safer Society*; Crime and Justice 19: 535–84, Chicago: University of Chicago.

Levi, R. (2000) 'The mutuality of risk and community: the adjudication of community notification statutes', *Economy and Society*, 29, 578–601.

Lonborn, K. (1998) 'The Illinois registration and notification system for sex offenders', *Proceedings of the Bureau of Justice Statistics*, National Conference on Sex Offender Registries.

Longo, D., Land, G., Schramm, W., Fraas, J., Hoskins, B. and Howell,V. (1997) 'Consumer reports in health care: do they make a difference?', *Journal of the American Medical Association*, 278: 1579–84.

Marshall, M., Shekelle, E., Brook, R. and Leatherman, N. (2000) *Dying to Know: Public Release about Quality of Health Care*, London: Nuffield Trust.

Merton, R. (1968, 3rd edn) *Social Theory and Social Structure*, New York: Free Press.

National Center for Missing and Exploited Children (1997) *The Constitutionality of Statutes Requiring Sex Offenders to Register*, VA: MCMEC.

Pawson, R. (2002) *Does Megan's Law Work? A Theory-Driven Systematic Review*, Working Paper 9, ESRC Centre for Evidence-Based Policy and Practice.

Pawson, R. and Tilley, N. (1997) *Realistic Evaluation*, London: Sage.

Petrosino, A. and Petrosino, C. (1999) 'The public safety potential of Megan's law in Massachusetts: an assessment from a sample of criminal sexual psychopaths', *Crime and Delinquency*, 45: 140–58.

Poole, C. and Lieb, R. (1996) *Community Notification in Washington State Washington: Decision Making and Costs*, State Institute for Public Policy, Olympia, WA.

Presser, L. and Gunnison, E. (1999) 'Strange bedfellows: is sex offender notification a form of community justice?', *Crime and Delinquency*, 45: 299–315.

Reynolds, M. (1992) *Uncollectable*, Salford: Greater Manchester Anti-Poll Tax Federation.

Roberts, K. (1977) 'The British insurance industry's criteria for vehicle security: a solution to escalating car crime', Paper presented to the *SAE Global Development Conference*, Detroit.

Rutter, M., Maughan, B., Mortimore, P. and Ouston, P. (1979) *Fifteen Thousand Hours*, London: Open Books.

Saunders, L. (1999) 'A brief history of educational "value added": how did we get there?', *School Effectiveness and School Improvement*, 10: 233–56.

Schram, D. and Milloy, C. (1995) *Community Notification: A Study of Offender Characteristics and Recidivism*, Washington State Institute for Public Policy, Seattle.

Shadish, W., Cook, T. and Levison, L. (1991) *Foundations of Program Evaluation*, Newbury Park: Sage.

Sutton, A., Abrams, K. and Jones, D. (2001) 'An illustrated guide to meta-analysis', *Journal of Evaluation of Clinical Practice*, 7: 135–48.

Thomas, S . (1998) 'Value-added measures of school effectiveness in the UK', *Prospects*, 28: 91–108.

Towner, E., Dowswell, T. and Jarvis, S. (1996) *Reducing Childhood Accidents – The Effectiveness of Health Promotion Interventions: A Literature Review*, Health Education Authority.

West, A. and Pennel, H. (2000) 'Publishing school examination results in England: incentives and consequences', *Educational Studies*, Vol. 26: 421–36

West, A., Noden, P., Edge, A. and David, M. (1998) 'Parental involvement in education and out of school', *British Educational Research Journal*, Vol. 24: 461–84.

2 Complex and contingent causation – the implications of complex realism for quantitative modelling

The case of housing and health

Dave Byrne

'The housing and illness literature is fascinating because it represents a key battleground on which social science has waged an empirical war upon its traditional enemies in the natural sciences.'

(Allen 2000: 49)

Introduction

The delineation of patterns of morbidity and exploration/explanation of the causal systems underlying those patterns is the central concern of epidemiology. However, epidemiology, in accord with the frequentist approach to statistics which underpins its major techniques, provides information not about the individual case confronting a clinician but about what will happen over the long run in large numbers of cases. It describes patterns in populations, not prognosis for the individual human being. This is always an issue in clinical science, but is particularly apparent when we are dealing not with biological assaults on an individual physiology – as with infection – but with the implications of general social conditions for morbidity and mortality.

The social programme in health, from its origins in the collation of mortality statistics and the association of these with living conditions by the early Victorian Healthy Towns movement, has dealt with population relations. Its key evidence base has always been the demonstration of an association between general social conditions and measured mortality/morbidity, coupled with the assertion or demonstration of some sort of mechanism which offers an explanation for that relationship. Given that such associations were observed *and acted on* prior to the establishment of bacteriological foundations for the doctrine of specific aetiology, social epidemiology necessarily dealt with complex and unobserved socio-ecological generative mechanisms. In essence social epidemiological explanation has always been realist.[1] However, in terms of statistical modelling there is a real problem for explanation here. Health, or absence of it, is a property of individuals, and population measures for health are simply founded on aggregations of events for individuals (especially death) or, more rarely, on assessments or self-evaluations of overall health in individual cases. The social properties are expressed at a different level – typically that of a defined geographical area on some scale.

Sometimes we can understand this level as representing an emergent property from aggregation – for example, the emergent character of the socially excluded area consequent on the concentration in it of socially excluded people. Note that this is emergent – it is more than just the aggregate sum of individual characteristics. Concentration produces something over and above this. We must also note that areal level properties can be properties of the area as a whole – for example, the design layout properties of a housing estate, the polluted environment of an industrial zone, the beneficent effect (we hope) of good primary health care facilities delivered on a spatial basis. However, there remains the considerable problem as to how we can relate causal mechanisms at levels beyond the individual to expressed effects in the individual case and consider how change at those levels might affect the individual case.

The major method proposed by statisticians to deal with this is multi-level modelling – an approach which deserves serious attention from researchers working in a realist tradition because it does try to come to terms with the actual way in which social processes work. Goldstein puts it like this:

> The multi-level modelling approach views the population as of potential interest in itself, so that a sample designed to reflect that structure is not merely a matter of saving costs, as in traditional survey design, but can be used to collect and analyse data about the higher levels in the population.
>
> (1995: 5)

Multi-level modelling has been proposed as a way of resolving the difficulties of cross-level relationships among individually expressed health and social conditions. This interesting approach does represent a genuine effort to confront problems which are central to the relationship between the collective and the individual. However, this chapter will argue that the approach remains unsatisfactory, precisely because it 'disembodies' both aspects of the complex individual and aspects of the complex social systems through which individuals lead their lives. It continues statistics' typical reification of the variable and assigns causality to relationships among variables rather than social relations among real complex systems. Let us begin by picking up two very different 'individual' centred approaches to the issue of housing and health.

The strange case of the clinician and the social constructionist – convergence from extremes

The general character of social explanations for individual health have recently been attacked from what would seem to be polar opposite directions. On the one hand, Allen, a sociologist with strongly social constructionist views, has advanced a realist critique of the 'housing and health' literature founded on that literature's treatment of human agents as 'physiological dopes' (Allen 2000). On the other, Le Fanu, a prominent writer on medical practice and health affairs, has asserted the primacy of clinical science and rejected the social account of health determination as misleading and founded on fundamental misconceptions (Le Fanu 1999). Le Fanu demands a return to specific aetiology. Here we have a social constructionist and an assertion of the bio-mechanical model agreeing in an attack on understandings of health as a collective property. An exploration of their arguments helps us to develop a realist method for approaching and understanding this crucial issue of the relationship between collective condition and individual case.

Allen's article is a sustained assault on the social epidemiological approaches to understanding the ways in which housing conditions and health are expressed in the individual human being. Moreover it is explicitly informed by 'the ontological doctrine of critical realism' (Allen 2000: 50) and thereby committed to rejection of any essentialist privileging of a single mechanism (here equivalent to cause) as opposed to understandings founded on attention to the 'relational dialectic' connecting phenomena in the social world. Allen's approach works by asking the question (to paraphrase): 'why if bad housing causes ill health do many people living in bad housing not become ill?' He answers this by asserting the 'autonomy' of the human subject, an interesting and important proposition to which we will return. However, for the moment I want to draw attention to a remarkable correspondence between the arguments of Allen – a convinced social constructionist – and Le Fanu (1999), who explicitly rejects probabilistic epidemiological reasoning about social causation of ill health and endorses instead both 'clinical science' based on detailed observation of disease processes in the individual case and through sets of individual cases, and 'disembodied' physiological experimentation and the laboratory-based construction of basic biomedical science. Actually, although neither refer to him, both Allen and Le Fanu share the unease about, indeed outright rejection of, probabilistic reasoning which led Znaniecki (1934) to propose the strategy of analytic induction. Moreover, although neither totally dismisses epidemiological approaches, both privilege the individual case as a locus of health and as the site in which significant health is determined.

These arguments offer us an interesting way into considering just how we might understand *and establish* the nature of causal processes when we are dealing with complex open systems and attempting to comprehend them from a realist perspective. Both Allen and Le Fanu, coming from very different starting points, assert an individualistic account. For them health is expressed in the individual. For Le Fanu individual bodies are the objects of knowledge of the clinician. For Allen they are autonomous agents 'choosing' or 'rejecting' disease causation processes. Neither Allen nor Le Fanu operate with a 'simple' or 'crude positivist' deterministic understanding[2] but both deal with the level of the case. For Le Fanu this is taken for granted. For Allen the 'collective experience' is written out of the picture. Neither has a theory of 'levels'.

Let us contrast this with the traditional concerns of public health – which concerns I am going to argue derive from two intersecting collectivist visions. The first of these is that of public health as 'veterinary practice' – public health in the service of a capitalism which, to quote a working class mother speaking to her college educated daughter in one of Marge Piercey's books, looks on the working class as 'laying chickens' – that is, as a herd which has to reproduce labour power. No vet ever treats an individual battery hen; it is the character of the group – the emergent character – which matters. Likewise the great working class programmes of municipal housing reform, a twentieth century process which utilized but did not derive from the elite concerns with public health initiated by Chadwick to which Allen (2000) attaches so much importance, were about collective health, although the people engaged in that programme knew about individual consequences.

The issue is central to any kind of probabilistic knowledge. Probabilistic knowledge describes long runs of events for large numbers of cases. There is a real, and in logical terms apparently insurmountable, problem about deriving any kind of prediction about the outcome of an individual case from population data, whilst at the same time that information is important in understanding the future trajectory of social collectivities. This difference of attention – the difference between the objectives of a clinician dealing with an individual patient and a Director of Public Health concerned with the health of the population of an administrative locality – is compounded by a profoundly individualistic bias in causal reasoning. Diez-Roux puts the issue very well, arguing that in contemporary debate:

> The study of causes of disease ... shifted from the environment as a whole to specific factors within the environment as a whole to specific factors within the environment (biological organisms) and to the behaviors of individuals. The model of disease causation shifted from a rather vague, holistic determination to the unicausal model of the germ theory and to the multicausal model (the 'web of causation') prevalent today, in which a variety of biological and behavioral risk factors are presumed to interact in the causation of disease. This process has been accompanied by progressive 'individualization' of risk (i.e. attributing risks to characteristics of individuals rather than to environmental or social influences affecting populations) ... This individualization of risk has perpetuated the idea that risk is individually determined rather than

socially determined, discouraging research into the effects of macro-level or group-level variables on individual outcomes. 'Lifestyle' and 'behaviors' are regarded as matters free of social contexts that shape and constrain them. This tendency by which disease patterns are explained solely in terms of the characteristics of individuals is analogous to the doctrine of methodological individualism in social science.

(1998: 216)

We have a twofold problem here. On the one hand, we have a politics of methodological individualism – a use of reasoning at the individual level to deny the significance of social structure and social change in relation to health outcomes. Le Fanu is an arch exponent of this position. On the other, we have the very real problem for clinicians and other case centred workers – what do I do with this person? Indeed the case can be any real entity, collective as well as individual. We can well argue that the change in a whole social ecology, predicated in large part on a working class programme of local social reform, was the factor which eliminated TB as a serious cause of death in urban industrial Britain.[3] We could equally argue that the re-emergence of TB in New York (Wallace, D. 1990; Wallace, R. 1991; Wallace, R. and Wallace, D. 1993) is a product of the new postindustrial polarized social order. That does not help the clinician deal with the case of TB coughing up on her. However, it does predicate a collective response to polarization.

Multi-level modelling

Diez-Roux turns to multi-level modelling as a way of resolving the explanatory dilemma – as a way of transcending both the ecological (reasoning to cases from data which describe aggregates) and atomistic (reasoning about collectivities on the basis of micro data describing component cases) fallacies and as a way of trying to disentangle effects at different levels in order to work out processes of causation across those levels. Yen and Syme describe the technique thus:

> This analytic approach acknowledges the nested or tiered nature of the data, such as individuals within census tracts. The model does not assume that the variation in the outcome comes only from the individual variation. Instead, another term is added to the error structure to account for variation from the second-level factors. These multilevel models allow for other processes that are presumed to have an impact on the individual beyond the effects of the individual-level variables.
>
> (Yen and Syme 1999: 301–2)

Multi-level modelling procedures were developed primarily to handle educational data (see Goldstein and Spiegelhalter 1996). The educational instances illustrate the approach rather well. If we are concerned with the educational achievement of children, then we want to be able to take account not only of the characteristics of the individual children, but also of the classes of which they are members, and the schools which contain those classes. Note that there may be distinctive properties of these 'higher' levels – the school may or may not be single sex. There may also be properties which 'emerge' from the characteristics of the aggregates. A school with a large proportion of high achieving children will focus its whole attention towards high achievement. One with a more 'middling' intake will, in the contemporary UK, devote a lot of attention to increasing the achievement of the large middle group, whilst in triage style leaving high achievers to 'get on on their own'. High achievers will do better in the former school, middle achievers in the latter. These are school level properties which emerge from the interactions of the components. As Diez-Roux remarks: 'Perhaps the most challenging aspect of multilevel analysis is that it requires a theory of causation that integrates micro-social and macro-level variables and explains these relationships and interactions across levels.' (1998: 220)

However, the approach remains variable centred. That is to say that it sees attributes at all levels as somehow independent of the cases – as having a reality of their own. I have criticized this approach extensively elsewhere (Byrne 2001) by drawing on Reed and Harvey's proposal (1992) of 'complex realism' – an approach that combines the philosophical ontology of critical realism with the scientific ontology of complexity. The essential contribution from complexity theory is an understanding that we are dealing with complex open systems which are nested[4] so that individuals are complex systems, nested within households, nested within neighbourhoods, nested within localities and so on (to use merely the spatial dimension of nesting). The important thing about complex systems is that they have emergent properties. They are inherently non-analyzable because their properties, potentials and trajectories cannot be explained in terms of the properties of their components. A most important word here is 'interaction'. When Yen and Syme say : 'any environment is the result of the continuing interaction between natural and man-made components, social processes and the relationships between individuals and groups' (1999: 288), they are recognizing the significance of emergence for our understanding of these issues. Multi-level models recognize the problem of explanation but not the complex character of the open systems with which they are trying to deal. Approaches more or less explicitly informed by realist perspectives offer another route towards explanatory adequacy.

Single case probabilities – figurations?

The issues of explanation in relation to the individual case have been addressed by Williams (1999) and Ulanowicz (1996) by reference to Popper's later work on single case probabilities. Popper argued for a notion of propensity in the individual case which was different from probability as understood in relation to the population as a whole. Higgs *et al.* (Chapter 4, pp. 93–4) draw on Lawson's (1997) discussion to address this issue, noting that whilst constant event patterns do not occur in open systems, 'partial' regularities – demi-regs in Lawson's terminology – do. It is worth repeating their quotation here: 'The patterning observed will not be strict if countervailing factors sometimes dominate or frequently co-determine the outcomes in a variable manner. But where demi-regs are observed there is evidence of relatively enduring and identifiable tendencies at play.' (Lawson 1997: 204.)

Another conceptual repertoire on which Higgs *et al.* draw is that of 'Logics, Relations and Figurations' (after Scambler and Higgs 2001). If relations, which derive from underlying logics, and in particular the logic of capital accumulation, manifest at the level of Bhaskar's real, then they are expressed in figurations (after Elias 1978), which I take here to represent processes of connection in specific contexts – the relation between housing and health in the polarized post-Fordist city as opposed to such relations in the Fordist city of stepped inequalities (see Byrne 2001).

All these frames – single case probabilities, demi-regs, figurations and multi-level modelling with its frequentist probabilistic foundations – are attempts to handle not only the problem of complex and contingent causation, but also that of relations among levels, relations which are crucial to the generation of useful understanding as the basis for both collective action and intervention in the individual case. The nature of the problem we encounter here has long been appreciated by geographers. Johnson put it like this:

> These investigations relating the 'contents' of social areas to the behaviour of the residents are termed areal studies of behaviour here ... Areal studies are not able to discern the operation of structural or neighbourhood effects, since they make no reference to the internal set of forces, what we might term the individual effects ... ecological studies require three data sets – referring to individual pre-dispositions towards certain behaviour, to the distribution of individuals with those pre-dispositions, and to resultant behaviour.
>
> (Johnson 1976: 119)

Even this is still individual centred. Johnson's approach allows for emergent properties which derived from the relative concentration of individuals with a given set of characteristics in a locale, but not for locale level properties which do not derive from emergence from aggregation. That is to say, it does not deal with structural properties which belong to the context itself. This is also the crucial problem with techniques of agent-based simulation (see Drogoul and Ferber 1994) in which the environment is essentially passive. Of course the environment may be the product of social actions undertaken by collectives of individuals but that is different from something which is the product of passive aggregation.

Le Fanu's discussion of the history of tuberculosis can be used as a target for the argument here. Le Fanu argues against McKeown's (1979) assertion that clinical practice made virtually no difference to the massive decline in tuberculosis in England and Wales from the mid-nineteenth to mid-twentieth century. Le Fanu quotes an unattributed historian(!!) to the effect that:

> McKeown mis-stated, or failed to understand, the point demonstrated with brilliant clarity in the classic book *The Prevention of Tuberculosis* published in 1908, namely that the effect of placing consumptive patients in poor law infirmaries was to separate them from the general populace and to restrict the spread of disease – the proportion of consumptive patients thus segregated corresponded to the progressive rate of decline of tuberculosis in England and Wales.
>
> (Quoted Le Fanu 1999: 320–1)

If this had really been the case, then we would be dealing with an emergent property which derives purely from individual aggregation. An apparent analogy is the concept of prevention of measles epidemics being contingent upon achieving a sufficiently high rate of immunization in the population. If enough individuals are immune, and this is a non-linear effect of course, then at a threshold point the disease cannot spread. And therein by the way lies the weakness of Le Fanu's point. As Bradbury (1933) was to note after more than twenty years of the sanatorium policy, in working class Tyneside everybody remained exposed to TB. The threshold for separation was never and could never be reached by anything short of a slaughter-on-diagnosis policy. The benign and kindly regime of the sanatoria was far removed from that! Le Fanu is of course confusing correlation with cause.

Let us consider a contrary argument. In the history of tuberculosis in urban industrial society we find a number of processes operating together and in interaction. One, undoubtedly, is biological selection of urban populations towards resistance to tuberculosis. Another is the general increase in standard of diet overall, consequent on the recasting of wage labour relations from the expropriation of absolute to relative surplus value after the mid-nineteenth century, which was consequent in large part on the organizational capacity of trade unions. Finally, there is a progressive (in a political rather than numerical sense) transformation of urban social ecologies achieved in particular by the development of good quality council housing and the generalization of sanitary adequacy. We have individual changes (selective resistance), aggregate changes (better fed individuals in the mass), and transformations of environment deriving from collective social interventions. To return to the abstract terminology which was discussed at the beginning of this section, we might regard the change in urban social ecology as a transformed figuration, the impact of complex genetic interactions as determining individual probabilities,[5] and different transformed 'demi-regs' as describing the relationship between exposure and TB infection in the different social ecological regimes.

The above historical account is essentially retrodictive. It is plausible and compatible with all off trend data, clinical understandings and popular social commitments. It is the last of these which is really the most interesting. A mix of people – experts in the form of public health doctors, working class politicians – originally and continuously local but at key points becoming national (especially John Wheatley, Labour's first Minister of Health), and working class publics who elected those politicians, were able to 'imagine' not some utopian future but a possible way in which urban industrial life might be transformed for the better, with the better including the effective elimination of tuberculosis as an endemic condition. The account fits all the records, most importantly the record of declared intention in this period. This is very far from trivial in itself because the way in which a politics based on both expert and lay understandings of disease causation underpinned radical and effective social change offers a general guide for future social action. The remaining question is how knowledge can contribute to such effective critical practice. Pawson (this volume, pp. 31–3) argues for the production of middle range context, mechanism, outcome configurations (CMOCs) and recognizes that contexts have multiple layers. We might regard the local practitioners of urban reconstruction from the 1920s through to the 1950s as people who both understood specific CMOCs and acted on that understanding. The interesting question now is how might we construct a CMOC for the relationship between housing and health in postindustrial urban society which corresponds to the effective understanding of 'pully string Hancock' in Gateshead in the 1920s?[6] In so doing we need to take account of Pawson and Tilley's (1997: 28) pertinent observation that: 'Similar outcomes may in principle be generated through varying mechanisms.' Are there any tools we might employ which get us beyond the necessary, foundational and important task of retrodiction and open up for us the possibility if not of prediction, then of some sort of account of potential future states which follow from contemporary actions?

Modelling multi-level complexity – some proposals

The problem with complex systems is that we cannot abstract from them in order to represent them. Cilliers (1998) demonstrates that for complex systems with emergent properties, abstraction renders any model simple and hence of minimal value as a method of determining possible future trajectories (the emphasized plural is very important) of the system. Let us see what the complexity problem is that we have to deal with here and think about how we might model the intersecting systems in a way which meets the CMOC criteria. Let us approach the issue by recognizing that it presents in different ways to different people at different levels. Collectively putative relationships between 'housing' and health matter because they have potential causal implications in relation to the most important manifestation of health inequalities in postindustrial societies – the massive differentials in premature mortality (which here can also stand as an index of extent of morbidity throughout the life course) among social classes. This is a problem for the collective politics and administration of health. Individually relationships between 'housing' and health manifest themselves at the case level for practitioners who want to deal with manifest morbidities as they present to them.

There has been a longstanding process of 'medical certification' for dealing with the problems of individual cases in relation to housing and health. GPs and housing managers have administrated a system in which 'points' for rehousing, originally from the private to the public sector and then primarily in relation to transfers within the public sector, were allocated on the basis of diagnosed morbidity which it was considered rehousing might improve. The uniquely individual manifestation of this is in relation to disability, where an occupational therapist can assess needs for aids and adaptations in relation to a particular case. This is uncontentious except in relation to major claims on resources. The historic role of rehousing of the tubercular was likewise not contentious. Let us deal with the contemporary by focusing on depression. It is important to note that even in the stable Fordist early 1970s Brown and Harris (1978) identified housing conditions as an important background factor in the multi-causal complex aetiology of clinical depression. Here we have to specify what we mean by 'housing conditions'. This term has to include not only the specific housing form, amenities and general condition of individual dwellings, but also neighbourhood effects in terms of general social character. Byrne *et al.* (1985) found that for Gateshead council tenants, in estates regarded as good and desirable by residents,[7] prevalence of depression as recorded by standard questionnaire assessment was much less than in undesirable estates. Brown and Harris's general account of the aetiology of depression is exactly realist in that it is complex and contingent. The generative mechanism is a combination of background misery and life coherence threatening event. We might well find that movement from a threatening, unstable and stigmatized locale to one which is safe, stable and better regarded is effective in reducing general depression at the individual level. The collective remedy is the development of an inclusive and empowering[8] collective strategy of housing transformation – an assertion of solidarity in general terms. Both of these statements are assertions, though plausible and supported by historical experience. Can we model them in a way which provides some quantitative foundation?

Case-based strategies – retrodicting and predicting individual trajectories

I want to focus on the impact of neighbourhood conditions on individual health, in terms both of retrodiction – i.e. the elucidation of the trajectory of individuals through their life course to the health status they now have – and of prediction – considering the possible future trajectories (again a very deliberate plural) from this time point. A key purpose of retrodiction across large numbers of cases is that it might lead us to understandings which inform actions which have a determinant effect on the future trajectories of cases. It is a way of finding out what has worked. Note that this implies a plurality of *different* routes towards a desired health status. Let us consider what we might be able to do given the availability of data sets which describe life trajectories through health provision systems.

The development of electronic databases for administrative purposes has generated accounts of the trajectories of cases through processing to outcomes with information recorded about the character of the cases on entry into the system, the content of each processing stage, and outcomes defined in terms of 'present state' of the case. An example is provided by the Mental Health Minimum Dataset (MHMDS), developed for the National Health Service to improve information on mental health services usage and need. The data set describes the care received by service users during each overall *spell of care* they receive. It is person-centred, so that all the care received by individuals can be studied, and includes details of clinical problems, treatments given, outline aspects of social care and outcomes. Geographic markers allow analysis by any type of health, GP or local authority administrative categories. Where individuals have more than one spell of care, the NHS unique patient identifier allows linkage. This source provides a large amount of richly detailed data about large numbers of individuals' service use which probably contains patterns that could be used, for example, to characterize differences in the type and quality of care provided by different clinical teams, or to flag up warning signs of impending relapse or other adverse clinical situations. Patterns of contact over time would probably be particularly useful in both respects, but are among the types of data which are highly complex to analyze.[9]

Mental health interventions are typical of the majority of social interventions in that what happens is the product of complex factors over long time periods. Some factors are external to the process of care (for example, loss of jobs or relationship breakdowns). Some interventions are the personal actions of human agents, such as nurses and doctors. Only a few (notably the administration of drugs) are to any degree reliably uniform in the way that simple controlled trial methods assume. While the objectives of these interventions are at first sight more clear cut (to change the state of the case – e.g. from mentally 'ill' to 'well'), in many more cases they are more complex – to maintain a state of optimal functioning and to minimize the frequency of relapse. Analyzing the success of care in this context is difficult as inevitably there are multiple interventions, begun and ended in response often to external circumstances rather than to any scheduled programme, over long periods of time with no clear cut start and end points. In this situation, methods are required for developing more individually tailored problem classifications and prognostic indices. These are likely to be based on the accumulating history of each subject's illness, circumstances and treatment. They are needed to produce greater clarity both in research about what works for whom, and in the subsequent application of its conclusions in deciding treatment strategies for future patients.[10]

The general import of the discussion of the relationship between housing conditions and depression is that housing circumstances, in the broadest sense, have import for mental health status. If we have a data set like the MHMDS, then we can look at how housing change, in association with a whole range of other factors, is associated with different trajectories towards present state. Traditional quantitative causal modelling based on developments of the general linear model cannot handle complex causation of this kind. Indeed the only serious social science treatment of the issues known to us is in the literature surrounding 'Qualitative Comparative Analysis' (QCA). Fielding and Lee (1998: 158) describe QCA thus: 'Unlike the data matrix in quantitative research, where the analytic focus is on variables displayed in the *columns* of the table, it is the *rows* which are important here. What is being examined for each row is the *configuration* of causes associated with the presence or absence of an outcome for the case.' There is explicit recognition of 'causal complexity' (Coverdill *et al.* 1994: 57), that is, of the possibility of multiple and/or different causal patterns associated with a given outcome. QCA is traditionally understood as a 'small N' method, i.e. as one which is appropriate when there are small numbers of cases, although we think that, run in tandem with numerical taxonomies, it might be applied to large data sets. We might also use neural net methods, Bayesian approaches, and time ordered and mapped numerical taxonomy procedures (based both on traditional clustering techniques and on using the classification potential of neural net methods) as ways of delineating the trajectories of cases and exploring patterns of cause associated with different outcomes for cases. These approaches accord with Byrne's (2002) proposal for retrodictive relational classification as a means towards intuitive induction.

Of course the above remains confined to the individual level and the MHMDS does not necessarily contain information about social area, although this can be derived from postcodes of addresses which the MHMDS will contain. The practicality of using the MHMDS for exploring housing as a component of transformation of mental health state remains to be established but the principle of exploration at the individual level remains the same if we employ other database data sets of this form, for example the records of a local authority housing management system in relation to case data.

Indeed a housing management data set would be even more appropriate because it would include information about higher levels than the individual household in the form of both aggregate and overall descriptive data relating to particular housing areas. We could certainly construct multi-level models in which 'health related transfer applications' might be treated as the dependent variable in a multi-level analogue of logistic regression. As an exploratory procedure that would be fine. Of course, Allen would remain unhappy with the odds ratio probabilistic knowledge generated. In contrast the case-based methods do address exactly the issue of individual determination and recognize its complexity, contingency and variate form. This is, however, not the same as saying that every case is ideographic and unique. As always we are after patterns.[11]

Collective transformations of urban systems

Here let me begin with an assertion which summarizes much of the argument of Byrne (2001). We cannot understand the position of discrete neighbourhoods in an urban system without understanding the character of the urban system as a whole. In other words, contemporary 'socially excluded spaces' (see Madanipour et al. 1998) in postindustrial cities exist because whole urban systems have become polarized, consequent upon a massive increase in income differentials and other inequalities in the urban system as a whole. This is a contention for the moment dependent on qualitative descriptions, but which is amenable to quantitative modelling in which data sets for many urban areas over a time period are collated, so that relative trajectories can be assessed in relation to the character of policy interventions through that period. Here simulation *may* offer some possibilities for retrodiction and prediction. The complexity theory concept of 'near neighbour' is interesting here. Basically – and the idea is in essence basic – systems which are like each other to begin with will have similar subsequent trajectories unless something changes the trajectory of one of them.

I am particularly interested in the transition from industrial to postindustrial cities. There is a general tendency for similarity here but I very much agree with Lovering (1997) that this is not so much a matter of a general global systemic determination as the product of local action based on representing outcomes as globally inevitable. In other words, there is much more autonomy in urban systems than urban elites will admit. The interesting places are those which are different and we can use these sorts of strategies to see why. Moreover we can look at how health conditions are expressed in space in relation to the character of different sorts of urban systems. If we are concerned to improve the health of urban populations, then we have to look at the whole urban system with which we are engaged and we need information about how other urban systems work as a guideline for what we might do – note guideline, not prescription. We can collect a range of quantitative and qualitative data which can be used to generate retrodictive comparative trajectories – to see what places were like and what they have become – and explore both quantitatively and qualitatively for factors which, in complex interaction or not, generated change. For example, we can explore, as I have already done in a preliminary way (Byrne 1998), the ways in which UK cities with different ethnic minority populations have developed in different ways. This is by no means merely, or even substantively, a matter of policy decisions but it does show how some things work out in a way which might inform the character even of communal aspirations and individual behaviours.

Multi-level modelling taken alone remains a story of linear determination of the individual case. Exploratory multi-time point classification allows us to examine the non-linear trajectories – we are always and rightly more interested in changes of kind than in changes of degree – of individual cases, *at all levels*. We can see how individuals, households, neighbourhoods and localities change together, and we can map the patterns of such changes as a route towards understanding their inter-relationships. Such an approach liberates us from the reification of variables and the enormous error of traditional statistics, including here multi-level modelling, of 'parcelling out' by abstracting from bodies and all other levels and assigning effects to constructed entities called variables which have no real existence. What matters, always, is embodied (here taken to be a term applicable at any level) interaction in real complex systems. TB is a function of exposure but not all those exposed (including the present writer who has a strong antibody reaction to a Heaf test) develop any clinical disease. That is a function, as Bradbury (1933) recognized, of the interaction in the body of genetic potential, diet and housing conditions. I think Allen is assigning too much to agency when he sees these individual contingent relations as taking an agent-based form (op. cit.).

However, agency there is at the level of the urban socio-ecological system. Here transformed urban ecologies – transformed for the better by fully paid up members of the human race like Councillor Hancock, transformed for the worse by the 'urban regimes' of postindustrial capitalism which have recreated the social polarization of the late nineteenth and early twentieth century in contemporary cities – have implications for the generative potential of disease beyond the individual human body. The significant agency is largely collective and social but agency there is.

Conclusion

Modelling reality using quantitative methods is an important part of any scientific practice. Such modelling must employ methods which in some way correspond to, represent, the reality being modelled. That means that the methods must take account of the nonlinearity which characterizes the social world and its inter-relationships with the natural, of the character of the multi-level and inter-penetrating complex open systems of the social and natural world, and of the significance of all of the micro, meso and macro levels of social structure and social interaction. The problems associated with assessing how housing and health are related at the micro scale of the individual case, the meso levels of neighbourhood and locality and the macro of 'welfare and environmental regime' demonstrate what any adequate modelling process must be able to deal with. Multi-level modelling is a genuine response to these issues but one which remains trapped in the linear probabilistic approaches of frequentist statistics. There are other ways to model which might avoid these issues. Really the issue is only in the first instance, although that instance matters, one of the isomorphism of representations with reality. Models are most important as tools for thinking with. Getting beyond multi-level modelling without having to resort to individual agency alone, as with Allen, or deterministic biomechanisms, as with Le Fanu, is a way to thinking coherently and relating individual condition to processes of collective reconstruction – the essence of a proper critical social research practice.

Notes

1   The status of realist codification of causal explanation as the product of induction – in other words as a coherent expression of the actual practice of scientists – is very well demonstrated by any serious consideration of those accounts of the relationships between social environment and patterns of infection which were written prior to the discovery of specific aetiologies. The social measurers of the first half of the nineteenth century were all realists in practice.

2   Le Fanu's rejection of genetic determinism and of the claims for the potential of genetic specification for the development of effective clinical interventions is clear and compelling.

3   Le Fanu's arguments to the contrary are risible in their ignorance of the actual social processes of life in inter-war Britain. Le Fanu seems unaware of the very important study by Bradbury (1933) which flatly contradicts his whole account.

4   It is very important to emphasize that the notion of nested systems *does not* imply that containing systems have some determinant priority over contained. All chains of causal influence are recursive – they run both ways.

5   To say this is not to license a simple specification of genetic determinism on the lines of a 'gene against TB'. Any genetic component will be complex and interactive at the genetic level, and interactive with physiological (especially diet) and social ecological environmental factors.

6   Councillor Hancock was the working class Labour Chairman of the Public Health Committee in Gateshead in the 1920s who used unemployment relief funding to achieve a massive transformation of sanitation in inner urban areas by replacing earth closets with water-borne sanitation and hence WCs and strings to pull (see Manders 1974). His nickname is amusing but it describes an effective critical practitioner.

7 Which assessment was absolutely validated by inspection of transfer patterns – the desirable estates had virtually no transfer out requests and many transfer in, with vice versa for the undesirable.

8 A word to be used with great caution – see Byrne (2001) for a discussion of this.

9 This description was prepared by Gyles Glover.

10 As 9.

11 This strategy owes a great deal to Wendy Dyer's approach in her PhD thesis (Dyer 2001).

References

Allen, C. (2000) 'On the "physiological dope" problematic in housing and illness research; towards a critical realism of home and health', *Housing, Theory and Society*, 17, 49–67.

Bradbury, F.C.S. (1933) *Causal Factors in Tuberculosis*, London: National Association for the Prevention of Tuberculosis.

Brown, G. and Harris, T. (1978) *The Social Origins of Depression*, London: Tavistock.

Byrne, D.S. (1998) 'Class and ethnicity in complex cities', *Environment and Planning A*, 30, 703–20.

Byrne, D.S. (2001) 'Partnership – participation – power: the meaning of empowerment in postindustrial society', in S. Balloch and M. Taylor (eds) *Partnership Working: Policy and Practice*, Policy Press, 243–61.

Byrne, D.S. (2002) *Interpreting Quantitative Data*, London: Sage.

Byrne, D.S., Harrison, S., Keithley, J. and McCarthy, P. (1985) *Housing and Health*, London: Gower.

Cilliers, P. (1998) *Complexity and Postmodernism*, London: Routledge.

Coverdill, J.E., Finlay, W. and Martin, J.K. (1994) 'Labour management in the Southern textile industry: comparing qualitative, quantitative and qualitative comparative analysis', *Sociological Methods and Research*, 23, 54–85.

Diez-Roux, A.V. (1998) 'Bringing context back into epidemiology: variables and fallacies in multilevel analysis', *American Journal of Public Health*, 88(2): 216–222.

Drogoul, A. and Ferber, J. (1994) 'Multi-agent simulation as a tool for studying emergent processes in societies', in Gilbert, N. and Doran, J. (eds) (1994) *Simulating Societies*, London: UCL Press 127–42.

Dyer, W. (2001) 'The identification of the careers of mentally disordered offenders using cluster analysis in a complex realist framework', Unpublished PhD: University of Durham.

Elias, N. (1978) *What is Sociology?*, London: Hutchinson.

Fielding, N.G. and Lee, R.M. (1998) *Computer Analysis and Qualitative Research*, New Technology for Social Research Series, London: Sage.

Goldstein, H. (1995) *Multilevel Statistical Models*, London: Edward Arnold.

Goldstein, H. and Spiegelhalter, D.J. (1996) 'League tables and their limitations', *Journal of the Royal Statistical Society – Series A*, 159, 3, 385–443.

Johnson, R.A. (1976) 'Areal studies, ecological studies and social patterns in cities', *Trans. Inst. of Brit. Geographers* NS, 1, 118–21.

Lawson, T. (1997) *Economics and Reality*, London: Routledge.

Le Fanu, J. (1999) *The Rise and Fall of Modern Medicine*, London: Little Brown.

Lovering, J. (1997) 'Global restructuring and local impact', in M. Paccione (ed.) *Britain's Cities*, London: Routledge, 63–87.

McKeown, T. (1979) *The Role of Medicine*, Oxford: Blackwell.

Madanipour, A., Cars, G. and Allen, J. (eds) (1998) *Social Exclusion in European Cities*, London: Jessica Kingsley.

Manders, F. (1974) *Gateshead: A History*, Gateshead: Gateshead County Borough.

Pawson, R. and Tilley, N. (1997) *Realistic Evaluation*, London: Sage.

Reed, M. and Harvey, D.L. (1992) 'The new science and the old: complexity and realism in the social sciences', *Journal for the Theory of Social Behaviour*, 22, 356–79.

Scambler, G. and Higgs, P. (2001) ' "The dog that didn't bark": taking class seriously in the health inequalities debate', *Social Science and Medicine*, 52(1): 157–9.

Ulanowicz, R.E.J. (1996) 'The propensities of evolving systems', in E.L. Khalil and K. Boulding (eds) *Evolution, Order and Complexity*, London: Routledge.

Wallace, D. (1990) 'Roots of increased health-care inequality in New York', *Social Science and Medicine*, 31, 1219–27.

Wallace, R. (1991) 'Social disintegration and the spread of AIDs', *Social Science and Medicine*, 33, 1155–62.

Wallace, R. and Wallace, D. (1993) 'Inner city disease and the public health of the suburbs', *Environment and Planning A*, 25, 1707–23.

Williams, M. (1999) 'Single case probabilities in the social world', *Journal for the Theory of Social Behavior*, 29(2): 187–201.

Yen, I.H. and Syme, S.L. (1999) 'The social environment and health: a discussion of the epidemiologic literature, *Annual Review of Public Health*, 20: 287–308.

Znaniecki, F. (1934) *The Method of Sociology*, New York: Farrar and Rinehart.

3   Realism and probability

Malcolm Williams and Wendy Dyer

Introduction

Although most discussions of methodological positions in the social sciences will cite realism alongside positivism and interpretivism, in empirical practice the first position is uncommon. The best-known realist programme in social science, Roy Bhaskar's critical realism, has many supporters yet, despite its commitment to scientific naturalism, it has had little or no impact on quantitative research in social science. The only important exception has been Ray Pawson's (1989) *A Measure for Measures*, which is a reconstruction of survey method along realist lines. Now there may be good sociological reasons for this lack of realist penetration into quantitative research, but there are also good ontological grounds for a rejection (by quantitative researchers) of critical realism as it currently stands. In this paper we will defend the overall project of scientific realism in social research, but we will be critical of its current principal manifestation (of critical realism) in one crucial respect, that of *necessity* and what this then implies for probability. We will claim that the particular view of necessity critical realists adopt leads them to criticise empiricist versions of probability, but to offer nothing back in return. We take it as axiomatic that quantitative research needs some theory of probability in order to be able to explain and predict.

The aims of this chapter are firstly to re-cast realism in a weaker contingent form that does not rely on natural necessity and secondly to re-introduce probability, albeit in a realist form that might reconcile realism with quantitative research. The third aim of the chapter is to show how contingent realism might be translated into empirical research. The version of realist probability we advocate here implies case rather than variable based analyses and we show, through a recent example of an investigation of Custody Diversion Teams in the North East of England, how such research might be undertaken using the technique of cluster analysis.

Reality and probability in quantitative research

Despite the absence of realist methodologies in quantitative research, there has been a long reflective tradition in empiricism about what it is researchers measure. One of the clearest expositions of this was the work of Hubert Blalock (1964). In the tradition of the logical positivists he took the view that 'science contains two distinct languages or ways of defining concepts, which will be referred to simply as the theoretical and operational languages' (1964: 6).

To measure crime or class (for example) is not to measure these as a real property of the world, but to create operational definitions that can stand in for them in a meaningful way. Blalock was not suggesting that any old thing can stand in for such concepts, but the derivation of these concepts should be driven by theory, though tempered with what can be measured. Blalock correctly believed this was how rigorous survey research proceeded. It didn't matter to Blalock whether something was real or not, or what that word could mean in respect of the social world, but on the grounds that some objects will have constant properties over time and that some events are very similar to others we can make causal inferences on the basis of comparing the probabilistic relationship of these to things that do change (1964: 7).[1]

Unfortunately, as Blalock recognised, in non-experimental research these assumptions rarely hold firm because of measurement error, the difficulties of replication and randomisation and crucially the tendency of the act of research fundamentally to change that which is being researched. The problem of operationalisation and the problem of open systems are impediments to strong causal claims in many of the natural sciences as well (see Nagel 1979: chapter 10), but of course things are much worse in the social world.

The only causal claims that could be made, according to the empiricist view, were the weak ones of constant conjunction, which at best can lead to an 'inference to the best explanation' (Lipton 1991) – that is, the most likely explanation, given the available evidence. Although a kind of simple ontological realism might be acknowledged (i.e. there is a real world with real effects), this is irrelevant to the empiricist programme – all that is relevant is the best possible description and explanation of the phenomena that can be measured.

A more recent example of this kind of causal claim is offered by Tacq (1997: 65), who describes a technique of path analysis to explain organisational mobility. The dependent variable (y) is the inclination towards organisational mobility and amongst the independent variables (e.g. satisfaction with community, research motivation, individual achievement) dependency is postulated; thus it is claimed that in several hierarchical steps causes of causes can be investigated in an additive model.[2] However, even in a method as sophisticated as this, the hypothesised causes are bounded by the number and specification of the variables in the model and their existence is probabilistically measured, with the inevitability of statistical 'outliers'. Although such a model allows deductive inference, it is not really a set of nested causes (in the sense of necessary and sufficient conditions), but a set of nested *probabilities* within an open system that may or may not hold other invisible, though contributing, 'variables'.

The realist critique

For empiricism, causality is an epistemological matter in which we can only make claims on the basis of that which we observe. We cannot have direct knowledge of unobserved events, though we can infer either logically or probabilistically to unobservables. But this is a finishing point and provisional at that. The starting point for realism is that there is a reality existing independently of our perceptions of it. However, scientific realism (and for our purposes we can regard critical realism as a sub-set of this) contains a stronger claim and it is broadly that science must *begin* from the principle of ontological realism and therefore permits the postulation of unobservables that are not directly testable. Its challenge is to devise a methodology to show how we can obtain knowledge of the reality it assumes. Only then can the empiricist complaint that realists make an unwarranted move from the metaphysical and general to the concrete and specific be refuted.

Once we accept the starting premise of ontological realism, it is but a small step to accept that there are hidden structures (or, as critical realists would have it, mechanisms) producing those things which we can observe, but the difficulty is that we do not know that what we know of *specific* structures or mechanisms is sufficient to explain their observable effects. As Bhaskar put it:

> things exist and act independently of our descriptions, but we can only know them under particular descriptions. Descriptions belong to the world of society and of men; objects belong to the world of nature ... Science, then, is the systematic attempt to express in thought the structures and ways of acting of things that exist and act independently of thought.
>
> (Bhaskar 1978: 250)

In empiricism probabilistic knowledge of constant conjunctions stands in for knowledge of structures. In empiricist social science (particularly the social survey) some knowledge of structures can be inferred from the relationship between three or more variables, but the variable to variable relationship, even within a nesting of variables, remains probabilistic. Critical realists are, however, more optimistic and believe in the existence of mechanisms, which must necessarily exist but may not be observationally available. This view is philosophically justified by them through reference to not just one ontological 'level', that of experience, but three: experience, events and reality. Events can occur without being experienced (Outhwaite 1987: 22), which would indicate that there must be something beyond the veil of appearance. That which we experience is contingent upon either our selection through theories, or by accident. The aim of the scientist, then, is to make clear the connectives between these levels. A full explanation is one that shows how experiences are produced by events and the relationship of these events to structures. In order to do this the scientist must propose theories which, if they were correct, would explain those underlying structures. The scientist's theories Bhaskar refers to as the 'transitive' objects of science. The world itself consists of 'intransitive' objects; that is, things exist and act independently of our descriptions (Bhaskar 1978: 250) and prior to investigation (and indeed possibly after) are not known to science. The aim of investigation is to achieve a correspondence between the two. Events are caused, not simply conjoined, and therefore probabilistic explanation can at best be seen just as provisional.

Probabilistic explanation presents three specific difficulties for critical realism. First, the demonstration of a probabilistic relationship does not permit a distinction between a necessary sequence of events and an accidental one (Bhaskar 1998: 10) because the experiences, though repeated, are just singular observational events. Their arrangement may also be a function of manipulation rather than nature. This goes deeper than the apocryphal story of storks and babies and is a concern with the active intervention of the scientist. In performing an experiment, Bhaskar claims, the scientist is 'forcing' nature, engineering constant conjunctions. By extension we could similarly speak of *post hoc* survey analysis, when the researcher establishes the existence of significant relationships between variables, or just as importantly the operationalisation of those variables in the first place. Although the process in which this happens may begin with a hypothesis, the hypothesis is modified in accordance with the relationships shown, or not shown. In a logistic regression model, for example, the researcher (as an alternative to a stepwise procedure) may well fit terms in different orders to produce the greatest reduction in scaled deviance. Thus the probabilistic relationships between variables within a statistical model stand in for the necessary relationships of nature, but this is according to realism an unwarranted assumption.

Second, in speaking of a probabilistic relationship the empiricist conflates the existence of chance or random elements with our lack of knowledge of them (Sayer 1992: 191). The consequence is that the empiricist researcher applies further and more careful observation and control in the search for regularities (Harré 1986: 344) that may or may not exist.

Third, critical realists claim, the postulation of mechanisms requires a stronger version of causality than the 'causal inference' of empiricism. Because it is only probabilistic association it lacks the categories of 'producing', 'generating' or 'forcing'. Consequently, 'according to the realist view of social causality *qualitative* analysis of objects is required to disclose mechanisms' (Sayer 1992: 179; emphasis in original).

Both empiricists and critical realists see probability as an epistemological matter and both accept it offers incomplete knowledge. Empiricists have learned to live with this defect and are happy to improve their explanations through improved technical application, whereas critical realists, for the reasons outlined above, are dissatisfied.

Critical realist closure

The problem of following Bhaskar's methodological injunction to seek agreement between intransitive and transitive objects begins with the problem of what will be seen as evidence for the former – what will represent them? If realism is to be a viable methodology, it requires a form of 'closure', the ability to measure the existence and the properties of transitive objects in order that we can infer the properties of intransitive ones.

Pawson (1989: 213) specifies three elements of 'realist closure'. First, an empirical relationship we wish to explain should be seen as resulting from the action of a generative mechanism. Second, the context in which this mechanism is expected to manifest itself empirically must be specified as part of the explanatory framework (as opposed to mere description of the circumstances). Finally, we must control for the effects of intervening and different mechanisms on the one in which we are interested. The model can thus be seen to operationalise Bhaskar's three levels of 'experience, events and reality'.

Though noting that there are no actually existing examples of realist closure in social research, Pawson shows how E.O. Wright's work on class structure can be reconstructed in such a way. Wright's work is concerned with how the forces of exploitation and domination in capitalism differentially determine the possibility of action in different classes. For Pawson, what is special about this work is not simply that Wright constructs models of empirical regularities which explain the interrelationships of the various properties, but crucially it defines the operational boundaries within which they should operate (Pawson 1989: 214–15).

Pawson's attempt at realist closure is a potentially useful strategy, but it does expose two core problems for critical realism:

1   How can the researcher know when she has discovered 'real structures'? The empiricist says that we cannot and the best we can do is to name those phenomena which we are able to measure. The ontological realist has folk psychological evidence for reality and that new and unexpected things are revealed continuously, but these are revealed contingently and simply hint at yet other layers of reality. Empiricists say that a scientific research programme cannot begin from this. Yet critical realism (and

scientific realism generally) wants more, aiming to discover underlying structures and mechanisms. The three elements in Pawson's closure suggest a nesting of data, whereby the specific is explained in respect of other elements, a strategy common enough in all multiple regression models (Tacq 1997: Chapter 3). Pawson advocates 'identifying those contexts where a particular mechanism operates producing certain observable regularities' (ibid.), which seems to be a good empirical strategy. However this does not free us of the need to name and specify the properties of a mechanism, such as class, so that we shall know that the observable regularities might be identified for what they are. In other words, the mechanisms themselves, unless they are to remain wholly in the realm of *a priori* metaphysical assumptions, must be capable at least of identification.

2   The second problem is that of what shall count as social reality and is altogether a much 'deeper' problem. In Wright's analysis class 'is the context of production which identifies the economic resources and coercive powers open to members of particular class positions' (Pawson 1989: 186) and is a generative model presumably *capable* of producing at least some congruence between intransitive and transitive objects. However, Pawson contrasts the Wright model with two other 'generative' models of class and although they 'show remarkable similarities in terms of their measurement strategies' (ibid.), they nevertheless suggest different possibilities of congruence between intransitive and transitive objects. John Hall (1996: 194) takes up this point and suggests either there is one fundamental, generative, real process or 'there may be manifold mechanisms, processes, recipes of action and other phenomena that are tapped by alternative measurements of stratification' (Hall 1996: 194).

Hall regards the former as unlikely for three reasons: that the complexity and heterogeneity of processes that underlie stratification are essentially chaotic (in the mathematical sense) and necessarily defy complete description; this complexity may overwhelm our abilities to investigate stratification, such that shifting value interests will dictate research programmes; finally, that because the processes underlying and salient to stratification are historically emergent, they may well outstrip our ability to identify their properties (1996: 195). Now whilst we do not share Hall's pessimism, for reasons described below, he does put his finger on one important facet of critical realist ontology, that of the question of necessity in social reality.

Necessity and the social world

Bhaskar is very clear about the centrality of necessity to his project: 'A sequence *A, B* is necessary if and only if there is a natural mechanism M such that when stimulated by *A, B* tends to be produced' (1998: 10).

However, if Hall is right, then there cannot ever be necessity in A, B. In the confines of the laboratory it may be possible to bring about such necessity, but in the social world (and indeed in much of the natural world) this would not be the case. In his first book Bhaskar anticipates this criticism (1978: 199–215), making an important point that logical necessity and natural necessity are not the same thing. Hall's first possibility of one underlying generative mechanism of class implies that the realist case is of a fundamental essence that makes observable properties logically inevitable. Hall, as we saw, does not believe this to be so, but neither does Bhaskar. Natural necessity is something quite different and involves, rather, the *potentiality* of a mechanism:

> if science is to be possible, there must be a relationship of natural necessity between what a thing is and what a thing can do and hence between what a thing is and what it tends to do, in appropriate conditions.
>
> (Bhaskar 1978: 202)

Bhaskar's necessity is actually nomic necessity. This involves the assumption that as the world displays regularity, it must follow that this does not come about by chance – though this is not to say that things must always happen in the same way on every occasion. However, as Papineau (1993: 198*n*) points out, the difficulty of postulating necessities in the physical (and we could add social) world is the difficulty of distinguishing what must necessarily be[3] from 'accidentally true generalizations'. To say something is necessary, but also contingent, is to try to have one's cake and eat it. Indeed, critical realists maintain that because the world is complex, we can talk only of 'tendencies', 'powers' or 'liabilities' (Bhaskar 1978: 172; 1998: 97–101) in relation to necessity. Now whilst all of this is consistent with nomic necessity, that is, that such regularity does not rule out counterfactuals, such as instances where (statistical) laws seem not to apply, it does not tell us how we can show how necessity is different from apparent contingency or separate out the necessary from the contingent, should both exist.

Given this, does it provide any added value over probability and logical necessity, or indeed must it translate as these in any empirical investigation? This seems to be the implication of what Pawson is saying. It is hard to see how this is avoidable. An analysis of the antecedents of voting Liberal, for example, would, if conducted far enough, result in a set of nested probabilities. At the aggregate level nomic necessity is indistinguishable from probability, even if we carried out Pawson's advice of specifying a generative mechanism and its context, as well as controlling for the effects of intervening and different mechanisms. Only at the individual level (or level of the unit of analysis) can we talk of necessity and this is logical necessity; for example, an individual could not vote Liberal, if she were not a registered voter for that particular election.

Nevertheless, it is right to say that whatever strategies we propose to investigate social reality need to be predicated on the ontological assumption that the social is always contingent, even if individual manifestations of it possess a logical necessity. All that remains is probability and logical necessity. For a realist this may first appear as a doctrine of despair, but in the next section we will consider a possible resolution of the problem.

Contingency and necessity

An empirically adequate realism must do more than present a plausible story to demonstrate how effects might have come to be; it must also show how real structures can be distinguished from mere epiphenomena. The pessimistic empiricists deny this is possible, because (to put it crudely) we can only measure that which we can see is there. The metaphysical part of critical realism is plausible, but the real problem seems to lie in its insistence on a distinction between contingency and necessity. Now we do not deny that at a 'local level' logical necessity operates, but we suggest that critical realism cannot show how contingency can be distinguished empirically from nomic necessity. The critical realists speak of contingency in relation to powers and liabilities, that the specification of a mechanism does not imply a particular empirical realisation. Indeed, at one point Sayer, in recognising this, points out that: 'contingently-related conditions are never inert, but are themselves the product of causal processes and have their own causal powers and liabilities' (Sayer 1992: 140).

It is assumed that by contingency it is meant that something could have been otherwise. Now apart from the aforementioned logical necessity, this seems to be almost always the case in the social and much of the physical world. Karl Popper (1979: 206–18) uses a nice analogy of clouds and clocks. Clouds are irregular, disorderly and more or less unpredictable, whereas clocks are regular, orderly and highly predictable. Of course, as he points out, clouds of gnats move in irregular ways, but their velocities do not show a very wide spread. They can be probabilistically predicted. Conversely, in speaking of the accuracy of a clock, we would need to specify a margin of accuracy, say plus or minus n minutes/seconds per day/week, etc. Social systems are nearer to clouds, biological systems also, but a little nearer to clocks, whilst physical systems are much more like clocks. Most social and biological systems seem to possess the properties of contingency, logical necessity and some form of order, but this order is only amenable to theoretical and probabilistic description.

Contingency and structure in realist explanation

What will count as a 'real structure' if we pull away the rug of nomic necessity? Let us re-focus on the individual agent. A real structure for the individual might be defined as that which is external to him/her but can play an enabling or constraining role. Such structures may exist as the result of the deliberate actions of other agents, civil/criminal laws for example, or they may exist as unintended consequences. Each has a level of contingency. Many US states claim to punish first degree murder with death to the perpetrator, but this punishment outcome is, as we know, contingent upon factors such as class, colour and access to competent legal representation. Any explanation of real structures is actually an explanation of a series of clustered probabilities. There is no Newtonian force there and the necessity of the law of homicide is only realised at the point of death of the alleged perpetrator.

Intransitive objects are not Newtonian forces, but processes which have necessity only in outcomes as realised. In saying this we must avoid thinking about outcomes teleologically, for this brings us straight back to the atomism of empiricist measurement. Variables are merely 'traces' (Byrne 2002: 32), evidence of those processes, represented as measured outcomes. An intervention (as measurement) at any point is an outcome and a realisation of logical necessity, but the intervention could have been elsewhere. For example, we might measure the number of executions in the United States over a five-year period. Each execution is a real outcome of social, then physical processes. Conversely we could measure acquittals in homicide cases over the same period. As the judge brings down her gavel, the same kind of logical necessity is realised, but at some point there has been a bifurcation of the process. Of course, there could have been many bifurcations and those we map are a function of the conceptual framework in which we intervene through measuring.

The lack of teleology in processes does not imply lack of intention. We aim towards states and may succeed, but our success (or otherwise) is both the result of processes compatible (or otherwise) with our intentions and the source of new processes. Our intentions and actions are nested in countless other actions, intentions, but most especially outcomes. This certainly does not dissolve the concept of structure (or mechanism), because some intentions, actions or outcomes produce stable patterns. The sexual division of labour in a society, for example, becomes a structure as a result of actions constrained by other actions (e.g. the prevention of women entering certain careers) and intentions shaped by the actions available. A woman cannot become a Catholic priest, so her action space is reduced to becoming a priest in a different sect, or not entering the clergy at all. For another woman to stay at home, be a housewife and have babies is not logically determined, as in the previous case, but may be the result of pressure from a partner, parents or peers.

The above agency–structure relationship has been more ably expressed by others (e.g. Archer 1995; Layder 1990; 1994), but it is worth restating to show how we can retain realism without a concept of natural necessity. When Archer, Layder or Bhaskar describe structures, they are usually describing abstract structures, or structures at a very general level, but if we wish to devise an empirical method of investigation of structuration, we need some sort of quantifier. Logical necessity just gives us bi-polar states, whether something 'is' or 'isn't'. This does not suffice (and especially in the social survey); we need some way of measuring the contingency, the potential for a state to be realised. We need a realist probability.

Realism and probability

The critical realist critique of probability in empiricism misses the most fundamental (and, we would insist, realist) objection that whatever the ontological status of the variable itself, the measurement of its presence (or absence) is nevertheless a measurement of a concrete instance of something, yet within a frequency distribution that measurement is subsumed under an 'ideal' relationship to the mean. A measurement of children's attainment at age 11, in relation to (say) variables of class, ethnicity and gender, will allow aggregate predictions for different groups of children, yet the predictive odds (could they be known) for any given child are likely to vary from that group of which she is a member. Yet as Karl Popper pointed out (1983: 356–7) if a frequency distribution is generated by the dispositional characteristics of its cases, then one would expect that the probability of the case would be equal to that of the frequency distribution. This statistical paradox has been long recognised and was noted by von Mises (1951). Frequency distributions are not just statistical facts, they have other ontological properties, yet the dispositional properties of cases have been confined to the realm of the unknowable in the operationalist methodology of empiricism (Gillies 1995: 105).

However, in the mid-1950s Karl Popper resurrected the issue (Popper 1957; 1959). He noted that the (standard empiricist) frequency interpretation of probability takes probability as relative to a sequence which is assumed, but of course frequencies are produced only through repetitions, which indicates that what is repeated must generate the sequence (say, membership of a class, ethnic group or one's gender). This must mean, Popper argues, that a singular event has a probability that arises from the same generating conditions that produced the sequence. Every single event has a probability, even though it may occur only once, for its probability is a property of those generating conditions. Even very unlikely events have some probability of occurrence unless they *necessarily* cannot happen (and have a probability of zero), e.g. the impossibility, at present, of a woman becoming a Catholic priest.

One further component of Popper's argument is a realist argument for the properties of single cases and their generating conditions. The dispositional properties that produce the sequence must reside in the single events. Now the single events must themselves have two properties: a) that they have the propensity to be realised, b) that the properties are real, not virtual.

a) Single events are themselves not determined, but are the product of the generating conditions and will have only a probability of occurrence. Nevertheless, unless the occurrence of the event is a logical impossibility (a probability of 0), they will have some kind of probability of occurrence, even if this is very small (Popper 1983: 356–7). There is a probability of zero of a woman becoming a Catholic priest, though a small, but non-zero, probability of a woman becoming an Anglican bishop. These probabilities change and in the social world zero probabilities can become non-zero ones (in this case as a result of a change in Vatican law).

b) The reality of propensities exists in their dispositional properties. In an experiment these are not inherent properties, but are relational properties of the experimental arrangement itself. Popper uses the (perhaps over) simple example of a dice. A tendency for it to come up 6 is not to do with its essential character, its 'diceness', if you like, but the dispositional properties of its weight distribution, its surface characteristics and those of the surface it is thrown on to, etc. Analogously, gender is not an essential characteristic but is composed of socially specific dispositional properties, such as divisions of labour, child-rearing roles, access to education, that will produce a propensity for one's gender to make a difference to outcomes.

The realisation, or what Mellor (1971: Chapter 4) called the 'showing', of the propensities can only come about as a result of a particular set of interactions. We can, for example, talk of common salt as having the dispositional property of dissolving in water, but this can only come about when salt is added to water. It is possible to imagine a world where this dispositional property is never realised or 'shown' (Popper 1959: 37). Sayer (1992: 105) speaks of the causal power of being able to work, speak, reason, reproduce, etc., but these causal powers may, or may not, be exercised and when they are, they will exercised in the context of other interdependent relationships. For Popper's dispositional properties, read Sayer's causal powers.

Realist probability and cluster analysis

The context of Popper's propensity interpretation was the controlled experiment, in which the generating conditions, though variable, would show a limited variation. In order to derive the relational properties of the individual experiment, he advocates the strategy of the repeated experiment. Though he doesn't specify the detail of this, it might be supposed that the scientist would aim to build a model in which the relative weights of the factors might be calculated in order to arrive at the 'weight of the weighted possibilities' (Popper 1959: 36–7). The social world is much more 'open' in character and the antecedents of individual properties much more complex and the strategy of the 'repeated experiment' not tenable.

The key premise of the propensity interpretation is that analysis must be case based, because the probabilities are the ontological characteristics of the situation and not an epistemological tool to stand in for lack of knowledge. Most forms of quantitative analysis are variable, not case based, because they begin from the assumptions of the frequency interpretation of probability. Certainly techniques such as factor analysis can be used to demonstrate multiple contingency amongst highly intercorrelated variables, but such techniques are epistemological techniques and can still provide only inference to the best explanation. The principal candidates for realist analysis are case based cluster analysis techniques.

A cluster analysis begins from the case, not the variable,[4] and determines whether given categories of a particular case are similar enough to fall into groups or clusters. Cluster analyses are essentially taxonomic and originally developed in biology to 'gather all possible data on organisms of interest, estimate the degree of similarity among these organisms, and use a clustering method to place relatively similar organisms into the same groups' (Aldenderfer and Blashfield 1984: 8). In a social setting the 'case', usually an individual agent, will at any given point in their life possess characteristics that can be classified to show where these are held in common with other agents. Unlike variable analysis one begins from the case and seeks characteristics held in common, rather than beginning with the characteristics and seeking their association with cases.

Clearly every individual will have a unique biography and there must be some prior notion of what will count as a classification, but this is not necessarily arbitrary, as we will show in the example below, and is usually driven by a particular contextual concern – say offending behaviour. Each offender will have a history of prior events that have shaped their current situation. Some offenders with the same characteristics will have similar antecedent states, some different. Conversely offenders with different characteristics may at some point in the past have shared characteristics. At a number of measurable points there will be bifurcations where things happen to an individual, or they make particular choices based on beliefs and desires. Many of the things which happen to individuals will be evidence of structures, where 'causal powers' are realised.

Clusters represent these bifurcations. Each case is first put into its own 'cluster', so in a data set of 1000 there will be 1000 clusters. At each level of analysis the clusters are combined, allowing us to trace antecedent conditions and their bifurcations into current states. The technique is therefore hierarchical.[5] It can be visually represented (as in Figure 3.1) as a dendogram.

Cluster analysis is based on the premise that the most accurate information is available when each case constitutes a group. Consequently as the number of clusters is systematically reduced from k, k -1, k -2 ..., 1, the grouping of increasingly dissimilar cases yields less precise information. At each stage in

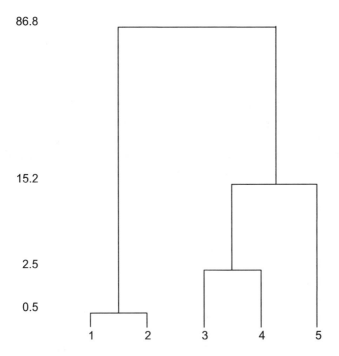

Figure 3.1 Clustering dendogram

Note: The usual form of graphic output from a hierarchical cluster analysis is a tree (dendogram). The tree provides a visual representation of the cluster structure of the hierarchy.

Source: Everitt 1993: 15

the procedure the goal is to form a group such that the sum of squared within-group deviations about the group mean of each profile variable is minimised for all profile variables at the same time. The value of the objective function is expressed as the sum of the within-group sum of squares (called the error sum of squares, ESS).[6] The probability of the single case can therefore be derived from the sum of the within-group sum of squares. Each reduction in groups of cases is achieved by considering all possible pairings and selecting the pairing for which the objective-function value is smallest. Each cluster of cases previously formed is treated as one unit. When the complete hierarchical solution has been obtained, the ESS values may be compared to ascertain the relative homogeneity of the groups formed. A sharp increase in the ESS indicates that much of the accuracy has been lost by reducing the number of groups.

In the next section we present a brief methodological case study of research using a two stage cluster analysis conducted by one of us (Dyer) in Cleveland, UK.

Cluster analysis and custody diversion teams: a case study of cluster analysis

Health and Social Service custody diversion teams were introduced in England at the beginning of the 1990s because of concerns about the prevalence of psychiatric disorder in the prison population (Gunn *et al.* 1991) and the possibility that the latter may be growing due to a process of transcarceration/criminalisation (Weller and Weller 1988). The aim of these teams was to divert mentally disordered offenders away from the criminal justice system and prison to care and treatment by the health and social services. The claim was that a policy of diversion was a positive step because it avoided the stigma attached to a prison sentence and the development of a long and perhaps notorious criminal career by ensuring people received the care and treatment they required. The question was: did the people referred to custody diversion teams exhibit evidence of exposure to a transcarceration/criminalisation process; and what impact did it have on the psychiatric and criminal careers of those referred?

The research was explicitly underwritten by a realist approach, particularly the need to identify underlying structures or mechanisms, and cluster analysis was initially chosen for its very practical advantages in identifying and mapping the different psychiatric and criminal careers experienced by people referred to the Cleveland Diversion Team and the divergent paths their careers took as a consequence of the team's actions. The processing of cases by the diversion team was observed through time in terms of a series of classifications of the cases at stages in their 'career' within the system. The temporal dimension was not calendar time but rather a stage in the process. The Cleveland Diversion Team, like other systems of this kind, 'processed' cases and what was interesting and important was what difference the processing made to the outcome for the case. It was possible to describe this using stage ordered classificatory procedures. Categories of entry could be distinguished – i.e. distinctions among original cases; categories of processing – differences in what was done to individual cases; and categories of outcome – what happened to the cases at the end of the process. Movement could then be mapped throughout the intervention process.

Three data sets were created representing the three career stages: 1) History, 2) First Referral and 3) First Referral Outcomes. To begin with, cluster analysis was undertaken within each of these quite separate data sets, thereby describing the state of the system at discrete periods of time. Each emergent cluster was a slice through the psychiatric/criminal career of an individual case, bringing into high relief each discrete time period used to describe careers but losing an overall portrait of longitudinal careers, which was necessary in order to evaluate the impact of the actions of the team. Researching the careers of mentally disordered offenders rendered inadequate any simple focus on clearly delineated and significant episodes. What was needed was a technique which uncovered the complex ways in which some individuals experienced one type of institutional career and yet others experienced another type, depending upon different circumstances and the actions of others – in other words, a method which could be used to trace the movements of cases from one state to another through a process of bifurcation, which was dependent on key changes in the magnitude of underlying causal variables. The process of bifurcation implied neither simple linear determination (constant conjunction where if A happened then B happened), nor random process where anything could happen. Instead what was implied was complex change, so that in the first bifurcation if A happened, then B *or* C happened depending upon small initial variations in the form of A. The observed states can therefore be seen as nested probabilities within a Markov chain (see Figure 3.2).[7]

The link between the discrete periods or slices through a criminal/psychiatric career was provided by the individual or the case referred to the team. Following cluster analysis, each individual was located in one cluster at the History stage, then in another cluster at the First Referral stage and finally in a last cluster at the First Referral Outcomes stage. The next step, which involved mapping or tracing the movement of people from one set of clusters in a discrete time period to the next using further cluster analysis and cross tabulations, brought into focus each complete career structure.

Five different types of career were identified (see Figure 3.3). Careers One and Two describe experiences of medicalisation – violent offenders with no psychiatric history who were referred, assessed and diagnosed but had no health or social care needs identified and were not referred again. Careers Three and Four describe experiences of criminalisation – violent offenders with a psychiatric history, half of whom (Career Three) were referred, assessed and diagnosed, had health or social care needs identified and were not referred again; the remainder (Career Four) were not assessed or diagnosed, nor did they have needs identified and consequently all were re-referred repeatedly. Career Five represents neither medicalisation nor criminalisation – individuals referred for information and for whom little else is known.

This two-stage cluster analysis uncovered and mapped the different psychiatric and criminal careers experienced by separate individuals and the different paths their careers took as a consequence of the team's actions, and

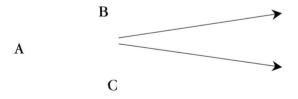

Figure 3.2 Probabilities within a Markov chain

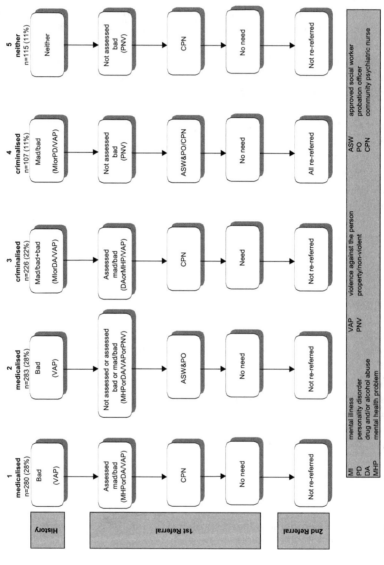

Figure 3.3 Career typology of individuals referred to the Cleveland Diversion Team for Mentally Disordered Offenders (n=1011)

then identified the shared experiences or types of career which could be used to group people together in order to generalise which actions had a positive or negative impact on which types of people. Changes could be mapped over time so that it became possible not to predict as such, but to act so that some things happened and others did not.

The methodology adopted permits the measurement of individual probabilities of different 'career' paths. The stability of patterns of outcomes common to individuals provides evidence of structure and indeed emulates, as far as one can, an open system. From an ontological perspective, the patterns of nesting and the contingency of antecedent states dissolve any notion of necessity, other than the logical necessity of the specific outcomes in individual careers. Crucially, however, they also demonstrate that the contingency is not random, but arises out of the differential realisations of earlier outcomes.

Conclusion

The heart of the dispute between empiricists and realists is ontology. Empiricists see it as a metaphysical distraction and put their faith in epistemology. Consequently their version of probability (and indeed the dominant version) is epistemological in character. Realists, on the other hand, begin from ontological assumptions. Now whilst this has got realism into trouble with empiricists, whose rejoinder is 'how can you know?', it is also potentially methodologically liberating in respect of thinking about probability. Frequentist probability is a measure of the world, or more accurately our ignorance of it, but the claim of realism must be that the world itself is probabilistic – a conclusion not logically open to empiricists. Thus far critical realism has avoided this claim because of its misunderstanding of probability. Yet in talk of 'powers' or 'liabilities' it has certainly implied that claim but has not given it methodological substance, and critical realism has instead retreated into qualitative methods. At a philosophical level we have argued that the removal of necessity (except logical necessity) and its replacement with contingency takes nothing from the critical realist case, but opens up the possibilities for realist quantitative methods.

In order to put methodological flesh on these philosophical bones we turned to some work Karl Popper undertook in the philosophy of statistics in the 1950s, where he argued for the replacement of a frequentist (empiricist) interpretation of probability with a single case (realist) approach. Popper's achievement was not just to produce an ontological theory of probability, but to specify an ontology that was probabilistic long before mathematical complexity had been demonstrated in open systems. In respect of realism it renders a methodological reliance on natural necessity as unnecessary and permits the reintroduction of probability, but as an ontological property.

Here we have tried to show how one methodological technique, cluster analysis, can emulate single case probabilities. Though the technique has been with us for some time, as far as we know this is one of the few times it has been used in realist analysis. Consequently the statistical and epistemological status of its results will no doubt be contested by empiricists. As Dave Byrne (2000) notes in an unpublished paper, frequentist statisticians are uneasy about clustering methods because in general they are not constructed around a central concern with inference from samples to universe. Of course this would be a fair criticism if adequacy of explanation equated with isomorphism of prediction – explanation, but, as we have indicated, realists want to go deeper to find explanations in structures (or mechanisms) and in this respect cluster analysis is a powerful realist methodological tool.

Notes

1   Blalock (1964: 36) notes that dependent and independent variables are algebraic equivalents, thus $Y = a + bX$ could equally be expressed as $X = -a/b + Y/b$. They are symmetrical and decisions about which to treat as the dependent variable involve inferences about the direction of causation.
2   The method used is that of LISREL (Linear Structural Relations). The model aims to produce causal models through the use of multiple indicators of latent variables and structural relations between those variables.
3   Papineau uses the expression 'physical laws', but extended to the social world we could speak of non accidental regularities.
4   Strictly speaking they can begin from a variable, but here we are concerned with case based cluster analyses.
5   There are other forms of cluster analysis that are not hierarchical. SPSS, for example, offers K-Means Cluster Analysis and Discriminant Analysis as well as hierarchical.
6   This can be expressed formally as

$$ESS = x_{\overline{i}}^{2} - 1/n \left(\sum x_i\right)^2$$

7   A Markov chain is a time series model (though not necessarily calendar time) where a given probability is dependent only upon the immediate preceding event. However, the approach described here differs from Markov methods, which usually take a 'black box' approach to preceding states of a system and are simply interested in prediction (see Byrne 2002: 122).

References

Aldenderfer, M. and Blashfield, R. (1984) *Cluster Analysis. Sage University Paper 44*, Newbury Park, CA: Sage.

Archer, M. (1995) *Realist Social Theory: the Morphogenetic Approach*, Cambridge: Cambridge University Press.

Bhaskar, R. (1978) *A Realist Theory of Science*, 2nd edn, London: Harvester Wheatsheaf.

Bhaskar, R. (1998) *The Possibility of Naturalism*, 3rd edn, London: Routledge.

Blalock, H. (1964) *Causal Inference in Nonexperimental Research*, Chapel Hill, NCA: University of North Carolina Press.

Byrne, D. (2000) 'What are we measuring when we measure?', Draft paper, ESRC Realism Seminar, Leeds, 16 February (unpublished).

Byrne, D. (2002) *Interpreting Quantitative Data*, London: Sage.

Everitt, B. (1993) *Cluster Analysis*, London: Arnold.

Gillies, D. (1995) 'Popper's contribution to the philosophy of probability', in A. O'Hear (ed.) *Karl Popper: Philosophy and Problems*, Cambridge: Cambridge University Press.

Gunn, J., Maden, A. and Swinton, M. (1991) 'Treatment needs of prisoners with psychiatric disorders', *British Medical Journal*, 303, 338–41.

Hall, J. (1996) 'Measurement and the Two Cultures of Sociology', in S. Turner (ed.) *Social Theory and Sociology: The Classics and Beyond*, Oxford: Blackwell.

Harré, R. (1986) *Varieties of Realism: A Rationale for the Natural Sciences*, Oxford: Blackwell.

Layder, D. (1990) *The Realist Image in Social Science*, London: Macmillan.

Layder, D. (1994) *Understanding Social Theory*, London: Sage.

Lipton, P. (1991) *Inference to the Best Explanation*, London: Routledge.

Mellor, D. (1971) *The Matter of Chance*, Cambridge: Cambridge University Press.

Nagel, E. (1979) *The Structure of Science: Problems in the Logic of Scientific Explanation*, Indianapolis: Hackett.

Outhwaite, W. (1987) *New Philosophies of Social Science*, London: Macmillan.

Papineau, D. (1993) *Philosophical Naturalism*, Oxford: Blackwell.

Pawson, R. (1989) *A Measure for Measures: A Manifesto for Empirical Sociology*, London: Routledge.

Popper, K.R. (1957) 'The propensity interpretation of the calculus of probability, and the quantum theory', in S. Körner (ed.) *Observation and Interpretation*, London: Butterworth Scientific.

Popper, K.R. (1959) 'The propensity interpretation of probability', *British Journal for the Philosophy of Science*, 10: 25–42.

Popper, K.R. (1979) *Objective Knowledge: An Evolutionary Approach*, Oxford: Oxford University Press.

Popper, K.R. (1983) *Realism and the Aim of Science* (from the Postscript to the *Logic of Scientific Discovery*), London: Routledge.

Sayer, A. (1992) *Method in Social Science: A Realist Approach*, 2nd edn, London: Routledge.

Tacq, J. (1997) *Multivariate Analysis Techniques in Social Science Research*, London: Sage.

von Mises, R. (1951) *Probability, Statistics and Truth*, 2nd edn, London: George, Allen and Unwin.

Weller, M.P.I. and Weller, B.G.A. (1988) 'Crime and mental illness', *Medicine, Science and Law*, 28, 38–49.

Part II

Applying realism

The two chapters in this section explore the possibilities of applying realist social theory to substantive areas of sociological interest and research which are currently dominated by other perspectives. Paul Higgs, Ian Rees Jones and Graham Scambler review the field of health inequalities, in which an empiricist search for correlations between variables is the standard approach. Bob Carter and Alison Sealey review sociolinguistics, where two main approaches have traditionally been hegemonic: an empiricist search for associations between variables (such as between particular variants in pronunciation and gender, class or age) and social constructionism (investigating the use of particular language markers for narratives of identity, for example). If empiricism is realist, it is so in a naïve and ontologically 'flat' sense (observables are real and inference is to links between them), while social constructionism tends to be irrealist to a greater or lesser extent.

Carter and Sealey take issue with narrow and reductive forms of realism – both with Saussure's structuralism and Chomsky's 'generative grammar'. In each case it is not so much the substantive content of the claims made about the nature of language that Carter and Sealey criticise as the methodological effects of over-extending these claims. They then consider social constructionist accounts of discourse, finding these unsatisfactory in their refusal to acknowledge the structural properties and powers of language itself. Where post-structuralist discourse theorists have reduced the social to language, Carter and Sealey insist that language is a cultural emergent property, the investigation of which is a crucial part of social research. Drawing on recent work in corpus linguistics, they go on to develop a novel and distinctively realist view of the relation between language, structure and agency.

Addressing the field of health inequalities research, Scambler, Higgs and Jones are frustrated by researchers' failure to look for the mechanisms which generate and reproduce health inequalities. Instead, most researchers use 'flawed models of class' to establish non-explanatory associations between 'class' and 'health inequalities' (Chapter 4, p. 91). 'While there is continuous confirmation of class based gradients, no conclusions about causation can be drawn' (Chapter 4, p. 95). Income differentials and other markers of class merely mediate the effects of exploitation in producing and perpetuating health inequality. In timidly fudging the extent of income differentials, the Acheson report obscured the mechanisms behind them, encouraging the attribution of health inequalities to the unwise life-style choices of individuals and groups. In its focus on putative mechanisms at the socio-psychological and evolutionary levels, Wilkinson's work similarly obscures the eminently social mechanism behind the polarisation of income.

The authors offer a realist critique of current sociological theories of class. They identify exploitation as the main mechanism which produces and maintains health inequalities, via its production of their more proximate causes. Like all mechanisms, it works through people's actions – here, the everyday decisions of people positioned in the 'capitalist executive'. 'The UK's widening health inequalities are the largely unintended consequences of the adaptive behaviours of its power elite' (Chapter 4, p. 102).

4 Class as variable, class as generative mechanism

The importance of critical realism for the sociology of health inequalities

Paul Higgs, Ian Rees Jones and Graham Scambler

Introduction

In Britain there has been a long tradition of empirical social research focusing on links between poverty, material deprivation and health. This research has played a key role in maintaining a spotlight on the health divides that arise from the enduring fault lines of class, age, ethnicity, gender and place (Acheson 1998). At the heart of this research, however, lies a puzzle. Despite appearing to confirm the continued importance of class divisions in society through the detailed and painstaking documenting of the relationship between mortality, morbidity and social structure, the research is largely reliant on flawed models of class. Indeed, much sociological research around such inequalities tends to approach the issues in a piecemeal fashion. This leads to sociological confusion and indeed to a failure of radical reform as insights are reified into policies which effect little change. We have argued elsewhere (Higgs and Scambler 1998; Scambler and Higgs 1999) that crucial elements are lost if social class is identified as just another (albeit potent) variable or cluster of variables in mapping the 'social facts' of modern societies. The focus on research that demonstrates correlations between health outcomes and various factors only serves to maintain individualised notions of social causality. In this chapter we will argue that a realist approach to health inequalities research is salient in two key ways. In the first instance, its stratified ontology and analytical separation of structure and action make particular demands of research. In the second place it can situate the social causes of health inequalities in the processes constituting social class in capitalist society. This requires us to look at the *logics*, *relations* and *figurations* in which and through which health is located in modern societies.

Realism and research

Realist social science is not new and, as Lawson (1997) points out, has an older pedigree than is sometimes assumed. However, it is in recent years that realism has begun to influence social scientists and social theorists working in the field of health and health care. In particular it has provided the platform for critiques of research addressing inequalities in health (Higgs and Scambler 1998). It has been used to counter postmodern approaches to the sociology of the body and to assert the role of modern medicine in mitigating pain and chronic illness (Williams 1999). It has informed critical perspectives on mental health and illness (Pilgrim and Rogers 1999). It has also been used as a theoretical underpinning for critiques of health services research and for attempts to develop realist research in the field of health and health care (Porter and Ryan 1996; Forbes and Wainwright 2001).

One way in which realism has underpinned this work is through its explicit theory of knowledge. Positivism, methodological individualism and variants of relativism are seen to be vulnerable to a number of fallacies which have limited their contribution to knowledge. Bhaskar identifies these as the epistemic fallacy (the view that statements about being can be derived from statements about our knowledge of being); the ontic fallacy (the reification of facts and the fetishism of their conjunction); and the linguistic fallacy (mistaking our language about being for being) (Bhaskar 1994). The use of social class in health research, despite its ability to reveal patterns of inequality, involves the epistemic fallacy. The classes in question are theoretically problematic: nominal schema which restate the data rather than explain it (Jones and Cameron 1984; Scambler and Higgs 1999). Equally with respect to the ontic fallacy, the reification of ethnicity as a risk factor for certain diseases (Senior and Bhopal 1994) has led to dangerous misunderstandings of the life world of different groups in British society (Sheldon and Parker 1992; Ahmad 1993). Research has shown that the complex interactions between health and social location will vary and develop over the life cycle (Vagero and Illsley 1995; Smith 1999). However, 'black box' research, which concerns itself only with inputs and outputs, may only distort our understanding of such complexity (Kreiger 1994). At least one critique of the Acheson report has highlighted the neglect of context in the framework employed (Birch 1999). By contrast, the postmodern relativist approach falls into the linguistic fallacy by suggesting that inequalities are socially constructed in language, and that there is no 'truth' concerning healthy and unhealthy bodies, only a multiplicity of discourses (Fox 1998; Bunton 1998). Such perspectives risk diverting attention from the effects of material inequality and the role of power relations in generating inequality (Sayer 1994).

Social realism begins from the position that human beings live in open systems and this has particular consequences for the ways in which we study social life. Social science is not reducible to the study of the behaviour of individuals and surface descriptions of the context in which they act (Lawson 1997). Social reality is dynamic, complex and characterised by interdependencies between agents and structures. Realism contends that the world is composed not only of events but can be better understood in terms of the *actual* (events), the *empirical* (experiences) and the *real* (generative mechanisms). Structures at the level of the real generate mechanisms that govern or facilitate events. As Lawson (1997) points out, events may be unsynchronised with the mechanisms governing them or may be affected by different, sometimes countervailing, influences. This means that events can rarely be 'read off' straightforwardly in terms of their governing mechanisms.

If society is viewed as 'both the ever present *condition* (material cause) and critically reproduced *outcome* of human agency' (Bhaskar 1989: p. 34–5), then social science should focus on the interaction of structure and agency over time and the resulting change and/or stability that is brought about by the causal influence of emergent properties (Archer 1995). The question then becomes how structures, generative mechanisms and emergent properties are identified. It is difficult for mechanisms such as relations of class to manifest themselves in terms of the regularities sought by neo-positivist researchers. In part this is a consequence of the fact that social phenomena exist in open systems where experimental closure is almost impossible to obtain. The techniques of *retroduction* and *abduction* offer a way of addressing this methodological problem. According to Lawson, a retroductive inference moves from a knowledge of events to a knowledge of mechanisms operating at a deeper level which contribute to the generation of those events. Abduction also seeks to identify mechanisms but involves a process of inference from lay accounts of the social world to sociological theorising about it (Blaikie 1993).

At this point, it is important to note that realist accounts are not dismissive of data produced by neo-positivist research. Although constant event patterns or invariant regularities may not occur in open systems, partial regularities do. Lawson calls these *demi-regularities* or *demi-regs* and defines them as:

> A partial event regularity which *prima facie* indicates the occasional, but less than universal, actualisation of a mechanism or tendency, over a definite region of time-space. The patterning observed will not be strict if countervailing factors sometimes dominate or frequently co-determine the outcomes in a variable manner. But where demi-regs are observed there is evidence of relatively enduring and identifiable tendencies at play.
>
> (Lawson 1997: 204)

Lawson attaches special significance to *contrastive* demi-regs that exist in great abundance in the social sphere, arguing that they can 'direct' social science research by providing evidence that potentially identifiable mechanisms are operating. Health inequalities research is an exemplar of a research paradigm saturated in contrastive demi-regs.

What are the implications of all this for researching inequalities in health and health care? In the first place we should be wary of assuming that material inequality and inequity derived from unequal power relations can be read off from what we know about patterns of inequality in health. This is not to say that the evidence on inequality is poor; rather it is to argue that what we can reasonably do with this evidence should be considered in relation to its ontological significance. Only when we have postulated mechanisms on the basis of the evidence can we make effective policy recommendations.

Class as variable

As we have seen, social reality is dynamic, complex and interrelational. Yet social life is highly routinised (Bourdieu 1990), being patterned by inequality and the acceptance of inequity. The retroductive or transcendental question we must ask ourselves is what must be the case for such a routinisation of social life to be possible. It is still the case that those with power, wealth and status are able to call upon social, cultural and economic capital as a basis for authority. They are able, as a result of their powers, to define what is authoritative, i.e. what counts in society, and this provides opportunities for *patterns* of domination, oppression and inequality to continue and to take on new forms. In a changing world, however, the problem becomes one of identifying relations of power within which generative mechanisms operate to reproduce *practices* of domination, oppression and discrimination.

The *Black Report* (1982), initially published in 1980, has been a major vehicle for the wide acceptance of the social causation of health inequalities in British society. The report had a profound effect on researchers, not least by demonstrating that there were still significant differences in mortality and morbidity between members of different occupational classes decades after the introduction of the National Health Service. This impact was deepened through the report's discussion of rival explanations for these inequalities and its advocacy of a 'materialist' approach to explaining them. Rejecting arguments that widespread inequalities were either the result of flawed data or social selection, the Black Report argued in favour of redistributing income as a solution to the existence of such health variations. While the materialist explanation proved contentious, it provided the impetus for rethinking the principles behind public health policy and its relation to the wider society (Blane, Brunner and Wilkinson 1996). The argument was subsequently supported by a number of large and small-scale empirical studies demonstrating that profound inequalities still persisted. A decade after the Black Report was published, Davey Smith *et al.* (1990; Blane *et al.* 1990) concluded that class related health inequalities had increased rather than diminished. This concurred with Black's own assessment (1993) as well as that of Whitehead (1992) and was confirmed by the Acheson Report (1998).

Most work on health inequalities has been epidemiological rather than sociological in design and mode of analysis. While this work has been significant in consolidating the view that social class is important in the explanation of health inequality, it has done so by identifying the particular circumstances and behaviours subsumed under social class. These circumstances and behaviours have become the principal focus for investigation and explanation. As Higgs and Scambler (1998) have written, this kind of research has thrown up a confusing welter of facts rather than explanations. Wadsworth (1997) systematically outlined a large number of factors and processes that could account for the inequalities in health. Some of these relate to life-style and behaviour, and some to the nature of the life events experienced by the successive cohorts studied. Problems of providing an explanatory account and developing any general synthesis continually emerge.

The recent work of Richard Wilkinson (1996) has focused upon the importance of income inequalities in different societies and has generated considerable debate. Wilkinson has built up a body of work suggesting that, above a certain level of income, countries with relatively large inequalities in income perform worse in terms of life expectancy. Many of the responses to Wilkinson's work have focused on the empirical shortcomings, and indeed more recent research has contradicted his findings (Mackenbach 2002). However, it is interesting to consider the explanation that Wilkinson puts forward for the patterns he finds in the data. Wilkinson focuses on evolutionary arguments, emphasising the harmful physiological effects that accrue through psychosocial pathways of living in the stressful conditions of exaggerated social inequalities. Beyond a certain level of prosperity it is the size of the gap between the rich and the poor in society that has most significance in the construction of health inequality. However, income inequality is an effect of the distribution of power in society (Muntaner *et al.* 1999; Lynch *et al.* 2000) and we would argue that there is a lack of structural explanation in Wilkinson's work. Similar problems exist in relation to debates about the usefulness of the class based data that provide the underpinning of the Black Report (see Illsley (1986)). Are the classes that provide the gradient real or significant? Indeed, there has been so much social change that the social class categories used by the Registrar General have not only been overhauled but replaced with a totally different schema by the British government's statistical department (Rose and O'Reilly 1998).

From all these approaches one main problem emerges: while there is continuous confirmation of class based gradients, no conclusions about causation can be drawn. The research seems blind to the experiential significance of class (Sayer 2002). This failure has implications for policy. Bartley, Blane and Montgomery (1997) pointed to the importance of understanding the effect of inequalities over the course of an individual's life, and in particular in relation to socially critical periods such as the transition to parenthood or job loss. They suggested that policy-makers could intervene by focusing on these points of transition. This approach was taken up by the 1998 Acheson Report, which presented thirty-nine recommendations to address inequalities in health. However, as commentators pointed out, these were not put in any order of priority; some were too vague or too general to be of any use, and none were costed. As a result the report had far less vision than that produced by Black. As Davey Smith *et al.* (1998) write:

> The fundamental role of inequalities in material circumstances in producing the inequalities in other exposures is therefore missed, and it is possible that many of the recommendations could be adopted – at least nominally – without addressing the underlying determinants of health inequalities
>
> (Davey Smith *et al.* 1998: 1465)

The scathing responses to the perceived timidity of the Acheson Report concentrated on its failure to address the question of income distribution. Obviously, fudging the issue of the distribution of income is one of the most blatant concessions to the sensibilities of the affluent and powerful. The notion that income distribution reflects the operation of class is probably more contentious, but such an explanation forms the hidden backdrop to what many critics are saying. While lip service is often paid to the importance of class, it is understood as a statistical variable rather than as real social relations. In this way its sociological importance slips further and further away.

Social class and exploitation

The necessity to locate the debate about health inequalities as a product of social structure has not been lost on some researchers, who have attempted to move beyond Acheson and much 'health variations' research. The work of Muntaner and Lynch (1999) and Muntaner, Lynch and Oates (1999) has made explicit the link between social structure, income inequalities and health inequalities. Praising Wilkinson for shifting the debate away from health behaviours, they nevertheless argue that his data-driven approach leads him towards social psychology when searching for the consequences of income inequality. While this has the benefit of concentrating on objective indicators of inequality rather than on subjectively perceived social ranking, it does not help explain the real processes at work. As Muntaner and Lynch point out (1999: 64): 'The "starting fact" for Wilkinson's model is that by some process (which he does not discuss) income is distributed unevenly and that this has consequences for health.'

Differential incomes are associated with different positions in the relations of production within capitalism. Muntaner and Lynch's explicitly Marxist approach centres on the importance of exploitation to the understanding of social class relations. As in classical Marxism, exploitation is underpinned by the labour theory of value (LTV), where rates of exploitation derive from the appropriation of surplus labour by an exploiting class of non-labourers. They argue that it is possible to quantify such exploitation through the ratio of appropriated surplus labour embodied in wages. In this fashion, income inequality is related to social processes creating social classes that end up having different outcomes in terms of mortality and ill health. However (and for Muntaner and Lynch this is an important caveat), the focus on income inequality hides as much as it reveals. On its own it cannot describe the 'economic and political processes that take place in the production of goods and services' (Muntaner *et al.* 1999: 703). They write: 'theories of exploitation provide social mechanisms for the emergence of economic inequality beyond income (e.g. wealth) and yield multiple measures that are empirically distinct from income inequality' (Muntaner *et al.* 1999: 703).

Fleetwood (2002) attempts to address theories of exploitation from a realist perspective in his discussion of the labour theory of value (LTV). He adopts a Marxist framework and asks what conditions and essential relations must exist to make the world we experience possible? Using retroduction, he moves to a set of underlying relations and connects these to their observable form. His analysis is facilitated by a method of contrastive explanation whereby the properties of a stylised capitalist system are compared with those of non-capitalist systems. His discussion falls short of a detailed and extensive movement back from abstract theory to concrete forms, but the contrast with the limited explanatory potential of deductivism is clear.

What is needed is a robust definition of what is meant by exploitation. Erik Olin Wright (1997), for example, considers exploitation as a specific mechanism generating inequalities. Exploitation can be conceptualised as a form of interdependence of the material interests of people. There are three conditions to this. First, the material welfare of the exploiters is causally dependent on the material deprivation of the exploited. Second, this is dependent on the exclusion of the exploited from access to productive resources. Third, this exclusion allows the exploiters to appropriate the labour effort of the exploited. All three conditions have to be in place for exploitative economic oppression to exist. For example, if the third condition does not exist, there is no interdependence and the result is non-exploitative. Wright uses the example of Native Americans to illustrate this point (see later).

How does exploitation operate as a mechanism for producing and perpetuating inequality? Charles Tilly (1999) has developed a theory of inequality based on the understanding that durable inequalities are built around categorical distinctions among people rather than on gradients derived from aggregate individual attributes. Tilly argues that we discover and rediscover paired unequal categories such as black/white, citizen/noncitizen. The division between these categories is usually incomplete because some people do not easily fit on either side, and in many situations the distinctions do not matter. However, where and when they are applied and institutionalised, such categories organise and produce durable differences in access to resources. These distinctions are generated and perpetuated by means of causal mechanisms - *exploitation* and *opportunity hoarding* - which are reinforced by two further mechanisms – *emulation* and *adaptation*. As noted above, exploitation is the extraction (by exploiters) of a proportion of the value of what is produced by the exploited. 'Opportunity hoarding' refers to the control of a resource and the systematic exclusion of others from access to it. 'Emulation' and 'adaptation' are mechanisms that enforce the position of exploitative groups or firms. Emulation refers to the copying of successful organisational models, while adaptation refers to the elaboration of valued social relations around existing divisions. 'Much of what observers ordinarily interpret as individual differences that create inequality is actually the consequence of categorical organisation' (Tilly 1999: 9), and the creation of categorical forms of inequality is a means of sustaining the tensions and contradictions that arise in organisational forms.

While there are a number of areas of Tilly's work that might be open to criticism, it does offer an alternative to views of inequality based around gradients of aggregate individual characteristics. The theory gives the concept of exploitation a fundamental role to explore the ways in which relations of class are expressed.

Class theory: realist and irrealist

Despite the promise of the approaches outlined above, a growing orthodoxy in sociology has deemed social class redundant as a tool of social investigation. Taking its cue from varieties of post-structuralist and postmodernist thought, this orthodoxy is now so entrenched that it has become what one commentator has deemed 'normal science' (Callinicos 1995). Turner writes: 'class theory and analysis, far from aiding the search for comprehension, has become its fetter' (Turner 1996: 261). Pakulski and Waters, whose book title *The Death of Class* (1996) neatly sums up their position, write:

> It is merely fideistic, to use Gramsci's term, to take the view that the class structure forms the dominant power grid, and is the key mechanism in structuring life chances, but that we cannot see it clearly because class formation or structuration is impaired. If structures do not manifest themselves and if there is no evidence that they are operational, then there is little point in clinging to the concepts that reference them. Most sociologists will accept that structures are historical, that they are formed and that they inevitably expire. Let class also rest in peace, respected and honoured, but mainly relevant to history.
>
> (Pakulski and Waters 1996: 152)

Such charges against the theory of class (including weaker neo-Weberian versions of class analysis) obviously have a potential bearing on our capacity to uncover generative mechanisms underlying inequalities in health. Wright (1985) offers currently the most influential example of an attempt to operationalise an explicit theory of class based on ideas of exploitation and conflicts of interest. As Gubbay (1997) points out, however, in also trying to introduce ideas such as credentialism Wright overloads his schema with too many classes, making it difficult for him to analyse capitalist dynamics in which class is formed. Similar criticisms can be directed at the neo-Weberian form of class analysis, best epitomised by the 'Nuffield programme' (Crompton 1996). This accepts multidimensional bases for stratification. If it privileges class, it also grants autonomous causal capacity to gender, ethnicity, religion, political arrangements and even to individual preferences. In Gubbay's terms it is an explicitly 'weak relational' or 'nominalist' approach. Goldthorpe's class scheme reflects the Weberian equation of 'market situation' with 'class situation' (Goldthorpe 1987; Erikson and Goldthorpe 1992). Noting the predominance of corporate rather than individual employers, he contends that, small employers apart, all are now employees. Employees are divided according to the extent to which they exercise delegated authority or special knowledge and expertise. Additional allowance is made for skill levels and for location in industry or agriculture. The result is a scheme of eleven classes, allowing for reductions to seven-, five- and three-class versions. Again it is difficult to see how such a schema can develop any sustained generative mechanisms to account for inequalities in health.

One response to this is to follow Esping-Anderson (1993), who posits a model of a post-industrial class structure, which he argues derives from post-Fordist work principles and allows for the growing salience of gender, race and age in accounting for social stratification. His scheme consists of four occupation-based classes and a fifth 'outsider' or surplus population group, which he regards as a significant new factor in postindustrial society. This fifth group is a product of labour market change and welfare policies, both of which encourage, for example, the formation of sectors of the long-term unemployed or early-retired.

For other theorists, however, class has considerably less explanatory potential than it possessed a generation or more ago and therefore needs to be re-thought. Bradley (1996), in describing the interest of some sociologists of postmodernism in social divisions, has distinguished three tendencies. The first, exemplified by Jameson (1991) and Harvey (1989), combines a postmodern account of culture with orthodox Marxist or neo-Marxist class theory. The second maintains that postmodern culture heralds an end to class inequalities. Beck (1992), for example, argues that distribution of risk is now more important than distribution of resources. Similarly, Crook and colleagues (1992) anticipate a decline in the salience of class and see future forms of stratification as 'fluid and chaotic'. The third of these postmodern tendencies holds that class remains relevant but now requires to be conceptualised more in terms of consumption than production.

Thus Bauman (1992; 1998) maintains that the core relation between capital and labour has altered, with capital now engaging labour in the role of consumers rather than producers. According to this view, the 'new poor', another version of Esping-Anderson's outsider or surplus population group, are not part of the labour reserve but 'permanently displaced'. This has not led, as might be expected, to social unrest because most people are seduced by the glamour of the new consumerism. The state may yet, however, have to take repressive measures to keep the new poor in order, for example by extending policing and surveillance and contracting citizenship rights. As Bradley puts it, 'seduction and repression become the twin axes of class domination' (Bradley 1996: 69).

Alan Warde (1997) offers a note of caution about the limitations of much postmodern thought in relation to consumption, pointing out that there are greater continuities and limitations in the processes of consumption than are often acknowledged. The accumulation regimes of capital are as dependent on the reproduction of patterns of consumption as they are on the reproduction of relations of production. As David Ashley (1997) contends, in its present form capitalism requires commodities not only to take on the dual form of use and exchange value but also the form of sign value. The symbolic value assigned to clothing labels, certain drinks, makes of car, etc. guarantees new avenues for extracting profits in ever shorter time periods. However, Ashley is careful to point out that new forms of hyper-commodification do not lead to a rupture between consumption and relations of production. Indeed the transformations he documents are the result of far reaching and intricate relations of social production and social consumption (Sayer and Walker 1992).

The health inequalities debate seems largely to ignore the possible effects on health of changes in relations of production and consumption. This may be due, in no small measure, to a general sense of helplessness and fatalism in the face of the forces of global capital. As Tony Smith (2000) points out, the 'new dawn' heralded by lean production, economic restructuring and labour market flexibility is underpinned by processes of exploitation, structural coercion and alienation. In a detailed analysis he highlights how, under lean production, workers appear to be working more intensively. In traditional Fordist plants the labour process took up approximately 45 seconds every minute, while in lean production plants this figure is estimated at 57 seconds. Smith argues that rates of exploitation are underpinned by mechanisms of 'divide and rule' such as competition between divisions, the maintenance of core and periphery, waged and contract staff, rivalry between teams and reserve armies of unemployed in the wider economy. These mechanisms draw upon existing inequalities of class, gender and ethnicity. They require new forms of management based on processes of governmentality, using increasing numbers of cultural intermediaries, or 'new professionals', to perform functions of affirmation and legitimation (Ashley 1997). These new forms of worker discipline are welcomed by advocates of lean production as life affirming, challenging, progressive, enabling and empowering. There is no thought for the possible insecurities, stresses and corrosive effects of such changes.

It is because realist social theories can theorise class relations as affecting health through mechanisms at various levels that realism is important for the understanding of health inequalities. To be able to use it to inform health inequalities research, we need to establish that class relations are objective realities. In terms taken from the earlier work of Bhaskar and invoking his transcendental realism (1989; see Collier 1994), we would see Marx as offering a 'transformational model of social activity' (in which society pre-exists individuals and conditions their actions, which in turn reproduce, modify or transform it), and a relational model of society. Clement and Myles (1997) have developed a useful neo-Marxist approach to class based on the idea that classes are formed at the point of production and reproduced throughout social life. Central to class formation are the issues of 'real economic ownership of the means of production' and the 'appropriation of surplus value' created by the labour of others, which Carchedi (1977) describes as 'the global function of capital'. Clement and Myles point out that exercising control and surveillance of the labour process is distinct from accomplishing 'co-ordination and unity' of the process of creating surplus value. The former is the role of what they describe as the *capitalist executive*, who have 'specific powers that are called real economic ownership' (Clement and Myles 1997: 13). This group has control of 'strategic decision making', while members of the *new middle class* are involved in 'tactical decision making'. The new middle class are separated from real economic ownership and in effect provide co-ordination and unity to the labour process and are therefore productive of surplus value. In their model, Clement and Myles also identify a role for the *old middle class*, who increasingly lose 'real' economic ownership of their means of production. Instead, they become dependent commodity producers 'experiencing proletarianisation without becoming proletarian' (Clement and Myles 1997: 15).

Logics, relations and figurations

We would argue that social class needs to be seen in the context of a threefold distinction between *Logics*, *Relations* and *Figurations*. These three elements contribute different parts to explaining an overall picture (Scambler 2001; 2002). The economy and the state are inscribed in their own 'logics', most significantly those associated with capital accumulation and regulation as appropriate. These logics require order and establish the parameters for 'relations'. This is, to use Bhaskar's terminology, the *real* level of social causality. It is these real relations which constitute or give rise to the generative mechanisms sought by critical realists in sociology. The most significant relations arising out of the logic of capital accumulation are those of class. Relations of class are expressed in networks or 'figurations', a term first used by Elias (1978) to connect time and space in interdependent chains of networks. Figurations are fluid and change over time and may be global as well as national or local.

To illustrate these points Graham Scambler (2001) has put forward what he terms the *greedy bastards hypothesis* or GBH. This combines the logics of capital accumulation and regulation, real relations of class and the figuration of the British nation-state. The GBH states that the UK's widening health inequalities are the largely unintended consequences of the adaptive behaviours of its power elite, informed by its capitalist executive. The distinction between the former and the latter is a consequence of global 'disorganised capitalism' that ensures that the capitalist executive is of necessity strongly globalised, while those involved in the 'command' functions of the state are as yet only weakly globalised. While there are functional differences between the two groups, the investigative work of George Monbiot (2000) suggests a large degree of overlap.

Scambler argues that strategic decision-making by the capitalist executive, facilitated by the power elite, is a key determinant of the changing patterns and distribution of labour and of income/social transfers in Britain. It is this decision-making that leads to the enduring and widening of health inequalities. Work destandardisation, the new individualism and what has been termed the 'new poverty' all have their origins in the adaptive behaviours of the capitalist executive as they participate in the transition from an organised to a disorganised capitalism.

The key relationship is that between the capitalist executive class and the *working class*. The working class has no command over the means of production, the labour power of others, or its own means of realising its labour. It is a class with only its labour power to sell. It is, in effect, the subject of capital. But more needs to be said to provide a full account of the dynamics of class. The missing dimension is exploitation, which generates social antagonism through social classes having differential access to the proceeds of surplus labour. Class is conditioned by processes connected to the production, distribution and control of social surplus (Gubbay 1997). Social class is essentially a relationship to exploitation and appropriation of surplus. Callinicos (1989: 52) summarises this position in classically Marxist terms: '[The] mode of surplus-extraction, or exploitation, in turn determines the class structure, so that classes are defined relationally, by their objective relationship to the means of production and labour power and to other classes. Exploitation in turn gives rise to class struggle.'

From this perspective, questions of inequalities in health are not primarily about particular factors associated with membership of a particular class *per se,* or indeed about changes in economic arrangements, but rather are related to relations between classes. It should not be surprising that collective welfare provision and a more egalitarian distribution of wealth mitigate against such inequalities because they represent, through the social wage, a successful articulation of working class interests against those of the capitalist executive. However, as has been noted by many writers (Gough 1979; Higgs 1993; Navarro 1994), such concessions were just that and were removed when the interests of capital accumulation were compromised. In this context, it is easy to see why inequalities widen, and why a shift towards budgetary restraint and individualistic solutions to health inequality occurs.

Alternative views of class relations

Using the model of class outlined above may offer a chance to connect existing demi-regs about health with generative mechanisms. However, such an approach is not the only game in town. The debate about the existence or not of an 'underclass' consisting of a sizeable outsider or surplus population of people chronically materially, and perhaps culturally, adrift is often seen as the key issue in modern social policy. The origins of concerns with an underclass are to be found in US policy circles, where there has been concern regarding the position of the predominantly black residents of inner city ghettos. Influential researchers such as those involved with the Nuffield project (Marshall *et al.* 1995) have been keen to refute the existence of such an underclass in Britain on the (unsatisfactory) grounds that it is impossible to separate out their views from those occupying conventional positions in the class structure (Morris and Scott 1995). Utilising attitudinal data as a way of explaining social processes leads to a misidentification of causal factors.

In terms of the US, a more theoretical approach is provided by Wright (1995), who points to the importance of examining the relational aspects of an underclass. In the US it can be established that there are groups permanently excluded from the workforce, or wider social contact and even social security. To explain this situation, Wright draws an analogy between the modern underclass and the experience of Native North American Indians. The latter became the victims of genocide during the nineteenth century because there was little interest in incorporating them into the formal economy. In a similar way, in more recent times, an underclass is perceived as having limited usefulness in terms of the wider economic system and therefore becomes an issue for social policy and containment. While in the US such a group may exist, in Britain it is much harder to identify. While there has been mass unemployment and the growth of long-term unemployment in particular regions, the case for a structural underclass has yet to be convincingly made. There is a displaced segment of the working class which has borne the brunt of most social re-structuring and which has the bleakest outlook of any group in society (Scambler and Higgs 1999). However, as current employment policy testifies, they are not seen as outside of society but rather in need of 'guidance'. In the US the underclass is seen as constituting an irremediable problem. In Britain, whilst ideas about an underclass may be journalistically popular, no one is seen as located outside of society. Social inclusion is now official policy precisely because social exclusion is unacceptable (Levitas 1990). All inequalities, it is suggested, stem from not being able to utilise the talents and capacities of each citizen. The state's role is to encourage self-development: the educationally disadvantaged groups should be encouraged to study; inequalities in health can be reduced by proper diet and exercise; good jobs can be gained by application, flexibility and the right attitude. Moreover, good parenting can provide a 'sure start' to life that removes some of the obstacles that have beset previous generations. This is not social democracy but meritocracy (Hattersley 2000). The generative mechanisms behind inequalities are thus by-passed by a focus on the behaviour and private circumstances of individuals. Many researchers into inequalities in health seem oblivious to the way their data fits in with this 'third way' approach. But making such connections between health outcomes and various individual and social factors results in misleading fragmentation of the social causality of health inequalities. It is possible in the world of research based policy to find arenas of intervention (smoking cessation being merely one example) that comply with statistical notions of effectiveness. Indeed, existing evidence tends to be clearer with respect to 'downstream' interventions that are focused on individual behaviour, while there is a paucity of studies evaluating the effectiveness of 'upstream' community or population based interventions (Macintyre *et al.* 2001). Some have argued that orthodox evaluative approaches prevent complex understandings of social life (Connelly 2001). This raises important questions about the appropriateness of evidence for public policy decision-making. For example, a study of an intervention that improves the presentation skills of job applicants may show a significant effect in terms of improvements in selection chances, but the intervention would have no real effect on the wider social economic forces that periodically lead to large increases in unemployment rates. By confining 'evidence based' assessment to individualised interventions, there is a disregard of interventions that address root causes (Smith *et al.* 2001). Inequalities are not changed, social causation is ignored and individuals are held responsible.

Political consequences

One of the problems involved in not explicitly stating a theoretical approach to class is an inability to state clearly a political position. Instead, key issues of social and health policy are being redrawn as issues of personal concern. The twin issues of 'risk' and 'governmentality' (Turner 1997) are mediated through discourses provided by health professionals and researchers (Lupton 1995). As an example, there is not only a concern with the individual's diet in terms of cholesterol levels, but there is an acceptance of the superiority of an 'internal locus of control' (where the individual deals with risk through their own efforts rather than relying on an external agent to do the job; see Pitts 1996). Identifying individual risks from aggregated data obviously benefits the individual if they manage to avoid, for example, a heart attack. However, applying these insights to populations through the medium of 'surveillance medicine' (Armstrong 1995) is a different matter. As with the case of smokers who may be refused cardiac surgery, factors associated with the individual's uptake of health promoting behaviour can form the basis for the institutionalisation of health service rationing. Research by Waterman (1997) has shown that people who identify themselves as working class have negative attitudes to such approaches. The lack of an explicitly theoretical approach to health inequalities helps to prepare the ground for individualisation of the problems in health policy and practice.

Since 1997 Labour governments have produced a deluge of green and white papers, all of which recognise the increase in relative poverty over the last 25 years. These documents are replete with the rhetoric of social exclusion, inclusion and opportunity and stand in stark contrast to the denial of inequality under previous Conservative governments. A closer look at government reforms, however, raises a number of questions about the extent to which policies address root causes of inequality or are located in a more complex relationship between state and capital. In July 1999 the government produced an action report aimed at reducing health inequalities (DoH 1999). This emphasised the government's focus on mothers and families and highlighted increases in child benefit, the national minimum wage and minimum income guarantees as interventions addressing family poverty. At the same time the government introduced Sure Start programmes to 'promote physical, intellectual and social development of pre-school children'. Following the publication of a national strategy for neighbourhood renewal by the Social Exclusion Unit in 1998 (SEU 1998), the government has introduced the 'New Deal for Communities', aimed at regenerating the most deprived neighbourhoods; a targeted Single Regeneration Budget; Health Improvement Programmes as well as Health Action Zones in 26 urban and rural areas. Other initiatives include the Healthy Schools programme, New Deals for Employment and the Healthy Workplace Initiative.

Many of these initiatives can be interpreted as extensions of governmentality and part of the development of the state as a regulator of citizens. In the meantime, the government has extended its approach to involving the private sector in public sector projects and restricts itself to the role of facilitator for the global needs of capital. The impact of such policies on the health of citizens is ignored because of the myopic nature of the dominant deductivist approach to health inequalities.

Conclusion

Research into class related inequalities in health has been one of the most successful areas of sociological research in the UK. The demonstration that morbidity and mortality are related to social structure remains an important pointer to the existence of a class divided society. It is ironic, therefore, that the major work done on class inequalities in health is reliant on models of class that are fundamentally flawed at a theoretical level. Not only do they conflate status and occupation, but also they find it difficult to move beyond the statistical associations created by their data. There have been a number of attempts to overcome some of these difficulties. However, a sociologically robust theory of the relationship between class and health has yet to emerge. This has led to the insights of sociological research often being utilised for health promotion campaigns based on individualism rather than being made the basis for more structural alternatives. The continuing relevance of sociological research into class based inequalities in health is dependent on moving research away from such epidemiologically based 'black box' explanations. Instead, there is a need to adopt a critical realist approach, one which starts from the processes and practices of social class that are constitutive of the dynamics of a capitalist economy. Only in this way can we hope to understand the persistence and changing nature of class inequalities in health.

References

Acheson, D. (1998) *Independent Inquiry into Inequalities in Health*, London: HMSO.

Ahmad, W. (1993) *'Race' and Health in Contemporary Britain*, Buckingham: Open University Press.

Archer, M. (1995) *Realist Social Theory: The Morphogenetic Approach*, Cambridge: Cambridge University Press.

Armstrong, D. (1995) 'The rise of surveillance medicine', *Sociology of Health and Illness* 17: 393–404

Ashley, D. (1997) *History Without a Subject, The Postmodern Condition*, Oxford: Westview Press.

Bartley, M., Blane, D. and Montgomery, S. (1997) 'Health and the life course: why safety nets matter', *British Medical Journal* 314: 1194–6.

Bauman, Z. (1992) *Intimations of Postmodernity*, London: Routledge.

Bauman, Z. (1998) *Work, Consumerism and the New Poor*, Buckingham: Open University Press.

Beck, U. (1992) *Risk Society: Towards a New Modernity*, London: Sage Publications.

Bhaskar, R. (1989) *The Possibility of Naturalism*, 2nd edn, Hemel Hempstead: Harvester Wheatsheaf.

Bhaskar, R. (1994) *Dialectic: The Pulse of Freedom*, London: Verso.

Birch, S. (1999) 'The 39 steps: the mystery of health inequalities in the UK', *Health Economics* 8: 301–8.

Black Report (1982) *Inequalities in Health*, Harmondsworth: Pelican.

Black, D. (1993) 'Deprivation and health', *British Medical Journal* 307: 163–4.

Blaikie, N. (1993) *Approaches to Social Enquiry*, Cambridge: Polity Press.

Blane, D., Brunner, E. and Wilkinson, R. (1996) 'The evolution of public health policy: an Anglocentric view of the last fifty years', in D. Blane, E. Brunner and R. Wilkinson (eds) *Health and Social Organisation*, London: Routledge.

Blane, D., Davey Smith, G. and Bartley, M. (1990) 'Social class differences in years of potential life lost: size, trends and principal causes', *British Medical Journal* 301: 429–32.

Bourdieu, P. (1990) *The Logic of Practice*, Cambridge: Polity.

Bradley, H. (1996) *Fractured Identities: Changing Patterns of Inequality*, Cambridge: Polity Press.

Bunton, R. (1998) 'Inequalities in late modern health care', in A. Peterson and C. Waddle (eds) *Health Matters: A Sociology of Illness, Prevention and Care*, Buckingham: OUP.

Callinicos, A. (1989) *Making History*, Cambridge: Polity Press.

Callinicos, A. (1995) 'Postmodernism as normal science', *British Journal of Sociology* 46: 734–9.

Carchedi, G. (1977) *On the Economic Identification of Social Classes*, London: Routledge.

Clement, W. and Myles, J. (1997) *Relations of Ruling: Class and Gender in Postindustrial Societies*, Montreal: McGill-Queen's University Press.

Collier, A. (1994) *Critical Realism: An Introduction to Roy Bhaskar's Philosophy*, London: Verso.

Connelly, J. (2001) 'Critical realism and health promotion: effective practice needs an effective theory', *Health Education Research* 16: 115–20.

Crompton, R. (1996) 'The fragmentation of class analysis', *British Journal of Sociology* 47: 56–67.

Crook, S., Pakulski, J. and Waters, M. (1992) *Postmodernization*, London: Sage.

Davey Smith, G., Bartley, M. and Blane, D. (1990) 'The Black Report on socioeconomic inequalities in health 10 years on', *British Medical Journal* 301: 373–7.

Davey Smith, G., Morris, J. and Shaw, M. (1998) 'The independent inquiry into inequalities in health', *British Medical Journal* 317: 1465–6.

DoH (1999) *Reducing Health Inequalities: An Action Report*, London: Department of Health.

Elias, N. (1978) *What is Sociology?*, London: Hutchinson.

Erikson, R. and Goldthorpe, J. (1992) *The Constant Flux*, Oxford: Clarendon.

Esping-Anderson, G. (ed.) (1993) *Changing Classes*, London: Sage.

Fleetwood, S. (2002) 'What kind of theory is Marx's labour theory of value?', in A. Brown, S. Fleetwood and J.M. Roberts (eds) *Critical Realism and Marxism*, London: Routledge.

Forbes, A. and Wainwright, S. (2001) 'On the methodological, theoretical, philosophical and political context of health inequalities research: a critique', *Social Science and Medicine* 53: 801–16.

Fox, N. (1998) 'The promise of postmodernism for the sociology of health and medicine', in G. Scambler and P. Higgs (eds) *Modernity, Medicine and Health: Medical Sociology towards 2000*, London: Routledge.

Goldthorpe, J. (1987) *Social Mobility and Class Structure in Modern Britain*, 2nd edn, Oxford: Clarendon.

Gough, I. (1979) *The Political Economy of the Welfare State*, London: Macmillan.

Gubbay, J. (1997) 'A Marxist critique of Weberian class analysis', *Sociology* 31: 73–90.

Harvey, D. (1989) *The Condition of Postmodernity*, Oxford: Basil Blackwell.

Hattersley, R. (2000) 'In search of the third way', *Granta* 71: 231–55.

Higgs, P. (1993) *The NHS and Ideological Conflict*, Aldershot: Avebury.

Higgs, P. and Scambler, G. (1998) 'Explaining health inequalities: how useful are concepts of social class?', in G. Scambler and P. Higgs (eds) *Modernity, Medicine and Health: Medical Sociology towards 2000*, London: Routledge.

Illsley, R. (1986) 'Occupational class, selection and the production of inequalities in health', *Quarterly Journal of Social Affairs* 2: 151–62.

Jameson, F. (1991) *Postmodernism, or the Cultural Logic of Late Capitalism*, London: Verso.

Jones, I.G. and Cameron, D. (1984) 'Social class analysis – an embarrassment to epidemiology', *Community Medicine* 6: 37–46.

Kreiger, N. (1994) 'Epidemiology and the web of causation: has anyone seen the spider?', *Social Science and Medicine* 39, 7: 887–903.

Lawson, T. (1997) *Economics and Reality*, London: Routledge.

Levitas, R. (1998) *The Inclusive Society? Social Exclusion and New Labour*, London: Palgrave.

Lupton, D. (1995) *The Imperative of Health: Public Health and the Regulated Body*, London: Sage Publications.

Lynch, J.W., Smith, G.D., Kaplan, G.A. and House, J.S. (2000) 'Income inequality and mortality: importance to health of individual income, psychosocial environment, or material conditions', *British Medical Journal* 320: 1200–4.

Macintyre, S., Chalmers, I., Horton, R. and Smith, R. (2001) 'Using evidence to inform health policy: case study', *British Medical Journal* 322: 222–5.

Mackenbach, J.P. (2002) 'Income inequality and population health', *British Medical Journal* 324: 1–2.

Marshall, G., Roberts, C. and Burgoyne, C. (1995) 'Social class and the underclass in Britain and the USA', *British Journal of Sociology* 47: 22–44.

Monbiot, G. (2000) *The Captive State: The Corporate Take-over of Britain*, London: Macmillan.

Morris, L. and Scott, J. (1995) 'The attenuation of class analysis: some comments on Marshall, Roberts and Burgoyne "Social class and the underclass in Britain and the USA"' *British Journal of Sociology* 47: 45–55.

Muntaner, C. and Lynch, J. (1999) 'Income inequality, social cohesion and class relations: a critique of Wilkinson's neo-Durkheimian research programme', *International Journal of Health Services* 29: 59–81.

Muntaner, C., Lynch, J. and Oates, G. (1999) 'The social class determinants of income inequality and social cohesion', *International Journal of Health Services* 29: 699–732.

Navarro, V. (1994) *The Politics of Health Policy*, Oxford: Basil Blackwell.

Pakulski, J. and Waters, M. (1996) *The Death of Class*, London: Sage Publications.

Pilgrim, D. and Rogers, A. (1999) *A Sociology of Mental Health and Illness*, 2nd edn, Buckingham: Open University Press.

Pitts, M. (1996) *The Psychology of Preventive Health*, London: Routledge

Porter, S. and Ryan, S. (1996) 'Breaking the boundaries between nursing and sociology: a critical realist ethnography of the theory-practice gap', *Journal of Advanced Nursing* 24: 413–20.

Rose, D. and O'Reilly, K. (1998) *Final Report of the ESRC Review of Government Social Classifications*, Swindon: ESRC .

Sayer, A. (1994) 'Cultural studies and the economy stupid', *Environment and Planning D* 12: 635–7.

Sayer, A. (2002) 'What are you worth?: why class is an embarrassing subject', Sociological Research Online, 7, 3, http://www.socresonline.org.uk/7/3/sayer.html.

Sayer, A. and Walker, W. (1992) *The New Social Economy: Reworking the Division of Labour*, Oxford: Basil Blackwell.

Scambler, G. (2001) 'Class, power and the durability of health inequalities', in G. Scambler (ed.) *Habermas, Critical Theory and Health*, London: Routledge.

Scambler, G. (2002) *Health and Social Change: A Critical Theory*, Buckingham: Open University Press.

Scambler, G. and Higgs, P. (1999) 'Stratification, class and health: class relations and health inequalities in high modernity', *Sociology* 33: 275–96.

Senior, P.H. and Bhopal, R. (1994) 'Ethnicity as a variable in epidemiological research', *British Medical Journal* 309: 327–30.

Sheldon, T.A. and Parker, H. (1992) 'Race and ethnicity in health research', *Journal of Public Health Medicine* 14, 2: 104–10.

Social Exclusion Unit (1998) *Bringing Britain Together: A National Strategy for Neighbourhood Renewal*, CM4045, London: HMSO.

Smith, G.D. (1999) 'Poverty across the life-course and health', in D. Gordon, M. Shaw, D. Dorling and G.D. Smith (eds) *Inequalities in Health, The Evidence Presented to the Independent Inquiry into Inequalities in Health, Chaired by Sir Donald Acheson*, Bristol: Policy Press.

Smith, G.D., Ebrahim, S. and Frankel, S. (2001) 'How policy informs the evidence', *BMJ*, 322, 184–5.

Smith, T. (2000) *Technology and Capital in the Age of Lean Production*, Albany: State University of New York Press.

Tilly, C. (1999) *Durable Inequalities*, California: University of California Press.

Turner, B. (1996) 'Capitalism, classes and citizenship', in D. Lee and B. Turner (eds) *Conflicts about Class: Debating Inequality in Late Industrialism* London: Longman.

Turner, B. (1997) 'On risk and governmentality', in A. Petersen and R. Bunton (eds) *Foucault, Health and Medicine*, London: Routledge.

Vagero, D. and Illsley, R. (1995) 'Explaining health inequalities, beyond Black and Baker – a discussion of some issues emerging in the decade following the Black report', *European Sociological Review* 11, 3: 219–341.

Wadsworth, M. (1997) 'Health inequalities in the life course perspective', *Social Science and Medicine* 44: 859–69.

Warde, A. (1997) *Consumption, Food and Taste*, London: Sage Publications.

Waterman, S. (1997) 'Survey of an inner city general practice population to examine attitudes to "risk", risk behaviour and the "risk society"', Unpublished MSc Dissertation, University College London.

Whitehead, M. (1992) *The Health Divide* (2nd edn), London: Penguin.

Wilkinson, R. (1996) *Unhealthy Societies: The Afflictions of Inequality*, London: Routledge.

Williams, S. (1999) 'Is anybody there? Critical realism, chronic illness and the disability debate', *Sociology of Health and Illness*, 21, 6: 797–819.

Wright, E. (1985) *Classes*, London: Verso.

Wright, E. (1995) 'The class analysis of poverty', *International Journal of Health Services* 25: 85–100.

Wright, E. (1997) *Class Counts: Comparative Studies in Class Analysis*, Cambridge: Cambridge University Press.

5 Researching 'real' language

Bob Carter and Alison Sealey

Introduction

Our starting point in this chapter is the interface between social theory and the study of language. Throughout its history, sociology has maintained an interest in language, although this has taken a number of forms, and the congruence between the concerns of linguistics and those of the other social sciences has shifted along with developments in the concerns of each area of inquiry. In this chapter, we briefly present some of the background to shared areas of interest and distinctive differences, before exploring the contribution which realist theory could make to empirical research into language and social action. We also suggest that social researchers seeking to implement a realist programme in their empirical investigations could benefit from a fuller awareness of advances in the description of authentic language data.

The social sciences and the study of language

Social theory has inherited from its founding figures particular sets of interests in language and its relation to social life. Broadly, these have informed the work of subsequent social theorists in three ways. Firstly, in the work of Mead and the symbolic interactionists, Goffman, and ethnomethodologists such as Cicourel and Sacks, language has been considered as a key element in social interaction. Here the concern with the role of meanings in the determination and interpretation of social action is important. Secondly, there have been those writers influenced by post-structuralism such as Foucault and social constructionists such as Harré, Potter and others who have emphasised the 'linguistic turn' in social theory. Finally, Habermas, Bourdieu and others have sought to develop a view of language as having systemic features as well as being a key source of creativity for people in social life. We shall not discuss these contributions to sociologically influenced theories of language in detail here,[1] devoting the greater part of the chapter to the language end of this notional language–sociology continuum, but it is worth pointing out that much contemporary social research involves itself with language when it highlights 'discourse'.

'Discourse' in social research

One well established approach to researching the social world is associated with qualitative methods which focus on actors' accounts of their experiences: data from interviews, focus groups and ethnographic observations, as well as documents produced in the course of various kinds of social interaction, are all, by definition, linguistic data. Interest in these linguistic products is often associated with 'the discursive turn' in the social sciences, where a particular view of the ontological status of language accords with a social constructionist epistemology.

Thus there has recently been an increase in studies involving analyses of the language of social actors, as well as in resources for students and researchers in the social sciences to guide them in their methodology (e.g. Silverman 2001; Wetherell *et al*. 2001). Coupland and Jaworski (2001: 148) suggest reasons 'why so many academic disciplines entertain the notion of discourse with such commitment', including 'geographers, philosophers, political scientists, sociologists, anthropologists, social psychologists, and many others'. Among these reasons is a recognition of the crucial role of language in social life, which several writers in the field interpret in a strongly social constructionist way. Potter (1997: 146), for example, states explicitly that his version of discourse analysis 'is characterized by a meta-theoretical emphasis on anti-realism and constructionism', while Coupland and Jaworski (2001: 134–5) assert: 'The theoretical position [discourse analysis] adopts can itself be called "constructivist" because it makes the radical claim that the realities we take to define our social circumstances, and our selves within them, are to a large extent socially constructed.'

Elsewhere, Potter (1996) elaborates on the role he believes discourse analysis can play in illuminating aspects of the social world. He gives priority to analysis of descriptions themselves, working with a metaphor of language not as a mirror but as a construction yard, and 'the idea that descriptions and accounts *construct the world*, or at least versions of the world'. He also claims that:

> [r]eality enters into human practices by way of the categories and descriptions that are part of those practices. The world is not ready categorized by God or nature in ways that we are all forced to accept. It is *constituted* in one way or another as people talk it, write it and argue it.
>
> (Potter 1996: 98)

This tradition of discourse analysis implies a close association between the use of language data in social scientific research and a theoretical orientation which is sympathetic to social constructionism. However, we argue that a focus within social scientific inquiry on empirical language data by no means entails a constructionist perspective on the social world, and in what follows we develop an alternative theoretical position. We suggest that the two areas do have much to offer each other, but that, in order to be consistent with the realist social theory developed in this book, social scientists would need to pay more attention to the systemic features of language itself than is the case with many studies which identify themselves as discourse analytic. We think it is important to explore the relationship between language and social action in a way which recognises the distinctive properties of each. This imperative is as relevant for research which is primarily concerned with the nature of language as for that whose point of departure is closer to traditional sociological concerns. Before illustrating this claim, let us sketch out a little of the background to some relevant debates within linguistics itself.

The study of language: contemporary debates

Like many of the disciplines whose subject matter is closely concerned with human beings, linguistics has had to struggle for its place in the academy. Its definition as 'the scientific study of language' would seem to be designed partly with this in mind, and traditional linguistics identifies its remit as the provision of a 'grammatical model' of a language, which is an attempt to represent systematically and overtly what the native speaker of that language intuitively knows. Linguistics is routinely acknowledged to overlap with many other disciplines, including psychology, philosophy, anthropology and sociology, and its concerns have included the identification and description of different languages around the world, the history of changes in language through time, the relationship of the sub-systems of language to each other (sounds, units of meaning, vocabulary, syntax) and so on. To some extent, linguistics has needed to distinguish its own field of study from other, cognate areas, and two of the key contributors to the discipline have been important in this respect. They are figures with whose work social scientists are likely to be familiar, and their ideas need briefly to be addressed in this chapter, because they are concerned with the nature of the real and with stratified accounts of language.

Language as a system

The structuralist Saussure is responsible for positing the distinction between *langue*, the underlying totality of the resources of a language, or the capacity of the grammatical system which is housed in the human brain, and *parole*, the act of language use by an individual in a specific context. Saussure was concerned with the formal properties of the linguistic system which make possible a potentially infinite number of combinations of individual units, according to a system of syntactic categories, each having distinct properties. Saussure's work thus introduces a stratified view of language, one that distinguishes between its actualisation by real speakers in specific social settings and a conception of it as a system of interrelated structures and mutually defining entities. Importantly, this opens up the possibility of an interplay between utterances and these systemic features; meaning, for example, is not only speaker derived, but for Saussure is also partly made possible by the arbitrary relation between signifier and signified.

The generativist Chomsky drew a distinction between *competence* and *performance* which parallels Saussure's *langue/parole*. In an often-quoted passage, he makes clear that linguistics is concerned with idealised representations of what are essentially unobservable mental processes. 'Linguistic theory,' he states:

> is concerned primarily with an ideal speaker-listener, in a completely homogeneous speech-community, who knows its language perfectly and is unaffected by such grammatically irrelevant conditions as memory limitations, distractions, shifts of attention or interest, and errors (random or characteristic) in applying his knowledge of the language in actual performance. This seems to me to have been the position of the founders of modern general linguistics, and no cogent reason for modifying it has been offered.
>
> (Chomsky 1965: 3–4)

Empirically observed language production is deemed to be of only marginal interest to this project, and research in this tradition sets greater store by the intuitions of native speakers' judgements as to whether or not a particular construction is grammatical in the language in question.

In both Saussurean and Chomskyan approaches to linguistics, the relation between the structural elements of language and their empirical manifestations in language-in-use is, in our view, rather one-sided. That is, people's actual language behaviour is contingent, 'imprecise' and ephemeral, whereas the systemic features of language are endurable, structured and consistent. These linguists' work thus tends to diminish the role in research of transient, empirically observable language use in favour of the stable, non-observable structural entities which are held to govern or regulate its use by individual speakers, and so encourages a view of *langue* or competence as autonomous entities. With its echoes of older philosophical claims about the distinction between 'appearance' (actual language use) and 'reality' (what underlies or generates actual language use), this is a form of realism from which we would wish to distance ourselves.

Linking language and society: sociolinguistics

This approach to linguistics has not entirely dominated the subject, however. One branch of the study of language, 'sociolinguistics', is concerned with the interaction between 'language' and 'society'. There are two types of emphasis within sociolinguistics. Some sociolinguists, in seeking to identify and explain the social significance of linguistic variation, are concerned primarily with the systemic properties of language. Their research investigates how speakers' choices from those available in the language system (particularly the sound system, but also its lexis and grammar) vary in accordance with their membership of particular social groups. The focus is on 'aggregate regularities in group performance' (Downes 1984: 16), and on 'the role played by language in conveying information about the speaker' (Trudgill 1983: 14). The goal of this research is improved understanding of the structure of language. At the other end of the continuum are sociolinguists whose interest in the relationships between language and society is aimed at improved understanding of the nature of society. For some writers, this emphasis identifies such researchers as 'sociologists of language' rather than 'sociolinguists' (e.g. Chambers 1995; Wardhaugh 1992).

During the 1970s it seemed that a sociology of language might indeed be developing, drawing on insights from both the kinds of social theory we have summarised above and the work of empirical linguists who were studying varieties of language around the world. This possibility was not fully realised, however, and the 1990s brought critiques of the sociological base of sociolinguistics. One such was that by Williams, who locates the 'flimsy epistemological base' (1992: 40) of contemporary sociolinguistics in 'early developments of sociology and linguistics during the nineteenth century' (1992: xiii). 'Variationist' sociolinguistics (associated particularly with Labov) has discovered robust correlations between social stratification and linguistic variation. The patterns Labov identified, such as the pronunciation of a particular sound in a particular way being a very accurate clue to class location, have been replicated in countless subsequent studies of various groups in different countries. His approach has been criticised both by Williams (op. cit.) and by Hasan for prioritising systemic aspects of language-in-use (variations in sound, words, syntax) while disregarding meaning, 'ignoring deeper issues of the role of language in the creation, maintenance and change of social institutions' (Hasan, 1992: 81).

If much sociolinguistics, then, is concerned with variations within the linguistic system, and 'autonomous' linguistics with intra-organism, cognitive and idealised linguistic phenomena, other branches of the discipline have developed in yet other directions. One very significant area is the more functional orientation, which asks questions about the communicative aspects of language, and the principles which contextualise observable linguistic behaviour.

Language as a social practice

While autonomous linguistics looks inwards, to the human mind, other aspects of the discipline are oriented towards language as an intersubjective, public phenomenon. Hymes, for example, advocates maintaining the link between linguistics and the social sciences, proposing the conduct of 'ethnographies of speaking', which draws on 'a theory of speech as a system of cultural behaviour' (Hymes 1974: 89). Hymes thinks that linguistics should move 'from what is potential in human nature, and elementary in a grammar, to what is realizable and realized; and conceive of the social factors entering into realization as constitutive and rule-governed too' (ibid: 93). He insists that the grammatical mechanisms considered by Chomsky could never account for appropriateness, and that speakers' actual knowledge of language involves their ability to implement that knowledge in performance. The properties involved in the social role of speaking are 'in part ... functions of the social organization of speech ... , in part they emerge in the actual events of speech themselves' (ibid: 97).

Halliday, likewise, characterises linguistics as a branch of sociology rather than psychology, developing the idea of language as 'social semiotic', where linguistic codes are 'symbolic orders of meaning generated by the social system' (1978: 111). For Halliday, 'meaning is a social act, and it is constrained by the social structure' (p. 160), so he rejects the theoretical position which relegates 'the social structure' to 'just an ornamental background to linguistic interaction', representing it instead as 'an essential element in the evolution of semantic systems and semantic processes' (p. 114). From this more functionally oriented view, 'language is as it is because of what it has to do' (p. 19), and thus 'the linguistic system is a sociolinguistic system' (p. 72).

Language and relativism

Another strand in the study of language itself concerns the relationship between language and perception. The Kantian proposition that human beings can only apprehend the world through synthetic, *a priori* categories or 'forms of sensibility' implies that things can only be known as they appear to us within such categories rather than as things in themselves. This carries a strong relativist implication, which appears in linguistics in discussions of the extent to which different languages bring about different perceptions of the world. The claim known as the 'Sapir-Whorf hypothesis' is that the distinctions encoded in different languages constrain the ways in which speakers can perceive the world. So when the colour spectrum is divided differently in two different languages, speakers of each will actually 'see' a different range of colours accordingly. The stronger version of the hypothesis has few adherents today, partly because of the fact that concepts can be translated, even though not always on a word-for-word principle. But its weaker form – the claim that to speak a particular language is to adopt a local conception of reality – has been widely influential, particularly in those areas of language study concerned with social and discursive practices. Similar ideas have, of course, suffused postmodern and post-structuralist social theory, where the shift has been from the claim that *thought* is relative to language towards the much more radical relativising position that *reality itself* is relative to language.

Language, society and human practice

In the previous section we considered various features of the approaches to the study of language and society. Some approaches constitute language and social structures as discrete, although related, entities or objects of study which can be readily demarcated. The more robust forms of structuralism suggest that meaning is a product of the relationship between signs, and is thus internal to the linguistic system itself. We would reject the disregard of human practice which is implied in this perspective. Archer, too, has exposed the downwards conflationism of Chomskyan linguistics, which reduces the independence of the socio-cultural level to 'its ingenuity in elaborating permutations of the code', denying to its users the potential to make any 'reciprocal contribution to altering the code itself' (1988: 39). On the other hand, the stronger versions of relativism suggest that all meanings are indexical: context-bound, and reducible to what human beings say. We would reject in this perspective the implied disregard of the constraints and enablements of language itself. Our position thus lies somewhere between these two extremes, recognising the importance of both elements, as the realist language philosophers Devitt and Sterelny also do:

> A word's relation to others in the language – *internal* relations – may often be important to its meaning; for example, the relation of 'pediatrician' to 'doctor'. But a language's relations to the nonlinguistic world – its *external* relations – are always important.
>
> (Devitt and Sterelny 1999: 263)

The conceptualisation of language as a form of human practice is in some senses a materialist position, recognising as it does that human practice in the world has temporal and logical priority over language. That is to say, that the human being comes before language: each individual exists in the world, and has material needs, before having access to language. Desires to do things in the world may precede the acts in which people engage, and precede the language used to accomplish those acts. However, in the linguistically saturated world inhabited by the contemporary human species, there is perpetual interplay between practice and language, with the existence of language representing a quantum leap in the human potential for practice in the world.

Language as a cultural emergent property

The interplay of language and practice to which we have just alluded rests not only on the assertion of the temporal priority of human practice, but also on the stratified social ontology of culture, structure and agency. As we have seen elsewhere in this volume, realists claim that the world is not directly produced or constructed by us, but is rather the complex outcome of the interactions between structural contexts and ourselves. They view social relations and structures as emergent properties of social interaction (Archer 1995). Since emergence is a key term in the vocabulary we shall be employing, we shall take a moment to explore it in more detail.

Emergence refers to the generation of new entities or phenomena from the combination of other entities or phenomena. Because the new entity is emergent from this combination, it possesses certain distinct features, namely: irreducibility to any of its constituent elements; autonomy from any of its constituent elements; ability to interact with any of its constituent elements. Thus languages are emergent products of the engagement of human practice with the material world: they cannot be reduced to any of their constituents (that is, languages are not merely what human beings say, nor are they simply an internal relationship between linguistic signs, nor yet a grammar which is grasped intuitively and is not corrigible by human intervention); they have a partial independence or autonomy both from human beings (we learn a language that pre-exists us) and from the material world (through language people create things, such as stories and characters which have no physical counterpart); and finally, language is itself a practice, capable of enabling people to act upon and modify the world (we do things with language), as well as to act upon themselves and others (language enables us to reflect upon, interpret and make judgements about ourselves and others). In short, we support Archer's description of language as a 'cultural emergent property' (Archer 2000).

Of course, if language is emergent in the sense outlined above, it is itself capable of combining with other elements in the social world to produce what Archer terms second and third order emergence. Thus, for instance, writing is a technology emerging from the combination of human practice with language. The invention of writing transforms the potentiality of language immeasurably by freeing language from its dependence on human interlocution. This is not a normative statement: we are not saying that literate societies are preferable to oral ones – and in any case few contemporary societies remain completely uninfluenced by the phenomenon of literacy. However, the central (realist) point is that language as a cultural emergent property has powers and properties, and that written language, as a second order emergent property from sound-based verbal economies, possesses a more extensive range of properties and powers. It is important to note, though, that these properties and powers are experienced as constraints and enablements by people only *in their practice* in the world. It is only when individuals or groups try to modify their circumstances, or resist the efforts of others to change them, that the properties of language become causally influential. But the causal influence is mediated through agency, through social interaction.

It follows from this that access to writing does not necessarily entail a restructuring of thought: it is an enablement which exists *in potentia*; its realisation depends on human practice, on people wishing to do things in the world. How people employ writing at any historical moment or conjuncture depends not on writing itself but on the circumstances of its use: the intentions of its users, their respective political and economic influence, their control of military and other resources and so on. To this extent we concur with the characterisation of literacy by Street (1984) as inherently 'ideological', rather than 'autonomous', since literacy is always literacy in use. Literacy is a matter of human practice first and foremost.

Nevertheless, as a second order emergent property, writing is not reducible to its constituents, and retains a *partial* autonomy from them. Amongst the core features of texts is their suitability for travel, especially once technological developments in typography made possible efficient reproduction. This allows texts, in marked contrast to embodied utterances, to move beyond their site of production, thus changing the communicative context dramatically 'both as regards the emitter and as regards the receivers, with consequent implications for the nature of the message' (Goody 1986). Thus one potential of written texts is that they can lead to abstract, analytic thought; by making memory more reliable they enable words to have histories, rituals to have rules, texts to have critics. Writing, as Goody has put it, is the 'technology of the intellect'. Above all, writing establishes an important condition for the development of what Popper (Popper and Eccles, 1977) has termed 'World Three', the emergent realm of the products of human consciousness.

The independence of the text, in this sense, makes possible certain transformations of the social and natural world. Constitutions can be written, legal systems can be codified, files can be kept and doctrines can be fought over as a result of writing. Moreover, the effects of writing are cumulative. Ideas, plans and traditions become ever more dense as textual commentary builds upon textual commentary and so place greater and greater pressure on those excluded from access to, and participation in, the ever expanding World Three of human knowledge. Interdiscursivity and intertextuality, both emergent properties of chirographic cultures, permit heightened forms of linguistic reflexivity as well as the commodification of language (Chouliaraki and Fairclough 1999).

As some of the discussion in our opening sections suggests, a social constructivist perspective often includes a formulation in which language/discourse and social action are mutually constitutive of each other. However, as Archer has indicated, formulations involving 'mutual constitution' may be associated with 'central conflation', and run the risk of implying temporal conjunction between the two elements, leading to an 'inability to examine the interplay' between them over longer periods of time (Archer 1988: 87). One advantage of an 'emergent property' view of language is that it can free accounts of speakers and the language they produce from the 'eternal present' implied in constructivist descriptions: speakers no longer have to be thought of as simultaneously bringing into being that to which they are responding. Texts (especially written texts) produced by long dead social actors are part of the cultural context within which the current inhabitants of the social world interact. In the next section, we consider further some of the properties of language itself which contemporary research identifies.

Identifying 'the real' in linguistics

It is perhaps unsurprising, in the light of the summaries of different aspects of linguistics which we have supplied, that the notion of 'the real' is important in contemporary debates in the discipline. 'Real language' is particularly salient in dialogue between 'pure' and 'applied' linguists. While the former are likely to claim that 'mainstream' linguistic work is – and should be – mainly concerned with I-language, that is, the cognitive system underlying the ordinary use of language, applied linguists, such as Brumfit, are more inclined to identify their priority as 'the theoretical and empirical investigation of real-world problems in which language is a central issue' (2001: 169). 'Real' is used in this debate with different shades of meaning. For autonomous linguistics, it concerns 'the mechanisms in the underlying linguistic reality which allow us to characterise these expressions [sets of sentences] as well-formed' (Carr 1990: 33). Applied linguists, on the other hand, tend to bring to the fore the 'real' world of sensory experience, so that 'real' can become a near synonym for 'empirical'. The 'real-world' problems with which applied linguistics is concerned include matters of practice and policy, such as teaching foreign languages, producing translations appropriate for specific commercial transactions, or applying knowledge about language in the development of government policies for education.

In this context, 'real language' is either the system 'underlying' actual utterances, making the latter of limited interest to linguists, or it is attested language, words which have actually been spoken by someone somewhere in the context of some socio-communicative purpose. It will be evident that, notwithstanding Chomsky's association with realism via the concept of generative mechanisms, our emergentist position is one which accommodates not only the unobservable systemic features of language, but also attested language use. This is partly because the Chomskyan project has in many ways failed the test of encounters with empirical data. As Beaugrande puts it, '"generativist" theory-driven procedures preclude the description of adequate data in practice' (1997: 35). Devitt and Sterelny (1999) provide a partial explanation of why this is so. A key criticism which they make of the generative linguists in the Chomskyan tradition is that they conflate two kinds of 'system'. On the one hand, there is the syntactic structure of linguistic symbols; on the other, there is speakers' ability to manipulate language to produce meanings. What Devitt and Sterelny wish to query is the assumption that these are a single phenomenon, demanding of a single explanation. 'Competence,' they argue, 'together with various other aspects of the speaker's psychology, produce linguistic symbols, but a theory of one is not a theory of the other' (1999: 116–17). Further, they claim that '[t]his conflation of symbol and competence is the first and perhaps the most important problem about current views of competence … Why suppose that a grammar explains competence at all?' (p. 167). They prefer to maintain 'a distinction between two sorts of rules, the "structure-rules" governing the products of a competence, and the "processing-rules" governing the production of those products, rules governing the *exercise* of the competence' (p. 171).

Devitt and Sterelny's position makes the enterprise of identifying the neuro-biological dimension of linguistics of far less central importance. They concede (as would we) that linguists' intuitions about grammaticality provide evidence about certain aspects of language, but it is indirect evidence. 'The direct evidence,' they continue, 'is provided by the reality itself, the sentences people produce and understand' (p. 183). This position is consistent with that of Pawson (who has contributed Chapter 1 to this volume), when he says that it is 'utterances [that] have to be the focus of any theoretical discussion of language' (Pawson 1989: 91). A growing number of linguists now take such a position, having recognised that '[l]anguage by itself can be described in "purely linguistic" terms only if it can hold firm and continue to subsist and operate upon its own internal, standing constraints' (Beaugrande 1997: 36). Evidence suggests that language, as a product of human beings engaged in social interaction, is shaped by much which lies beyond its own internal constraints, a point which we will develop in what follows.

It will be a claim familiar to readers of this collection that only an acknowledgement of the distinctive properties of culture, structure and agency makes possible consideration of the interplay between them. Translated into the specific concerns of this chapter, we would point to the importance of identifying: how the linguistic system itself constrains and enables the communicative intentions of speakers, and, as a cultural emergent property, manifests a partial autonomy from them; how speakers maintain their agential capacity to exercise choice, particularly at the level of situated interaction; and how social structures constrain speakers' choices (which is of central concern in sociolinguistics).

Empirical research: corpus linguistics

Despite the dominance in many quarters of the generative, Chomskyan approach to the study of language, the more socially scientific, Hallidayan tradition has been strengthened by developments in technology which have enabled the methodological realisation of this alternative epistemological position. The linguist Firth (much of whose work precedes that of both Chomsky and Halliday) recognised the role of context in meaning, not only at the level of internal structural relations, nor yet merely the level of speakers' situated intentions, but also in relation to the patterns of distribution found in 'observable, objective textual evidence' (Stubbs 1996: 174). Firth, working in the 1930s, as Stubbs points out, 'lacked the computational resources to carry out such an analysis'. Within the past twenty years, however, computer technology has made possible the collection of large, digitally stored databanks of naturally occurring language – referred to as language corpora – and the tools to search them. Of particular interest are recurring patterns, since, given that they are products of the many different speakers whose utterances and writings have contributed to the corpus, they would seem to reveal tendencies in language itself.

It is probably not appropriate to present here too many examples of the extensive and detailed findings of corpus linguistic studies, but it may be helpful to indicate the kinds of trends which have been identified. The basic technique for the computer-assisted analyses is to use a program known as a concordancer, which retrieves all examples of a word or phrase from the corpus being studied. (The largest of these include the Bank of English, which currently stands at several hundred million running words of writing and transcribed speech.) The output from this process is typically a list of all occurrences of the target feature, which can be presented so that its collocates – words with which it co-occurs – are made visible and calculated statistically, taking into account (as far as is technically possible) the relative frequency of the different items in the language as a whole. One phenomenon to emerge from this analytical process is 'the idiom principle', which derives from evidence of frequently found strings in discourse. Sinclair (1991) proposes that, rather than selecting utterances on a word-by-word basis, speakers make use of prefabricated 'chunks' in the linguistic repertoire, a view which undermines the received wisdom that syntax and vocabulary are separate phenomena. Thus:

> [t]he model of a highly generalized formal syntax, with slots into which fall neat lists of words, is suitable only in rare uses and specialized texts. By far the majority of text is made of the occurrence of common words in common patterns, or in slight variations of those common patterns.
>
> (Sinclair 1991: 108)

This is by no means to deny speakers any freedom of choice about what they say, but merely to suggest that the humanly produced cultural resource of 'language' acts back upon its speakers in particular ways, one of which is to reduce the degree to which they are obliged to make choices when in the act of constructing discourse. Subsequent studies into 'the company words keep' (Firth), with the aim of 'identify[ing] what is central and typical in the language' (Sinclair 1991: 17), have contributed an increasingly convincing weight of empirical evidence which is often at odds with the intuitions relied on for so long by linguists in the generative tradition.

Finally in this section on this one aspect of empirical research in linguistics, it must be noted that corpus studies provide us with direct evidence of the second order relations within language, and the further emergent properties which realist theory would predict. Sinclair discusses, for instance, the word *set*, which frequently occurs in combination with other common words to make phrasal verbs such as *set about, set in, set off* and so on. When viewed in the context of multiple occurrences, generated not in the abstract but by many speakers in actual communicative situations, it becomes apparent that the meaning of the combined 'chunk' is not reducible to either of its constituents. Few speakers would probably be aware of *set* or *in* as having any particular connotations, either positive or negative, but what emerges from a corpus analysis is that the collocates of *set in* (that is, the words repeatedly occurring close to this 'chunk') often denote something unpleasant. The kinds of thing which 'set in' are 'drought', 'rain', 'depression', 'rot' and so on. Thus as Sinclair says, '[t]he co-occurrence of two quite common little words can unexpectedly create a fairly subtle new meaning that does not seem to be systematically related to either or both of the original words' (Sinclair 1991: 68). (See Figue 5.1.)

Another example is provided by Beaugrande, who looked at collocations for the verb *warrant*. His analysis encompasses morphology, lexis, semantics and syntax, and he reports how, when seen in the context of many examples together, 'seemingly general or neutral lexical items ("circumstances, conditions, occasion, operation, qualities, situation") that would not have values as a part of their own core meaning also carry values in most of my corpus data' (1997: 48). In other words, the evaluative connotations of certain items of vocabulary are emergent from the discourse contexts in which speakers deploy them. These nuances are not reducible to the words themselves, but, significantly, nor are they reducible to the single occasion of their utterance or writing, since patterns like this are revealed only when examples of language are temporarily extracted from the immediate context and seen together with others of their kind. That is to say, meanings are reducible neither to individual words (since such meanings are partly derived from the effects of being placed in a string or sentence in relation to other lexical items) nor to individual utterances or instances of use (since such meanings are not personal and idiosyncratic, but shared in a discourse community). Corpus linguists are not advocating this decontextualising process as absolute, or an end in itself, but as one perspective from which to view empirical language data.

From this very brief outline, then, it becomes apparent that the actual process of describing language has begun to benefit from the incorporation of methodological approaches which are, at least implicitly, entirely consistent with the realist social theory with which this book is concerned. There are also developments in the study of language and social groups, i.e. sociolinguistics, which accord with this position.

vestors reach the PP at the same time, *panic* **sets in**; Tulip believes this could be November, o

xperiences, it is also creating them. *Night* **sets in.** Lazy, hazy crazy Laos Nobody knows w

arket debt to rush for the exit. When *panic* **sets in**, lenders are often inclined to lump countries

off at any second. Elsewhere, *claustrophobia* **sets in** as the road squeezes between residential tow

phor as *a physical reality of Russian life* – **sets in** after a five-month winter. The snow and ice

attention for some while, *fatigue* eventually **sets in.** Rather than shocking, the "monstrous" denou

oppressive boss goes missing. *Chaos* **sets in** when he unexpectedly reappears to

the familiar feeling of pointlessness **sets in.** If you have finished with the

that *this wordless reserve* so often **sets in** between fathers and sons, or is

of several republics. As *hardship* **sets in**, they hold on to their assets and

food and other urgent aid as *winter* **sets in.** His motive is not only

use of credit. Is it any wonder *panic* **sets in** when income suddenly falls or

effect has worn off, *depression* **sets in.** Eventually, greater and more

the temperature falls and *tepidity* **sets in.** Why should that be? Because we

becomes harder and bumpier as *winter* **sets in.** They took the most positive step

autumn, or when *severe cold weather* **sets in**, a number of the thousands of

Beale are stayers *disenchantment* soon **sets in.** No matter Sir Claude and the new

of control. That's where *the anxiety* **sets in** [p] But Carolyn English, the head
a stab in the back until *rigor mortis* **sets in**, often finding themselves waking
When you get to 350 and *tiredness* **sets in**, it's statistics that keep you
under John Major. [p] If *the panic* **sets in** after the local elections, you
can overwhelm her. 3. *Denial* **Sets in** Just as in active addiction, she
the ship free before *rough weather* **sets in**. Assaro says the Hundi Number 12
with a lack of interest. *Panic* **sets in**, the deal is sweetened, which,
onset of symptoms. If *your condition* **sets in** and develops into a cold, a

Figure 5.1 Concordance lines for 'sets in'

Note: The 'target phrase', 'sets in', appears in bold and is centred, which means that the text to both sides is incomplete. In each line, the subject is italicised, to make clear what is being described as 'setting in'.

Empirical research: sociolinguistics

The overlap between these two areas is highlighted by Beaugrande (1999), when he advocates that greater attention should be paid by sociolinguists to the developments in corpus linguistics. He draws attention to the interplay, again, between culture, structure and agency when he writes:

> The *standing constraints* persisting on the plane of the system (e.g. the English article going before the noun) interact with the *emergent constraints* being only decided on the plane of the discourse (e.g. the lexical choices appropriate for a job interview). The interaction of multiple local constraints that are essentially simple generates the rich global complexity of real language data...
>
> (Beaugrande 1999: 131)

Furthermore, we have elsewhere (Carter and Sealey 2000; Sealey and Carter 2001) suggested various ways in which sociolinguistics could benefit from the insights of contemporary developments in social theory such as those discussed in this volume. One aspect of this is in recognising the distinctive properties and powers of speakers and of language, which we have discussed above. In relation to sociolinguistic research, this would involve an assertive maintenance of speakers, rather than language itself, as the originators of language change, but in a model which does acknowledge, as we have said, the possibility of some partial autonomy of the linguistic system.

Once again, it is possible to identify currents in the prevailing research which can be classified as giving more or less significance to culture, to structure and to agency. Variationism, in the tradition pioneered by Labov, is primarily interested in the linguistic system and how it changes. Hence the charges brought against this approach by functional linguists: that it neglects the agential power of speakers and the significance of social practice. There is then a danger that when probabilistic tendencies are identified – such as that female speakers tend to adopt the prestige variety[2] to a greater degree than male speakers do – this correlation comes to substitute for an *explanation* of speakers' differential behaviour. That is, patterns of correlation based on linear models of variables exclude complexity and emergence, in which case the phenomenon which is to be explained is used as the basis of the explanation: for example, being female can come to be given as a reason for using those forms which females are more likely to use.

This perspective is modified by the inclusion of more ethnographic and interview data in sociolinguistic studies, such as those used by Eckert, for example. However, it is a further implication of stratified ontology that many aspects of the social world are indifferent to the discursive understandings of actors. (Thus, as Archer (1995) points out with reference to economic realities, inflation reduces fixed incomes irrespective of whether or not actors understand the reasons for this.) Given that there are limits to people's discursive penetration of the social world, then, asking informants about their attitudes to their social networks and to local language varieties may not necessarily reveal the complex of factors operating to link membership of a particular social category with use of a particular linguistic variable. So the supplementing of quantitative work by qualitative interviews only partially offsets the limitations of variationist accounts.

A further complication of sociolinguistic research is that the quest for correlations between speakers' choice of language variety and their category membership relies on the identification of social categories. These categories are theoretical descriptions, and, as the social constructionists remind us, such descriptions are constituted through language itself. How far are these categories self chosen, and how far are they objectively derived and impervious to speakers' own understandings of who they are? We have argued elsewhere (Sealey and Carter 2001) that there is something to be gained, analytically, from distinguishing between those social categories which are constituted by involuntaristic characteristics, and those characterised by some degree of choice on the part of the people who belong to them. The first kind of category can be termed (following Greenwood 1994) 'social aggregates': groups – such as the poor, the unemployed, women over 50 – whose only common feature is the property identified as salient by whoever is employing the category – such as those responsible for benefits policy or for selling insurance to over-50s. Aggregates do not imply shared conventions and norms to which people can be party. The second approach to categorising groups of people identified by Greenwood is with reference to their membership of 'social collectives'. These are descriptions of those groups in which members must be party to sets of conventions and norms. It seems to us that if research were to distinguish quite explicitly between these two kinds of category, and to explore the meanings for speakers of both kinds, a more emergentist kind of empirical research would be possible. It is likely that neither commonsense social categories nor social scientific ones will correlate categorically with the linguistic variables identified, because, firstly, language is always language in use and, secondly, the mechanisms bringing about linguistic variation and change are likely to be complex and multiplicative, rather than linear and additive.

Conclusion

Our central purpose in this chapter has been to demonstrate the potential for the study of language of a realist view of the social world. Whilst such a view is far from being methodologically prescriptive, it is clear that it carries methodological implications. To begin with, our ontological claims about the stratified nature of social reality, and the place of language within this, entail that researching language be regarded properly as social research. That is to say, our realism compels us to see language as an aspect of human practice:

language is never encountered 'on its own', either 'in there' in the intuitions of ideal speaker-listeners or 'out there' in autonomous systems of meaning. Furthermore, the notion of language, written and spoken, as emergent from the engagement of human practice with the world challenges variationism, the view that language change may best be understood in terms of the effects of discrete variables, such as social class or gender, on speech patterns. Instead, emergence encourages a view of the social world as open, complex and non-linear in which empirical phenomena provide 'traces' of the non-observable (Byrne 1998). A central methodological task is thus the development of what Layder has termed 'concept-indicator links', that is to say, establishing models and theories which specify clear linkages between concept and empirical indicator and which judge concepts with regard to the stratified nature of social reality (Layder 1998; see also Pawson 1989). The empirical always tells us something about the social world and theory is essential to telling us what this might be.

However, this requires a theoretical perspective able to keep the interplay between the different domains of social life (Layder 1997) always within view, a perspective whose concepts not only reflect agency and structure, but one which also recognises that the effects of agency and structure on social activities and practices are variable and depend upon the relative influence of the different social domains. This, in a nutshell, is the potential offered by recent realist writers for the study of language: an approach which is able to see a role for speakers and their intentions, which acknowledges the weight of history on present action, and which also accommodates the partial autonomy of language.

Notes

1   For a more thorough treatment of this topic, see Sealey and Carter (in press).
2   Many sociolinguistic studies have found that when women use more of a particular linguistic form (i.e. pronunciation, vocabulary item or grammatical construction) than men do, they usually favour the prestigious variant. When men use a particular form more than women do, it is usually a vernacular form.

References

Archer, M. (1988) *Culture and Agency: The Place of Culture in Social Theory*, Cambridge: Cambridge University Press.

Archer, M. (1995) *Realist Social Theory: A Morphogenetic Account*, Cambridge: Cambridge University Press.

Archer, M.S. (2000) *Being Human: The Problem of Agency*, Cambridge: Cambridge University Press.

Beaugrande, R. D. (1997) *New Foundations for a Science of Text and Discourse: Cognition, Communication, and the Freedom of Access to Knowledge and Society*, Norwood, NJ: Ablex.

Beaugrande, R. D. (1999) 'Linguistics, sociolinguistics, and corpus linguistics: ideal language versus real language', *Journal of Sociolinguistics* 3, 1: 128–39.

Brumfit, C. (2001) *Individual Freedom in Language Teaching: Helping Learners to Develop a Dialect of Their Own*, Oxford: Oxford University Press.

Byrne, D. (1998) *Complexity Theory and the Social Sciences*, London: Routledge.

Carr, P. (1990) *Linguistic Realities: An Autonomist Metatheory for the Generative Enterprise*, Cambridge: Cambridge University Press.

Carter, B. and Sealey, A. (2000) 'Language, structure and agency: what can realist social theory offer to sociolinguistics?', *Journal of Sociolinguistics* 4, 1: 3–20.

Chambers, J.K. (1995) *Sociolinguistic Theory: Linguistic Variation and its Social Significance*, Oxford: Blackwell.

Chomsky, N. (1965) *Aspects of the Theory of Syntax*, Cambridge, MA: MIT Press.

Chouliariki, L. and Fairclough, N. (1999) *Discourse in Late Modernity: Rethinking Critical Discourse Analysis*, Edinburgh: Edinburgh University Press.

Coupland, N. and Jaworski, A. (2001) 'Discourse', in P. Cobley (ed.) *Semiotics and Linguistics*, London: Routledge.

Devitt, M. and Sterelny, K. (1999) *Language and Reality: An Introduction to the Philosophy of Language*, Oxford: Blackwell.

Downes, W. (1984) *Language and Society*, London: Fontana.

Goody, J. (1986) *The Logic of Writing and the Organization of Society*, Cambridge: Cambridge University Press.

Greenwood, J.D. (1994) *Realism, Identity and Emotion: Reclaiming Social Psychology*, London: Sage.

Halliday, M.A.K. (1978) *Language as Social Semiotic*, London: Edward Arnold.

Hasan, R. (1992) 'Meaning in sociolinguistic theory', in K. Bolton and H. Kwok (eds) *Sociolinguistics Today: International Perspectives*, London: Routledge.

Hymes, D. (1974) *Foundations in Sociolinguistics: An Ethnographic Approach*, London: Tavistock Publications.

Layder, D. (1997) *Modern Social Theory: Key Debates and New Directions*, London: UCL Press.

Layder, D. (1998) *Sociological Practice: Linking Theory and Social Research*, London: Sage.

Pawson, R. (1989) *A Measure for Measures: A Manifesto For Empirical Sociology*, London: Routledge.

Popper, K. and Eccles, J.C. (1977) *The Self and Its Brain*, Berlin: Springer.

Potter, J. (1996) *Representing Reality: Discourse, Rhetoric and Social Construction*, London: Sage.

Potter, J. (1997) 'Discourse analysis as a way of analysing naturally occurring talk', in D. Silverman (ed.) *Qualitative Research: Theory, Method and Practice*, London: Sage.

Sealey, A. and Carter, B. (2001) 'Social categories and sociolinguistics: applying a realist approach', *International Journal of the Sociology of Language* 152, 1–19.

Sealey, A. and Carter, B. (2004) *Applied Linguistics as Social Science*, London: Continuum.

Silverman, D. (2001) *Interpreting Qualitative Data: Methods for Analysing Talk, Text and Interaction*, London: Sage.

Sinclair, J. (1991) *Corpus, Concordance, Collocation*, Oxford: Oxford University Press.

Street, B.V. (1984) *Literacy in Theory and Practice*, Cambridge: Cambridge University Press.

Stubbs, M. (1996) *Text and Corpus Analysis*, Oxford: Blackwell.

Trudgill, P. (1983) *Sociolinguistics: An Introduction to Language and Society*, London: Penguin.

Wardhaugh, R. (1992) *An Introduction to Sociolinguistics*, Oxford: Blackwell.

Wetherell, M., Taylor, S. and Yates, S.J. (eds) (2001) *Discourse as Data: A Guide for Analysis*, London and Milton Keynes: Open University and Sage.

Williams, G. (1992) *Sociolinguistics: A Sociological Critique*, London: Routledge.

Part III

Reflexivity and realist research

The contributors in this section are all concerned with reflexivity in social science research. For Wendy Olsen, 'methodological triangulation' is a tool for reflexivity. By framing a research problem in terms of different theories, and following each methodologically as long and as far as their practical unity can be sustained and their juxtaposition proves fruitful, researchers can enrich their initial perspective by viewing it from another standpoint. For Angie Hart, Marnie Freeman and Caroline New, unless reflexivity is an integral aspect of professional practice, professional interventions are likely to have unintended and unwanted consequences. Reflexivity is also built into the research design they propose by the use of differently skilled researchers working with different, but interacting, groups. For Tim May, to disregard reflexivity in social science opens the door to 'the revenge of positivism'.

Olsen reports on two pieces of interdisciplinary work into grain markets in South India. In the first, she used both neo-classical and Marxist political economy perpectives to frame an investigation into farmers' 'distress sales' of grain, enriching and counterposing survey data with ethnographic research. In the second, she and her co-researchers jettisoned the neo-classical category of the household and drew on feminist political economy approaches to conceptualise intra-household dynamics. The research design used the Indian Marxist political economy approach to design a complex survey of local class relations, triangulating this with interviews following the feminist tradition in methodology. The data they collected revealed (among other things) various forms of women's collective activity which had been invisible to the Marxist approach alone. Through the use of these consecutive studies, Olsen explores the process of meta-analysis, through which researchers reflect on their findings and categories and reconceptualise the field. Her work is relevant to the realist assertion that it is possible to make rational judgements between two theories purporting to explain the same or overlapping phenomena. Putting the theories to work in the same piece of research provides practical evidence of their capacities and limitations.

Hart, New and Freeman outline a research proposal which originated in Freeman's reflections on her own professional practice as a health visitor. They begin with a puzzle related to health inequalities – whether health visitors' targeted interventions with 'disadvantaged' parent-clients do reduce health inequalities by improving the health status of their children, or whether they actually tend to reproduce the status quo. Their preliminary model identifies possible mechanisms at several levels: the construction, through professional training and practice, of the discursive category 'disadvantaged'; the asymmetry of power in the relationship between professional and client; and the emergence of health visitor–parent-client relationships with emergent properties of their own which influence subsequent interaction. Their proposed design is longitudinal, consonant with Archer's methodological recommendation to bring time into the investigation of the relationship between structure and agency (1995). The research methods they propose are consciously related to the level and type of phenomena under investigation (Danermark *et al.* 2002), including focus groups to explore professionals' understanding and constitution of the category of 'disadvantage', separate researchers to observe the interaction between parent-clients and health visitors and to hear each party's account of episodes of intervention and their own consequent decision-making. This sort of qualitative research into the dialectic between structure and agency has the power to illuminate the actual mechanisms driving (or sabotaging) social policy interventions.

May considers the implications of ideas about reflexivity for social scientific research. Noting that the discussion of reflexivity has a long history in social science, he argues that recent emphases on 'multiple readings' of texts and the perspectival nature of knowledge tend towards a paralysing relativism. However, in May's view there is no necessary connection between reflexivity and relativism. Rather, by focusing on three key dimensions of knowledge production – need, degree and consequence – an alternative view of reflexivity can be developed. This task is more urgent in the light of efforts (from quarters as disparate as academic postmodernists and the funding councils) to deny epistemic authority to social science research into social reality, rendering its knowledge questionable and making its research agendas vulnerable to political manipulation. Drawing on the work of Bourdieu, May argues that a realist social science requires reflexivity, since as social scientists we are always in some position or other in relation to what we are researching. Acknowledging our positionality does not preclude the production of valid social scientific knowledge. On the contrary, May concludes, reflexivity 'is not a tool to undermine science, but one that provides for a more realistic science through its contribution to a realpolitik of scholastic reasoning in the service of epistemic gain' (Chapter 8, p. 186).

Reference

Archer, M.S. (1995) *Realist Social Theory: A Morphogenetic Approach*, Cambridge: Cambridge University Press.

Danermark, B., Ekstrom, M., Jakobson, L., and Karlsson, J. C. (2002) *Explaining Society: Critical realism in the social sciences*, London: Routledge.

6 Methodological triangulation and realist research

An Indian exemplar

Wendy Olsen

Introduction

Triangulation is widely recommended as a way of doing social research (Bryman 1996; Bryman *et al.* 2003; Denzin 1970; Flick 1992; Gilbert 1993). It involves looking at the research question from several viewpoints rather as mappers will place instruments on three hilltops to get overlapping data sets concerning the valley or plain below. The best known form of triangulation, data triangulation, uses multiple data types (e.g. qualitative and quantitative) to investigate the research question. Triangulation becomes a series of steps associated with changes in the researcher's conceptual map of the terrain (Gilbert 1993; Bryman 2001; Olsen 2003). Bryman and colleagues (2003) describe the result of multi-method research strategies as 'convergent validity'. Increasingly, quantitative and qualitative techniques are integrated (e.g. Robson 2001). A great deal of common ground then emerges between social constructionist and realist research techniques, despite the epistemological differences.

This paper describes the use of data triangulation in my research into grain markets in India, but it goes further and offers examples of methodological triangulation as well. Where data triangulation brings together research methods sometimes associated with conflicting methodologies, methodological triangulation actually attempts to use profoundly contrasting methodologies, while keeping in mind their differing epistemological and ontological assumptions (Denzin 1970). The methodologies considered might correspond to two competing theories in the chosen research area, each of which is given a role in some part of the conceptualisation and design of the research.

At first sight, methodological triangulation might seem incompatible with realism. Certainly it can raise difficulties of interpretation when the epistemological norms and ontological assumptions of different methodological schools are at odds with each other (Bryman 1998). Walby describes such deep differences of opinion as 'epistemological chasms'. She shows how it is still possible to reach dialogue or debate by focusing on the social origins of conflicting theories rather than their points of conflict

(Walby 2001). Similarly, methodological triangulation allows researchers to engage with contrasting theories, and to discover in practice what they can and cannot do and show in relation to a particular research question.

Social realists are fallibilists, aware that their theories, models and concepts may be misleading, partial or wrong as characterisations of reality (Lawson 1997). These are, after all, social constructions – but realists differ from strong social constructionists in their claim that it is possible to make rational (though fallible) judgements about the relative value of competing theories, models and concepts. While data triangulation allows us to reach more complex models, methodological triangulation allows us to compare theories and methodologies by applying them, yielding important information about their practical adequacy (Sayer 1992).

Triangulation does not merely validate claims or strengthen data sets. It also offers ways to enrich data analysis. In other words *the map changes* rather than getting *more perfect* within a single, narrow perspective. Triangulation is not primarily about accurate or unbiased measurement. It is about learning.

In the following sections I introduce the case studies and then take up more general issues of methodology. The paper concludes with some rules of thumb for realist research.

Case study 1: distress sales in Indian grain markets

The research question of my doctoral research (1984–88) was why 'distress sales' of foodgrains occurred among peasant farmers in southern India (Olsen 1993; 1994a). Fieldwork took place in Andhra Pradesh, where the upland plateau experiences just eight days of rain per year on average yet has widespread field agriculture, including rice, millet, groundnut, tomato, mango and lentil production. Animal husbandry is practised in conjunction with field crops. A shift towards 2–3 rice crops per year was widely experienced when wells and pumps became prevalent and so-called 'green revolution' crop varieties were introduced from about 1978. Two contrasting fieldwork villages, 3 km apart, were chosen in the sub-region known as Rayalaseema. The study area was chosen as being typically diverse in its castes and agrarian structure (Olsen 1996).

Marketisation and commercialisation of farm households, corresponding in part to their shift from peasant farming towards industrialised farming, have been seen as associated with price risks when farmers move from subsistence to market-oriented production. 'Distress sales' occur when farmers sell grain only to buy the same grain back later at very high prices (Kahlon and Tyagi 1983). Price seasonality in rice and other markets has historically been very high in India. Farmers' distress could be measured using proxy variables in large-scale surveys. One could record the month of sale, which would show a discriminatory low price existing for those sales that occurred just at harvest time. Large national surveys covered farmers' selling dates, but asking the price directly was sometimes difficult (because of variations in types, local measures, weighing procedures and the amount of bran or shell included with the edible crop). Separate records of monthly arrivals and daily prices were kept by the government of India at each registered wholesale marketplace precisely because seasonal crop prices have such wide social effects in India.

The two main theoretical/methodological approaches

There are two main approaches to distress sales. The first one is based on neoclassical economics (henceforth NCE). Older work in this school offered a descriptive analysis of patterns of crop marketing among the farmers in each region. By remaining at the level of description, these works tended to 'explain' simply by saying that these things happened. Nevertheless, the terms 'compulsive selling' and 'distress sales' entered into policy discourse. The later work in this school of thought argued that each sale must be rational and optimal for the seller at the time of sale, and that apparently compulsive selling might be rational in the context of multi-market relationships in which the crop-seller voluntarily chose to engage. You might, according to this view, buy fertiliser from a merchant who also lends you money, and then sell your crop to that merchant for a lower price than an anonymous, unconnected seller.

A second approach to distress sales derives from Indian Marxist political economy (henceforth MPE). This approach sees farmers as residing in a class structure which in turn helps to shape the credit market and the land-rental markets of each region. For the MPE approach, the class structure evolves in conjunction with the success or failure of social classes to exploit other social classes and economic opportunities. Distress sales of grain often occur as a direct result of indebtedness of a poor farm household. The causal chain involved is complex. The resources available to households are patterned by class differences, which in India are further exaggerated by the caste structure and castes' political power. To compensate for low earnings and for pauperisation through their loss of land over time, poorer households borrow from landlords to whom they are already linked by relations of obligation, protection and so on. Richer households, on the other hand, either reinvest profits or borrow from banks to make investments. Indebted farm households make distress sales of grain, often under duress.

Both approaches recognise that there may be a connection between crop sales and credit. 'Tying' became a topic for debate in the late 1980s between NCE scholars, who tended to assume that peasants make rational choices, and MPE scholars who argued that exploitation was taking new forms under capitalist commercialisation. The feelings of obligation and pressure associated with a given sale are omitted completely from the neoclassical economic framework (Braverman and Stiglitz 1982; Binswanger and Rosenzweig 1984; Rosenzweig 1988). In this paradigm, households are seen as idealised, rational actors choosing an optimal set of market exchanges (Ellis 1988).

Thus the dynamics of capitalism enter into the Marxist political economy explanatory framework and not into the neoclassical commercialisation framework. In realist terms, the MPE framework is ontologically stratified, seeking mechanisms at a deeper level, while the NCE framework is ontologically flat. For the MPE approach, a debt is seen as a *proximate* cause of the distress sale of grain, immediately after harvest, by a poor farmer at a low price (Bharadwaj 1986; Bhaduri 1983). Another issue dividing the two theoretical schools was whether to consider each market independently of the others. The NCE literature on grain markets had tended to treat them separately from credit markets, using a demand and supply model, and not to mention land markets at all (e.g. Kahlon and George 1985). NCE economists showed the impact of government price-setting in the grain market but placed the grain market in isolation from relations of indebtedness and from land ownership – i.e. from class and credit (Roemer 1986). My research, in contrast, explicitly linked the credit market conditions to the decision about the timing of sale (Olsen 1996).

I wanted to analyse the whole market in its historical trajectory. Here the literature again had two prongs. The NCE approach focused on specific sales and the profits from storage (e.g. Kahlon and Tyagi 1983; Newbery and Stiglitz 1981). The MPE literature rooted in research in northern India pointed to a different, much broader agenda (Bhaduri 1983; Bharadwaj 1986). The local markets illustrated the gains which one or two social classes were making either *at the expense of* poorer classes, or in the context of the green revolution and new irrigation facilities, through increased production per acre and per person.

Research design: methodological triangulation in case study 1

The empirical agenda in my field research was to examine the social class structure among households in two villages, record the production, purchase, sale and storage of all crops over a twelve-month period, and test for price discrimination in farmers' sale prices, whilst also examining the occurrence (and causes) of distress sales (if any). The aim was to link macro and micro causal processes in order to contextualise single sales.

The research used a mixed technique strategy led by a core questionnaire. Survey techniques were important to measure accurately the extent of commercialisation of the farmers (NCE approach), whilst qualitative techniques were used to relate these measures to class relations (MPE approach). Methodological triangulation implies data triangulation, but not vice versa; this study did both since each of the competing approaches influenced a part of the design.

Random sampling of seventy-one households in two contiguous villages was complemented by interviews with about sixty individuals (including bank employees and civil servants at the district and state level) over the course of a year. With the help of two local enumerators, I made ethnographic field-notes and local observations over a twenty-month period; recorded forty family histories; and analysed policy documents and government reports at all-India and state level. The core questionnaire was filled in during a monthly face-to-face interview over thirteen months. It covered each household's crop production, assets, consumption, storage of crops, labour-time allocation, borrowing and lending, and demographic changes. This was complemented by varying additional survey questions regarding topics like voting, irrigation, price expectations, daily eating habits, ritual food-giving to other families (one topic each month). Detailed notes and stories were collected at the same time.

In this case study, 'markets' were assumed to include non-monetary forms of exchange as well as commercial exchange, and 'farmers' were assumed to be 'households' – ignoring gender relations within households. These stipulations worked well enough for the research to progress. Equating farmers and households made the survey easier to do, but was a crude way of operationalising 'farming'. I was to return to this issue in the second case study.

Since I was using an NCE methodology as well as drawing on the MPE approach, hypothesis testing played a role in this research. My sample was not big enough to allow me to do a regression analysis, and the caste structure differed too much between districts to allow inference from my sample. One hypothesis which interested me is so basic to the neoclassical approach that it is not even seen as a hypothesis, but as self-evident: that farmers of all social classes acted to maximise their revenue from grain sales, i.e. acted rationally in economic terms. NCE economists simply assume this axiomatically. Their assumption supports the Duhem-Quine claim that empiricist hypothesis-testing never tests the whole theoretical and discursive underpinnings of a thesis (Boylan and O'Gorman 1995: 157). I tested this basic assumption (H1) through interviewing the people in my sample. When the grain market was considered on its own, the hypothesis turned out to be untrue; that is, farmers' sales of grain did not always result in revenue maximisation. If the assumptions were widened to recognise the interlocking of markets, it became possible to see the rationality of the decisions farmers did make – but these were conditioned upon their class locations and social relations with other castes. I also tested the hypothesis that distress sales occurred (H2). Having hypotheses at two levels implied a depth ontology in which I was not only observing outcomes (H2) but also investigating the underlying mechanisms which might have led to these outcomes (H1).

The research thus combined techniques from NCE-style empirical hypothesis-testing (the structured survey; rigorous checking and correction of data; careful operationalisation of the concepts of 'distress sales' and 'class') with techniques from the anthropological and political-economy traditions. The MPE tradition is more ontologically complex than the NCE approach, leading to a wider range of data-collection techniques. The diverse social objects studied included: discourses of dependency; local, regional and state variation in governance structures and policies; caste as a structure intersecting with the social class structure; markets as interlinked structures rather than as a series of isolated sites of exchange; and social relations as having a complex history rather than being the basis of simple, rational, optimising decisions. Triangulation is inherently appropriate to political-economy studies, whereas the neoclassical economic tradition tends toward single-level, methodological individualist research at the household level.

In the research design considered as a whole, the narrow explanatory focus of the NCE approach fitted within the wider perspective of the MPE approach. Thus each local loan was examined to see whether the lender was tying the borrower, and whether the borrower routinely depended upon this lender either for land-rental or for other services (e.g. buying food from their shop; selling crops to them). In other words several neoclassical questions were encompassed within the realist MPE approach.

Results of case study 1

Distress sales were indeed found. They occurred in the sale of the major local cash-crop, groundnuts (peanuts in the shell; Olsen 1993; 1996). Poor households grew peanuts but sold at harvest time at prices far below what rich farmers received later in the year. Merchants, too, bought up the crop, stored it and sold it at huge profits of 40 to 60 per cent, even 80 per cent if they sold peanuts during the next growing season when they were scarce both as seed and as food. Documenting these sources of revenue for landlords and merchants was an important part of the field research.

Distress sales were not found in the rice market; instead, due to good local credit-market conditions and especially the competitive presence of a bank branch in one village, people were able to store their rice for up to six months and then eat it. In exploring the distress sales of groundnut, I created a typology of tied social relations grounded in the local conditions. The typology stressed that merchant class households (all of merchant caste) tied local peasants into exploitative relationships, whilst the landlord class (of varying castes) tied local workers who then struggled with the dilemmas of dependency. My results thus tended to support the exploitation interpretation of the MPE approach, since they showed that each year households were becoming polarised into strongly differentiated classes.

The research also went beyond this typology towards the realm of meaning. What did these sales mean and how did the sellers relate to the buyers? Unequal social relations between households might create all sorts of pressures. I discovered that ritual food-giving by the rich was an important way to express one's benevolent attitude towards a tied household. For workers to resist accepting the ritual food implied a huge social shift towards 'free' inter-household relations. Breaking the tied relation would mean losing access to the plot of rented land in future. It might also mean losing access to emergency loans from the richer household. In discussion, two types of talk about this situation emerged. One discourse accepted dependency and expressed gratitude and acceptance of the unequal social relations, whilst the other discourse resisted dependency and stressed that the poor household needs a mixture of livelihood activities rather than tied transactions with one grain-buyer.

Feelings ran deep about such matters. Among the poor these social relations were the primary topic of discussion (along with drought) when I visited respondents for interviewing. People in the social classes that rented in land (especially the 'landed workers' and the 'petty commodity producing farmers') felt strongly that they were losing economically within their dependency relationships. Whilst most farmers could identify 'their' landlord, there were many who denied any dependency relation upon them, especially in the more commercialised of the two villages. These social relations were not simply archetypal patron–client relationships. They had been changing during the rapid growth of capitalist social relations locally.

The importance of trust and the symbolic role of 'their' landlord did not extend to relations between farmers and the money-lending merchants. Instead, relations with merchants existed on a less trusting, non-dependent basis rooted in a 'promissory note' held by the merchant. Promissory notes were binding on the borrower.

These dependency relations rooted in caste and class do not figure in the narrow NCE agenda. To explain distress sales it was necessary to go beyond hypothesis-testing, and to ask: 'Why were these findings observed?' Whereas in neoclassical and in the more recent new institutionalist research hypothesis-testing generally arises in a deductive logical framework, realist frameworks use retroduction. Retroduction is a mode of inference from observations to what must have been the case in order to bring about the observed events; it is about moving from one thing (empirical observation of events) and arriving at something different (what conditions and properties must exist for these events to be possible) (Danermark *et al.* 2002; Lawson 2003). Applied to distress sales, it led to a clear grasp of the interactions behind the researcher's 'true' and 'false' decisions on specific hypotheses (Boylan and O'Gorman 1995).

However, retroduction required triangulation, since the survey data on its own was too limited. For example, in one of the monthly survey rounds I asked people on each farm to forecast crop prices forward up to the next season. Over half the respondents could not answer this question at all. I saw these 'missing values' in the survey data as an event which must have specific causes. I looked at how respondents formulated their answers, and thought about why so many people did not answer this question. These gaps led me to reflect on the limited engagement with markets of many farmers, especially tenant farmers. Specific sustained patterns in the social-class holding of stocks were revealed.

In my book I focused on power relations among the classes of the village, as mechanisms involved in generating distress sales. I argued that

> any study of exchange must begin by looking at the productive structure [p. 24]. . . . compulsive involvement in markets occurs through the subtle manipulation of cultivators by the whole system of relations in a capitalist society. They are 'forced' to sell their crop by circumstances, some of which may be consciously defined by their moneylender . . . The cultivator may be aware, or unaware, or even deny, that any coercion is involved.
>
> (Olsen 1996: 24 and 35)

Other researchers in southern India have done similar work (Harriss 1982; Ramachandran 1990). Social class relations in India vary over localised regions, and caste in each locale interacts with the class structure (Balagopal 1998). Throughout southern India, local fieldwork-based monographs have been critical in developing a knowledge-base for policies for grain-market management. The methodological triangulation of my research confirmed the superiority of the MPE approach; the narrow neoclassical agenda, which would try to explain a specific sale's timing or a specific crop-choice decision, was not of sufficient breadth or depth to explain their complex patterns.

Case study 2: the impact of structural adjustment programmes

Distress sales are just one part of the story of class polarisation and people's struggle against a difficult climate in semi-arid upland southern India. A decade later, during 1995–6, further fieldwork in the same district revealed that the process of commercialisation was having dramatic long-term effects on poverty, wealth and class relations. The aim of this second research project, funded by the UK Department for International Development, was to investigate the impact of liberalisation on two Indian villages after the 1991 Structural Adjustment Programme. The SAP began in 1991 and had had little effect up to 1996, due to resistance from both rich and poor classes. The project aimed not only to explore the role that markets play in people's lives, but also to examine attitudes to the liberalisation of markets. On the whole, attitudes to the government were still populist and statist in the villages in 1995, but other attitudes (regarding gender and caste) had changed remarkably since the mid-1980s.

Case study 2 described the gendered nature of poverty and the heterogeneity of women even in a small community (Olsen and Johnson 2001). This time the research was overtly triangulated.

Theoretical approaches within Indian political economy

Case study 2 responded to a growing sense that political economy needed to be more empirically grounded and more feminist. The Indian Marxists of the political economy approach quoted earlier tended towards a deterministic view of capitalist history and some even mathematised their schemas to make them convincing to neoclassical audiences. By contrast another stream in political economy would take issue both with determinism and with mathematisation: this approach can be labelled feminist political economy. This time, the methodologies triangulated were the Marxist political economy (MPE) and feminist political economy (FPE) approaches.

Kabeer (1994) reviews the FPE approach, arguing that Marxists have sometimes been too structuralist and underestimated the role of agency. This is certainly true of many Indian academic Marxists. In addition Kabeer, like other feminists, values historically grounded narratives and in-depth qualitative analysis. Her own work on micro-finance uses methodological triangulation in a highly rigorous way. In Indian political economy both MPE and FPE strands must be taken seriously. They both take issue with neoclassical and neoliberal theorisations. The 1995–6 research attempted to use a transformational model of social action to examine local grass-roots organisations and civil society, and their effects on local markets and social relations, during a time of policy change.

Research design in case study 2

In the 1995–6 research I no longer equated farmers and households (in the NCE manner). Instead, as feminist methodology prescribed, intra-household dynamics were investigated, in relation to decision-making about taking loans and other issues. Records of labour use and the use of government services (e.g. banks and buses) were complemented by interviews with local women in two selected villages.

The survey was set up with several units of analysis incorporating different levels of the social world: persons, farms, households, loans, plots, wells, relations with moneylenders, and days of work. Sixty households were randomly chosen in each of two villages. A member of each household was approached once for an introductory meeting and a second time to fill in a questionnaire. Twenty in-depth interviews were carried out, linked to this household data. Finally, secondary data on local agriculture and the composition of about six villages was gathered.

In addition to the work of data-gathering, writing ethnographic notebooks created an opportunity to reconsider theories of liberalisation. Based on the earlier 1980s' research, a meta-critique was conducted in two stages. First, the absences in each existing theory were identified. The neoclassical economic approach notably lacks a theory of coercion. Marxist theory has its own weaknesses, especially when mathematised (as seen in Bhaduri 1983). In both cases, it appeared that only qualitative research could improve on the standard research designs. Using the FPE approach in the 1995–6 research generated new findings not usually allowed for in the NCE and MPE theoretical frameworks. For instance, women's self-help groups were accessing bank loans without collateral, and these groups had effects on women's consciousness generally (Olsen and Johnson 2001). Both traditional theoretical frameworks had not made these developments visible.

In the second stage of meta-critique, theory is developed which incorporates and goes beyond existing theory (Bhaskar 1993). In this research, apart from theorising 'power', it was also important to re-theorise 'development' itself. The encompassing theories I drew on were Nussbaum's theory of 'human development' (Nussbaum 1999; Nussbaum and Glover 1995) and feminist empowerment theory (Kabeer 1994). There is not space here to explore these schools further, but in my view both are consistent with critical realism (Hutchinson *et al.* 2002; Thomas 2000).

Results of case study 2

There is no space here to go into all the results of the 1995–6 research. I shall touch on two which emerged as a result of the triangulation of the MPE and FPE approaches.

In 1985 I had discovered that women often hid stocks of grain, particularly seeds of groundnut, until the sowing time came around again. In the later research this pattern was reconfirmed amidst much laughter and sometimes men's embarrassment. The differentiation of persons within households, who often disagreed about the timing of sale of crops, had been hidden in the household-based analyses of the earlier research. Asked about their farming decisions in 1995–6, women often showed much anger as they described the competing demands they felt were made upon them. They talked about their lack of mobility, their inability to use bikes or get out of the village much, and their use of local grass-roots organisations. Men took physical mobility and tearoom chat for granted, but we found that women needed to construct situations which strengthened their ability to operate in public spheres (Harris-White 1999). Whereas the MPE approach did give rise to ethnographic methods (as in case study 1), it was when these were supplemented by FPE-inspired interviews that gendered aspects of poverty and household decision-making were highlighted.

Elements of the survey data showed a further weakness in the MPE approach. Tenants were a special case not fitting easily into a Marxist class structure. The fieldwork showed explicitly, through the qualitative interviews, that men and women in poor households felt excluded from bank loan services and were thus 'financially excluded' (Olsen and Uma 1998). This was particularly true where the farmers were tenants rather than landowners. Financial exclusion (in the sense of social exclusion from *formal sector finance*) was found to occur both by gender and by class. Caste was inherently part of the system of relations that supported social exclusion. A new finding that arose unexpectedly was that tenants were constrained from using bank credit. Their subjective view was that they deserved bank services but were denied them due to a lack of firm collateral. There was little hope of tenants getting better access, and the research concluded that a form of social exclusion was occurring in which landowners had privileged access to formal sector credit and tenants were forced to use informal sector credit.

Methodological triangulation and meta-critique

Both case studies made it clear that the notion of a 'farmer' being a 'household' was misleading. The individuals within households in such villages were agents in their own right, (a) actively working in labour markets, and forming cross-class households; (b) experiencing conflicts of interest and acting in secret and/or independently of overt household strategies at certain crucial times. Thus a 'household' is a structure which interacts with the class structure.

Thus in several ways, summarised in Olsen and Johnson (2001), people need to be understood within the context of their household, their family and their caste, that is, within a stratified social ontology. There is another dialectic here between structure and agency: the person influencing society influencing the person, as illustrated in the Transformative Model of Social Action, or TMSA (Bhaskar 1979; Archer *et al.* 1998). Realism's opposition to methodological individualism is supported by feminist arguments for reflexivity (May 2000; Ribbens and Edwards 1998; New 1996). The research which comprises case study 2 followed these principles in its self-conscious awareness of gender relations, of values, and of the choice of conceptual frameworks.

Three rules of thumb for realist research

Three *rules of thumb* began to emerge from this research (see also Olsen 1999 and 2003).

1   Use a stratified ontology

In the 1980s the neoclassical literature appeared to forget that there are multiple levels in society, as if society consisted merely of a bunch of atoms, all separable and comparable, without differentiated sub-structures and without the emergence of larger structured units. As Fay (1996) put it, reductionism occurs when the world is simplified to a reduced set of (ontic) assumptions or things, and atomism is a particularly serious case of reductionism. Atomism may be appropriate as a temporary way of organising a single data set (e.g. a survey data set) but even then it is unnecessary to reduce everything to a single level. Data sets can have multiple levels, and the data set from south India had ten types of cases: loans, labour-days, crops, plots, people, households, transactions, sales, purchases and stocks. Reductionism thus involves a strong commitment to a very simple ontology. Even the neoclassical literature has moved away from looking simply at farmers; it now considers labour-tying relationships, government and other actors.

Whilst the critique of reductionism is obviously trenchant, it is not always clear what to do about it. A good first cut is to move up and down levels and to try to relate what is observed from each level to the other levels. In case study 1 this strategy involved interviewing individuals whilst constructing survey data at the household level. In this study the random sample was augmented with a sample of landlords chosen from a wider geographic area precisely in order to widen the explanatory power of the survey data from the villages (described in Olsen 1996, Appendix, and in Olsen 1994c).

2   Value analysis rather than pretended neutrality

Empiricist social scientists often aim for value neutrality, whereas critical social scientists attempt to incorporate the analysis of values into their research strategies. Critical realists therefore reflect on the values implicit or explicit in theoretical frameworks as well as in empirical data.

Value neutrality is part of empiricist epistemology. It enables logical inferences to claim authority and legitimacy; it grounds the notion of 'the facts'. Sandra Harding, in contrast, suggests the term 'strong objectivity' for research approaches that engage overtly with the ethical frameworks of both researcher and the things/people being researched (Harding 1991; see also Lacey 1999; 2002).

Two examples illustrate the impossibility of value neutrality. In one village, because I had walked around the dalit people's section and eaten in the houses there, I was shouted at by a 'higher' caste woman. She insisted I would never be allowed to enter her house again. I had offered to help her carry a bucket of water from the pump to the house, but when my hand touched the water she threw it down on the ground and walked away. This incident affected my later ability to interview her husband, a prominent moneylender. A choice between contacting all sections or affiliating with one or the other is pressed upon researchers engaging with Indian villagers. Certain workers approached me wanting my support and involvement in their anti-oppression grass-roots organisations. The collection of scientific data was coloured by these experiences and can hardly be called 'non-interventionist' given that I was perceived as being politically aligned with the dalit people. There was no doubt that the research activities had an impact on the local class relations.

Most social research is inherently a social activity in ways like this, and to pretend otherwise undermines the contribution research can make to knowledge. Following Harding, I recommend being open about the values of researcher and researched and the impact of the research.

3 Use retroduction

The grain- and credit-market research required measures of magnitude but the most interesting findings were about what lay behind the numbers. Careful recording made comparisons possible by class, by season and by crop. While social relations were represented categorically, the numerical measures were not treated as though they exhausted the findings or obviated the need for theoretical analysis.

Realists argue that a causal model may be more complex and involve more factors than can ever be represented in a set of mathematical equations (Sayer 1992) or by a specific set of data (Olsen 2001). The theoretical causal model is not the same as the model one specifies for empirical estimation. In case study 1 a single equation summarised the important tendencies of farmers to sell crops (a) when they could get a good price, (b) allowing for storage costs but (c) also allowing for their credit-market conditions through the marginal implicit interest rate (Olsen 1996: 151–2). Further discursive analysis based on case study 2 (using interview data) introduced the important role of tenants' dependency on the landlords, government crop-buying patterns, the rice subsidy, and local banks which affected interest rates. Retroduction is rarely expressible in mathematical terms, but, as this chapter has shown, causal mechanisms can be traced in relation to one another through wide-ranging types of data.

Conclusion

This chapter has shown how, in the first case study, Marxist political economy exposed the limitations of the neo-classical model. In contrast to the hypothesis-testing of neoclassical economics, which invariably fails to admit or test its own assumptions, retroduction allowed me to identify mechanisms at the level of class and caste relations which provided a fuller explanation of the patterns of data. The question of why neoclassical theories and assumptions are so widespread in the economics of farming is another retroductive task that falls outside of this chapter.

In the second case study further research based on primary fieldwork enabled feminist insights to be added to the Marxist political economy model. Retroduction from the absence of women as agents in case study 1, and in Structural Adjustment economics generally (which is based on neoclassical theories), led to new insights about mechanisms of exploitation, both at the level of gender relations and at the level of ideology. In both case studies methodological triangulation resulted in a richer description than either approach could have yielded on its own, and produced evidence for judging the relative value of competing theories.

References

Archer, M., Bhaskar, R., Collier, A., Lawson, T. and Norrie A. (eds) (1998) *Critical Realism: Essential Readings*, London: Routledge.

Balagopal, K. (edited by G. Haragopal) (1998) *Probings in the Political Economy of Agrarian Classes and Conflicts*, Hyderabad: Perspectives.

Bhaduri, A. (1983) *The Economic Structure of Backward Agriculture*, London: Academic Press.

Bharadwaj, K. (1986, 3rd edn 1994), *Classical Political Economy and Rise to Dominance of Supply and Demand Theories*, Delhi: Universities Press (distributed by Orient Longman).

Bhaskar, R. (1979) *The Possibility of Naturalism: A Philosophical Critique of the Contemporary Human Sciences*, Brighton: Harvester Press.

Bhaskar, R. (1993) *Dialectic and the Pulse of Freedom*, London: Verso.

Binswanger, H.P. and Rosenzweig, M.R. (eds) (1984) *Contractual Arrangements, Employment and Wages in Rural Labour Markets in Asia*, New Haven, Conn.: Yale University Press.

Boylan, T.A. and O'Gorman, P.F. (1995) *Beyond Rhetoric and Realism in Economics: Toward a Reformulation of Economic Methodology*, London: Routledge.

Braverman, A. and Stiglitz, J. (1982) 'Sharecropping and the interlinking of agrarian markets', *American Economic Review* 72, 4: 695–715.

Bryman, A. (1996, original 1988) *Quantity and Quality in Social Research*, London: Routledge.

Bryman, A. (1998) 'Quantitative and qualitative research strategies in knowing the social world', in T. May and M. Williams (eds) *Knowing the Social World*, Buckingham: Open University Press.

Bryman, A. (2001) *Social Research Methods*, Oxford: Oxford University Press.

Bryman, A., Lewis-Beck, M.S. and Liao, T.F. (eds) (2003) *Encyclopedia of Social Science Research Methods*, London: Sage.

Da Corta, L. and Venkateshwarlu, D. (1999) 'Unfree labour and the feminisation of agricultural labour in Andhra Pradesh, 1970–95', *Journal of Peasant Studies* 26, 2–3: 71–139.

Danemark, B., Ekström, M., Jakobsen, L. and Karlsson, J.C. (2002) *Explaining Society: Critical Realism in the Social Sciences*, London: Routledge.

Denzin, N.K. (1970) *The Research Act in Sociology: A Theoretical Introduction to Sociological Methods*, London: Butterworths.

Ellis, F. (1988) *Peasant Economics: Farm Households and Agrarian Development*, Cambridge: Cambridge University Press.

Fay, B. (1996) *Contemporary Philosophy of Social Science: A Multicultural Approach*, Oxford: Blackwell.

Flick, U. (1992) 'Triangulation revisited: strategy of validation or alternative?' *Journal for the Theory of Social Behaviour* 22: 169–97.

Gilbert, N. (ed.) (1993) *Researching Social Life*, Sage: London.

Harding, S. (1991) *Whose Science? Whose Knowledge? Thinking from Women's Lives*, Milton Keynes: Open University Press.

Harding, S. (1995) 'Can feminist thought make economics more objective?', *Feminist Economics* 1, 1: 7–32.

Harriss, J. (1982) *Capitalism and Peasant Farming: Agrarian Structure and Ideology in Northern Tamil Nadu*, Bombay: Oxford University Press.

Harriss-White, B. (1999) 'Introduction', in B. Harriss-White (ed.) *Agricultural Markets from Theory to Practice: Field Experience in Developing Countries*, London: Macmillan.

Hutchinson, F., Mellor, M. and Olsen, W.K. (2002) *The Politics of Money: Toward Economic Democracy and Sustainable Society*, London: Pluto Press.

Kabeer, N. (1994) *Reversed Realities*, Delhi: Kali for Women and London: Verso.

Kahlon, A.S. and George, M.V. (1985) *Agricultural Marketing and Price Policies*, Calcutta: Allied Publications.

Kahlon, A.S. and Tyagi, D.S. (1983) *Agricultural Price Policy in India*, Delhi: Allied Publications.

Kalpagam, U. (1994) *Labour and Gender: Survival in Urban India*, Delhi: Sage.

Lacey, H. (1999) *Is Science Value Free? Values and Scientific Understanding*, London and New York: Routledge.

Lacey, H. (2002) 'Explanatory critiques and emancipation', *Journal of Critical Realism* 1, 1: 1–31.

Lawson, T. (1997) *Economics and Reality*, London: Routledge.

Lawson, T. (2003) *Reorienting Economics*, London and New York: Routledge.

May, T. (2000) 'A future for critique? Positioning, belonging, and reflexivity', *European Journal of Social Theory* 3, 2: 157–73.

New, C. (1996) *Agency, Health and Social Survival: The Ecopolitics of Rival Psychologies*, London: Taylor & Francis.

Newbery, D.M. and Stiglitz, J. (1981) *The Theory of Commodity Price Stabilization: A Study in the Economics of Risk*, Oxford: Clarendon.

Nussbaum, M. (1999) 'Women and equality: the capabilities approach', *International Labour Review* 138, 3: 227–46.

Nussbaum, M. and Glover, J. (eds) (1995) *Women, Culture and Development: A Study of Human Capabilities*, Oxford: Clarendon Press.

Olsen, W.K. (1993) 'Competition and power in rural markets: a case study from Andhra Pradesh', *Bulletin of the Institute of Development Studies* 24, 3: 83–9.

Olsen, W.K. (1994a) 'Random sampling and repeat surveys in South India', ch. 4 in Devereux and J. Hoddinott (eds) *Fieldwork in Developing Countries*, Brighton: Harvester Wheatsheaf.

Olsen, W.K. (1994b) 'Researcher as enabler: an alternative model for research in public health', *Critical Public Health* 5, 3: 5–14.

Olsen W.K. (1994c) 'Distress sales and rural credit: evidence from an Indian village case study', in O. Morrissey and T. Lloyd (eds) *Poverty, Inequality and Rural Development*, London: Macmillan.

Olsen, W.K. (1996) *Rural Indian Social Relations*, Delhi: Oxford University Press.

Olsen, W.K. (1999), 'Village level exchange: lessons from South India', in B. Harriss-White (ed.) *Agricultural Markets from Theory to Practice: Field Experience in Developing Countries*, London: Macmillan.

Olsen, W. K. (2001) 'Stereotypical and traditional views about the gender division of labour in Indian labour markets', *Journal of Critical Realism* 4, 1: 4–12.

Olsen, W. K. (2003) 'Triangulation, time, and the social objects of econometrics', in P. Downward (ed.) *Applied Economics and the Critical Realist Critique*, London: Routledge.

Olsen, W.K. and Johnson H. (2001) 'Understanding livelihoods and lived experiences', in *Poverty and Inequality* (course book for U213, International Development), Milton Keynes: Open University.

Olsen, W.K. and Uma, R. (1998) 'Preparing for rural adjustment', Development Paper No. 2, Development and Project Planning Centre, University of Bradford.

Ramachandran, V.K. (1990) *Wage Labour and Unfreedom in Agriculture: An Indian Case Study*, Oxford: Clarendon Press.

Ribbens, J. and Edwards, R. (1998) *Feminist Dilemmas in Qualitative Research: Public Knowledge and Private Lives*, London: Sage.

Robson, C. (2001, 2nd edn) *Real World Research*, Oxford: Blackwell.

Roemer, M. (1986) 'Simple analytics of segmented markets: what case for liberalisation?', *World Development* 14, 9: 429–39.

Rosenzweig, M.R. (1988) 'Risk, implicit contracts and the family in rural areas of low-income countries', *Economic Journal* 98: 393.

Sayer, Andrew (1992, 2nd edn) *Method in Social Science: A Realist Approach*, London: Routledge.

Sayer, Andrew (2000) *Realism and Social Science*, London: Sage.

Thomas, Alan (2000) 'Meanings and views of development', in T. Allen and A. Thomas (eds) *Poverty and Development into the 21st Century*, London: Open University Press.

Walby, S. (2001) 'Against epistemological chasms: the science question in feminism revisited', *Signs* 26, 2: 485–509.

Health visitors and
   'disadvantaged' parent-clients
   Designing realist research

Angie Hart, Caroline New and
Marnie Freeman

Introduction

This chapter offers an example of realist research design. Its starting point is
the well-known, well-documented, seemingly intractable problem of health
inequalities and their reproduction. The researchers proposed to carry out a
stratified study of the interaction between health visitors and parent-clients,
to explore the possibility that this professional–client relationship has the
power to affect the health status of the families involved.[1] In other words, the
research begins with a model of the interaction within this relationship as
itself causally powerful, mediating other more generally recognised
mechanisms such as information transmitted and surveillance exercised. The
core of the research design was a longitudinal study over 18 months of a
sample of parents and health visitors.

The research design shows how the notion of a stratified social ontology
can be operationalised in social research. This particular example also shows
that social realism can both recognise and investigate the reality and power
of social constructions.

The researchers were unsuccessful in their application for Economic and Social
Research Council (ESRC) funding, so the proposal has not been carried out. Later
in the chapter we consider some of the referees' reasons for rejecting it.

Health visiting and health inequalities

In the past decade, academic researchers and policy makers have been
debating the causes of health inequalities rather than whether they exist
(Acheson 1998; Department of Health and Social Security 1980; Wilkinson
1997). Such debates draw on geographical, epidemiological, sociological and
psychological perspectives, but without bringing them together within a
single stratified social ontology. While relationships between lifestyles, social
class, age, race, gender, occupation and geographical location have been
discussed in the health inequalities literature (Bartley *et al.* 1998), there has
been little consideration of the complex interface between public sector
professionals and the clients with whom they work. This is the case even

within the substantial literature on psychosocial approaches to understanding health inequalities (Wilkinson 1996). However, whatever causal powers professional interventions have must be mediated through the relationship with clients. The research design discussed in this chapter takes as an orienting concept the likelihood that the professional–client relationship has emergent properties, including powers to affect in/equalities in health and in health care provision, whether by reproducing or changing them.

It used to be argued that health inequalities could partly be explained in terms of the 'inverse care law', which meant that some more 'advantaged' sections of society receive more and better health care than others (Titmuss 1968; Tudor-Hart 1971). On this model, which is indeed often the one implicitly used by health care professionals themselves, more health care provision will result in better health, and a better distribution of health care services represents a step towards equality. But in some cases, notably psychiatric services, the 'inverse care law' is inverted. Working class, poor and minority ethnic groups receive more than their share of services. But since clients of psychiatric services diagnosed as 'seriously mentally ill' are usually treated as chronic (hopeless) cases who must become permanent (ex)patients, this extra attention cannot be seen as alleviating health inequalities (Siegler and Osmond 1974).

Since the late twentieth century, health visiting has become increasingly targeted at families whose children are seen as having 'special needs', because they are ill or impaired or have learning problems, or because they are seen as 'disadvantaged' and vulnerable by virtue of their family context. 'Targeted' health visiting attempts to compensate for the lower uptake of preventive health care intervention by those socio-economically disadvantaged individuals who, statistically, have the poorer health (Benzeval et al. 1995). This additional involvement is interpreted as an increase in 'care', but the precise relationship between professional involvement and professional care is a complex one.

It is still unknown whether targeting, as done in the UK, improves health outcomes for the families who receive it (Roberts 1996; Elkan et al. 2000). A satisfactory evaluation study would have to use a complex and nuanced notion of health that included more than data about injuries, morbidity and mortality. It would need to be sensitive to the misery and struggles which, whether or not they are precursors of diagnosed illness, mean the absence of well-being. We would argue that the mental health of parents is crucial to their children's health and development. Doyal and Gough (1991) see *autonomy* as a 'basic' need (along with physical health), as one of the internal conditions for choice and action commonly conceptualised as 'mental health'. As used in their theory, autonomy implies the ability, confidence and resources to make and carry out reasoned strategic decisions. Since health visitors cannot bring up the children, parental competence requires a degree of autonomy in the parent or parents. But, Doyal and Gough argue, autonomy also requires external conditions which permit significant action.

These could be hard to attain under conditions of poverty, or indeed of surveillance. A second relevant concept, 'attachment', refers to the quality of the parent–child relationship, since secure attachment relationships are arguably necessary for the development of healthy children (Chase Stovall and Dozier 1998; Svanberg 1998).

Our proposed research did not aim at an overall evaluation of targeted health visitor interventions, although we would argue that an exploration of client/professional relationships would be a crucial element in such an evaluation. The current policy of pathologising the health needs of specific 'disadvantaged groups' by targeting them for interventions, while simultaneously confirming the health beliefs and behaviours of structurally advantaged social groups, may serve only to widen the gap between them and, by dint of association, between professional and client. Thus the professional accrues more authority and the client gains only more powerlessness (Hart and Freeman, in press).

One dubious feature of the current policy is the very process of targeting the 'disadvantaged'. The criteria used are presented as objective and unproblematic, but are shot through with prejudice and discrimination (Hart *et al.* 2001). The construction of 'social disadvantage' constitutes the rationale for the subsequent relationship, and thus is likely to affect the relationship itself. Secondly, the 'commonsense' assumption is made that health visitors have objective knowledge of what constitutes a healthy lifestyle (Turner 1998/9; Cowley 1999). But even if we assume that the educative intervention of health visitors is capable of leading to more 'healthy lifestyles' as the policy intends, it is less likely to do this effectively if delivered in a way which threatens the autonomy of a client group, or is perceived by them as so doing. Thirdly, surveillance that may protect (a small number of) children from gross abuse may nevertheless be deleterious to their developing attachments. In all these respects, the nature of the professional/client relationship may itself be a mechanism affecting health outcomes.

Professional intervention, then, may not be equivalent to professional care. Some commentators have forcefully argued that much intervention by health care practitioners is counter-productive, serving primarily to reinforce the elite role of the professional and the subordinated role of the client (House 2000; Illich 1977). However, such claims have rarely been the subject of careful empirical exploration. The complex way in which the dynamic between professionals and clients affects clients' lives, in material, physical, social or emotional terms, forms the basis of our proposal. A targeted health visiting service aims to alleviate health inequalities. Can it do this, given the power imbalance within the health professional/client relationship, which is not always currently addressed in health visitor preparation?

Targeted health visiting: contrasting scenarios discussed

The following vignettes, which describe real clients, give some idea of the issues involved. The first demonstrates the difficulties that can arise for a health visitor (here, one of the authors) trying to initiate a meaningful process of support.

The client was a young woman of 21 living on benefits, in a bed-sit, with a small child of 14 months. As a child, the woman was physically abused by her father, and her mother had left the family home. As a result she didn't have any contact with either parent, nor did she seem to have any friends. She presented as a very isolated person, defensive and monosyllabic. Although her child was always alert, active and generally happy, the woman interacted very rarely with her, and when she did it was rather brusquely. From my first visit when she moved into the area it was clear that the woman and her child fell within the criteria for a targeted service. This provides additional input to the regular health visiting service. It means that a care plan is developed with the family, and there is regular monitoring of the family's progress within the scope of that plan.

I visited the woman on several occasions, about every 3–4 weeks, but she was extremely difficult to engage with in order to discuss how she could best be supported. My visits were hard to prolong beyond about 20 minutes as conversation was largely one-sided and I could see she was agitating for me to leave. What I did understand from my exchanges with her was that she didn't like 'authority figures', and didn't want the support. She understood about the targeted service and wanted to know why she had been identified for additional input. I explained as best I could, but I was aware that despite all the talk about support the woman recognised that underpinning my visits was the requirement for me to monitor for child abuse. She commented that she felt I was watching for any sign of her hurting her child so that I could act.

Although I was in the position of being able to offer this woman a number of services which might have helped her to make friendships in the locality, and develop her skills in parenting, it was very difficult to have the discussion which could have led to this outcome. I was aware that taking what was offered might have compounded feelings of lack of self worth, in that she could construe that she was obviously a bad parent because she was being offered parenting skills sessions. My problem as a health care professional was firstly how to establish a meaningful dialogue with the client, and then how I could offer these sessions without making the client feel patronised or under duress.

In a world where health visitors are in short supply and workloads very heavy, making a consistently concerted effort to gain this woman's trust could be hard to achieve. Indeed the dynamic of the professional–client interaction may become closed if resources, information and advice are offered but not accessed or agreed with. Inevitably health professionals are likely to become tokenistic in their visiting, knowing that they have only to hold the case until the child is 5 years old. Providing a supportive and enabling service may be untenable in these circumstances, and indeed all that may be achieved is a validation of stereotypical beliefs on both sides of the relationship. We could contrast this scenario with that of another needy family.

> The clients were a young, moderately affluent mother and father with a 3-year- old child. This family was also receiving a targeted service but both parents willingly accepted the health professional input. Their child had been diagnosed with autism, a diagnosis which had initially been hard for the parents to accept, but in time they had been prepared to embrace the range of services that could be offered. They readily sought information from me and wanted access to all the support that was available. My visits to this family were often demanding, mainly because of trying to help the mother manage her child's often difficult behaviour. However, neither parent was defensive about being on the receiving end of a more intense professional input. We had long conversations about the child's behaviour, we discussed strategies for managing the behaviour, and I investigated, with other professionals, how the child could progress into education.

This second scenario illustrates how different can be the responses from a family where it is recognised that no judgement is being made about the parents' skills in caring for their child – even though support is required in terms of strategies to deal with the child's difficult behaviour. Although this family's progress was being monitored just as closely as that of the mother in the first vignette, the notion of surveillance for child protection was not of primary concern for either the family or the health visitor. The focus of concern was the nature of the child's behaviour, not the parents. Had this family been bringing up their child in the late 1970s, their response to the visits might not have been so positive. At that time it was thought that autism was a product of poor parenting – 'refrigerator parents' was the term used. Now, however, it is accepted that there are physiological antecedents to the condition, possibly genetic in origin. This shift in beliefs takes the emphasis off surveillance as a major aspect of the health visiting input. These parents were likely to have felt, and actually to have been, more powerful in the relationship than the woman in the first scenario.

The scenarios show clearly how readily notions of blame can creep into the professional/client dynamic, creating defensive responses from the client and unhelpful reactions from professionals. Surveillance forms a major part of the health visiting role in situations where mothers and fathers are under stress and limited in their ability to respond to their child's needs appropriately. Where the focus for the surveillance is the adequacy of the parents' caring skills, rather than the development of the child, it is easy to understand how the professional/client relationship can be constrained, limiting the outcomes of any health intervention. Of course, in both scenarios, parental neglect or ill treatment may be the outcome for the child – however, it could be argued that access to supportive services as a result of the development of a positive relationship would be likely to reduce the possibility of the need for child protection. Furthermore, whilst accessing supportive services would not remove health inequalities (there is no cure for autism, for example), amelioration of disadvantage would be possible.

We fully recognise the reality of disadvantage. People are positioned in ways which disadvantage them, constraining their agency by limiting their options, in all or some social contexts; for example being in poverty, belonging to ethnic minorities, or having a learning difficulty. The actions of health care professionals are not always causally relevant to how a person comes to experience health inequalities. But whether or not a person is 'disadvantaged' in practice will often depend to some extent on outcomes brought about *through a set of relationships* between a client, health care institutions and health care professionals, rather than directly on the client's own personal identity and social position. In other words, the effects of structure are mediated by agency. For instance, there is evidence to suggest that the *interaction* which develops between professionals and their clients influences the way in which health care provision is accepted and acted upon by clients (Cunningham and Hengeller 1999; Bloor and Macintosh 1990).

The health inequalities research has neglected the power of relationships to affect health outcomes. It treats health outcomes, which are events, as if they resulted directly from another set of events, health interventions. This is a Humean, constant conjunction notion of causality, widely criticised by realist social theorists (Bhaskar 1989; Sayer 1992). In fact health interventions must be understood as actions by professional agents, the causal power of which can only be exercised and sometimes realised through interaction with clients. It is the interaction, not the health intervention per se, which is the mechanism affecting outcomes, and over a long period of time repeated interactions between the same parties constitute a relationship with emergent properties. (The relationship between the particular health visitor and clients itself affects the nature – and degree of 'success' – of particular interactions, because it affects how each party interprets the words and doings of the other.)

The health visitor–parent-client relationship is asymmetrical in terms of authority and access to resources. The professionals are influenced, though not determined, in their side of the interactions by current understandings (for example, of disadvantage) and policies (for example, of targeted health visiting). Their interventions might take the form of advice-giving, of offering access to resources, of instruction in some aspect of parenting, but all depend for their effect on the responses of the clients (the other, differently positioned, agents in the relationship). Clients are structurally positioned as potential recipients of services intended to bring about an officially recommended aim (maintenance or improvement of the child's health status, as defined by the health visitor) in approved ways (through the clients following certain courses of action). However, the clients may not see the end as desirable or even if they do, they may not find the approved process an acceptable means of reaching it.

Popay *et al.* (1998a: 60) comment that much of the epidemiological or empirical social research on inequalities in health has 'tended to regard health, implicitly if not explicitly, as a category of the phenomenal world that is ontologically detachable from both power and experience'. They suggest that there is much to be gained from adopting an historico-sociological perspective which understands inequalities in health as taking place *within human relationships* (Popay *et al.* 1998a: 60, our emphasis). Exploring the way in which individuals are constructed as (and hence come to be) 'dis/advantaged' in human relationships with health care professionals is a central concern of the research proposal.

Client–professional interaction

While health inequalities research tends to ignore the possible causal influence of client–professional interaction, elsewhere in sociology such work has an impressive legacy. The relationships between health professionals and their patients/clients have been studied in terms of elite knowledge and authority, and lay and professional constructions of illness identities (e.g. Illich 1977; Bowler 1993; Clark *et al.* 1991; Kendall 1993; Lupton 1994; Aranda and Street 1999). Numerous studies have highlighted the problematic nature of the relationship between parent-clients and health care professionals (e.g. Turner 1998/9; Cowley 1999; Edwards 1995; Edwards 1998; Oakley 1992; Popay *et al.* 1998b). If, as Foucault has it, surveillance is a technique of power, then no wonder there seems to be a fundamental dilemma *vis à vis* the professional/client relationship within health education provision (Bloor and Macintosh 1990).

Accepted understanding among health visitors and previous research (e.g. Blaxter 1990) both suggest that the very people health visitors seek to target are the ones who frequently opt not to be involved. Does the service fail to match client needs, or does the manner in which services are provided alienate clients? If you were being offered a service which clearly identified you as lacking in parenting skills, whilst making it obvious that those professionals who were offering the service had the answers, perhaps you would respond in the same way. Macintosh's (1986) study of Scottish health visitors and their clients showed how perceptions of surveillance appeared to be pivotal in terms of clients' disclosures to health visitors and acceptance of their advice and information.

Although disadvantage is real, identifying people as 'disadvantaged' in relation to targeting health care provision means that a complex range of people with very different needs are grouped together as if they had a common identity (c.f. Stubbs 1993 for discussion of the grouping of ethnic minorities). This encourages over-generalised assumptions about appropriate practice, and also inhibits flexibility and the development of adaptive practices in relation to specific clients. Beliefs about a single 'other' are likely to become subsumed by general beliefs about the group to which he/she is assigned (Tajfel 1981). This is particularly relevant for health visitors whose proactive role in care provision requires them to seek out 'disadvantaged' people and 'apply solutions' to the problems they have. Pathologising the health needs of specific 'disadvantaged groups' through targeting them for interventions simultaneously confirms the health beliefs and behaviours of structurally advantaged social groups. This may serve only to widen the gap between them and, by dint of association, between professional and client.

Health care professionals *themselves* play a part in constructing the category of 'disadvantaged' and deciding who matches the identified criteria. Professionals are not instruments which can objectively apply equal treatment, but products of the values and norms inculcated in becoming a health care professional, operating in organisational structures which support or inhibit particular forms of professional action. Both health care professionals and parent-clients are gendered individuals with complex cultural and personal identities. All this, and their internal reflections on past and present experience, affect how health visitors act towards their 'disadvantaged' parent-clients and how these clients respond (Popay *et al.* 1998b).

Psycho-dynamic factors may also be salient to the way in which professional/'disadvantaged' client relationships develop. Some commentators draw on critical social psychology and psychoanalysis to explore relationships to subordinate others (e.g. Menzies-Lyth 1960). Considerable empirical research has been conducted in the United States of America in the field of therapeutic interventions with families who have been traditionally pathologised by services (Cunningham and Hengeller 1999). This research suggests that using a multi-systemic approach and actively avoiding the pathologisation of clients leads to more positive outcomes for clients. Such practice requires professionals to be systematically self-reflexive, but consideration of anti-discriminatory and anti-oppressive practice is rare in health visiting literature. Although health visitors have for decades been working with some of the most 'disadvantaged' members of society (Ministry of Health 1956; Botes 1998), there has historically been a dearth of public commitment on their part to reflect on their own practice within anti-discriminatory frameworks.

This discussion of the reality of health visiting, and the necessarily abridged version of the empirical and theoretical background which fuelled the development of our ideas, make clear the issues which concerned us when writing the proposal. We now devote the remainder of the chapter to the underpinnings of our research approach, a summary of what we proposed, the difficulties that were encountered by the referees in dealing with our proposal, and what we learned from this process.

Approaching research design

It is probably clear by now that the usual ways of researching health inequalities are unlikely to illuminate the causal powers of the health visitor–client relationship. The qualities of relationships, the power differences, the intentions, mutual constructions and assumptions, and interaction between people over a period of time, are difficult to reduce to a set of variables. Health visitor interventions could be evaluated by describing large numbers of clients in terms of such variables as class, age, family type, income, marital status and housing; while categorising interventions in terms of whether the client was considered disadvantaged and therefore targeted, frequency of contact, resources mobilised, some indicator of client affect, level of client co-operation, and number and duration of interactions. These variables would then be cross-tabulated to find out whether and in what combinations they were associated with a range of outcomes such as child health status, morbidity, family functioning and so on. At the most, such single snapshots in time would give us clues about where to start looking for the causal processes involved, but they would certainly not be explanatory in themselves. If, for example, targeted health interventions were associated with better outcomes for single-parent households than for dual-parent households, we would have no idea as to why this was the case. Modelling the possible causal processes involved within a complex interpersonal system is needed in order to get to explanation.

Such modelling is itself shaped and informed by the researchers' existing understanding and professional experience. Reflected upon and summarised, this prior knowledge justifies certain conceptual *abstractions,* which are 'formed when we – albeit in thought – separate or isolate one particular aspect of a concrete object or phenomenon; and ... abstract from ... all the other aspects possessed by concrete phenomena' (Danermark *et al.* 2002: 42). This conceptual work oriented the research and influenced its design.

Layder (1998) identifies 'orienting concepts' as the initial means of organising data and subsequently developing theory. These may be drawn from extant theory (general or substantive) or simply from their wide use as ideas within certain bodies of knowledge. The concepts are provisional: 'the initial orienting concept may turn out to be a temporary means of imposing order on the data and may be supplanted or modified later on'; the data might later require re-coding around different categories (Layder 1998: 109). But long before the stage of data analysis or even data collection, the orienting concepts allow us to 'generate new perspectives on particular problems ... one can begin to group or cluster concepts around the specific empirical problem in question' (1998: 120).

Surveillance is one of the orienting concepts used in this research proposal. It gives rise to a series of exploratory questions: what form does surveillance take in health visiting? To what extent is it like or unlike the surveillance carried out by the police, by prison officers, by mental health nurses, by schoolteachers? Is it formally recognised as an aspect of professional practice? If so, how is it presented, described and justified? If not, what concepts are used in its place? What is the content of surveillance by health visitors? What criteria could there be for its operation? How would we recognise an intervention in which it was present or absent? Similar questions could be asked about 'professional discourse', and about the 'construction' of clients as 'disadvantaged' within such discourse. From the sociology of professions come concepts of professional identity, professional power, professional closure, and professional boundaries. Of equal importance are wider theories of processes of social exclusion and inclusion, and concepts of therapeutic alliance, attachment and trust which have their roots in psychodynamic theories.

Social realists differ in their theoretical and methodological approaches, but one of the points of agreement is that explanation in the social sciences involves linking structure and action. As Layder puts it, an effective theory (he calls it 'adaptive theory')

> always represents an attempt to depict the linkages between lifeworld and system elements of society. That is, it centralizes the interconnections between, on the one hand, actors' meanings, activities and intentions (lifeworld) and, on the other, culture, institutions, power, reproduced practices and social relations (system elements). In this respect adaptive theory focuses on the ties between agency and structure in social life and the connections between macro and micro levels of analysis. Thus adaptive theory represents a methodological approach which takes into account the layered and textured nature of social reality (its ontological 'depth').
>
> (Layder 1998: 27)

The proposed design did just this. Abstracting from their many concrete forms, Hart and Freeman assumed that structured relationships between health visitors and parent clients share certain properties. Policies and regulations arising from the macro level determine the distribution of power between the parties, the construction of 'disadvantage' which sets the relationship up, and the norms of professional practice. They proposed to investigate how, in concrete instances, particular health visitors and parents draw on their own beliefs and values and experiences to decide what this relationship is, what it means for them, and how to act within it. We would expect the meaning of the relationship for each party to affect how they respond to each other at any particular time, to influence whether the 'official' mechanisms (education, access to resources and information, and surveillance and protection) are exercised, and to mediate their effects. Following Archer, we can see the relationship as a structure with emergent properties of its own, some of which pre-exist the interaction of the agents involved. In fact, the emergent properties of the relationship condition how the people within it act in response to each other and – importantly with respect to the parent-clients – in relation to others, such as their child or children. Over time the interaction between the parties to the relationship may reproduce the structure or possibly elaborate it (Archer 1995).

The research proposal

Over eighteen months of fieldwork, we aim to explore and compare health visitors' involvement and 'interventions' with two specific groups of parents, identified as 'disadvantaged' or 'non-disadvantaged' by the health visitors at the start of the research. We intend to discover how professionals think about and act in relation to parents identified in these ways. We also want to discover how parents think about their health and lifestyle, and how they view professional involvement in relation to these issues. The perspectives of clients and professionals in relation to the same events and interventions will be systematically compared. The research will use methods of data collection that recognise the power relationships between professionals, researchers and 'disadvantaged' parents, including the use of one researcher to explore professional issues and a separate researcher to work with clients.

Which participants should we approach first? This decision will have significance for the subsequent research process. We propose to recruit parent-client participants via health visitors, thereby negotiating initial access via the institutional setting. Such a 'top down' approach will have the advantage of minimising gate-keeping issues, given the access to the institutional worlds of health visitors afforded by our professional identities and past health professional and research careers. Beginning with health visitors will allow us to explore their own constructions of disadvantage and subsequent identification of clients. Furthermore, since health visitors provide a 'universal service' they carry a diverse caseload, automatically visiting all families with small children, and this will enable us to make comparisons of health visiting practice between two groups of clients ('disadvantaged' and 'non-disadvantaged'). The use of a separate researcher for all data collection that includes clients will help to overcome 'loading' of information from health visitors related to specific clients. The 'client' researcher will be chosen for their skills in working with 'disadvantaged'/vulnerable people, using an ethnographic approach. In this way we will have, as part of our research team, both an 'honorary' health visitor and an 'honorary' client. This will allow us to explore within the research team the different ways in which we have the potential for 'going native'.

The following research questions have been developed from the orienting concepts that guided the research. In relation to the health visitors' side of the relationship, we ask:

1 What constructions of 'disadvantage' and 'need' are used by health visitors in their professional interventions with parent-clients with children under school age?
2 How are health visitors' definitions of, and actual, practices influenced by these constructions?
3 In what ways are the interventions of health visitors and relationships with clients not identified as 'disadvantaged' different?
4 Do health visitors feel that the practices they actually engage in are reflective of their preferred approach to practice?
5 If not, what influences hinder them from practising in the way they want?

In relation to the parent-clients' side of the relationship, we want to know:

6 What are parent-clients' constructions of their needs and of the professionals' role in meeting these needs?
7 How do these affect the ways in which parent-clients engage with health visitors in terms of interventions to meet their needs?

And overall:

8 Do these professional/parental interactions develop reflexively over time through changed perceptions and behaviours? If so, in what way?

Methods of data collection

We follow Layder's recommendation of a multipronged approach to data collection in order to identify how the processes of interaction shape and are shaped by the correspondence and contradiction between the beliefs, values and behaviours of professionals, and those of their clients (Layder 1998). Three focus groups will be conducted with health visitors from each of three community trusts in the south east of England. All health visitors from one of the trust areas with a high incidence of economic and social deprivation will be further interviewed in depth. Subsequently, in-depth, longitudinal studies will be conducted over eighteen months in order to follow patterns of health interventions with twenty-four parent-clients identified by a further six health visitors working in a similar context but different location. Each health visitor will identify one 'disadvantaged' client and one 'non-disadvantaged'. All participants will be visited regularly over a period of eighteen months. During that time non-participant observation, informal and formal semi-structured interviews, and analysis of relevant documentation will be used as methods of data collection.

1 Focus group interviews

Three focus groups of between six and ten health visitors will be conducted in order to identify the ways in which health visitors construct concepts of 'disadvantage' and 'non-disadvantage'; how these shape constructions of health visiting practice; and what actual practices are employed when working with clients identified as such.

2 Taped semi-structured interviews

Individual interviews will be conducted with twenty-four health visitors (from one trust involved in the focus groups) to explore in depth the issues raised in the focus groups. Subsequently, six further health visitors from a trust with a similar socio-economic make-up, but in a different location, will be invited to participate in the longitudinal aspect of the research. Six interviews will be conducted individually with each health visitor and three with the identified parent-clients over the eighteen-month period (by the appropriate researcher). In the initial interviews with health visitors they will be asked to explore: the past history and development of their professional involvement with the parent/s; actions that have been taken; the basis on which those actions were taken; and reflection on critical incidents which helped to shape the relationship and actions.

They will also be asked to reflect on perceptions of 'disadvantage' and 'non-disadvantage' (that is, why parents were so identified and in what way they are differentiated), and their practices with both groups. In this respect they will be asked to consider how they approach parents, negotiate access, develop a relationship with them, and decide on courses of action with parents, and with what outcome.

Interviews with parents will explore the history of the relationship with their health visitor. Parents will be asked to reflect on their understanding of health visitor practice in relation to the approach, relevance, anticipated outcomes and usefulness of interventions. They will also be asked to think about themselves in relation to the professional input, how they felt about their own situation, and their health needs in relation to health beliefs. Paired telephone and/or face to face interviews will also be conducted around specific health visitor visits (with the 'health visitor' and 'parent/client' researchers interviewing their respective health visitor or client). In this way, interpretations of specific aspects of the interaction can be examined to determine critical events and incidents that led to desired outcomes as perceived by both members of the dyad.

3 Observation

Interactions between health visitors and parent/clients will be observed by the 'parent/client' researcher, paying specific attention to: the identified purpose of the visit and professional expectations; the process and structure of each visit; the dynamic between the actors; the language used; the negotiation in relation to the aim of the visit; and the outcome of the visit. Discussions and behaviours relating to potential or actual health visitor interventions will be recorded in field-notes. Drawing on ethnographic methods, this researcher will also be responsible for spending time with identified parent-clients in both public and private spheres. Participant observation with parents will cover informal interactions between them and other parents in contexts such as family centres, schools and homes. Discussions relating to health care involvement will be particularly noted.

Observation of health visitors' team meetings will be conducted by the 'health visitor' researcher, who will also make contemporaneous field-notes. She will pay attention to how health visitors discuss their clients; the terms used; the interventions debated; the potential difficulties engaged in conducting these interventions; and how health visitors' individual perceptions are influenced by other team members.

4 Documentation analysis

This category includes client notes, care pathways, policy and procedure guidelines, and promotional literature. All relevant documents will first be analysed for evidence of the levels of awareness and understanding of the specific issues pertaining to each parent, and of both professional and organisational recognition of anti-discriminatory and anti-oppressive approaches to practice. Secondly, parent notes will be examined for evidence of incidents, and actions based on those incidents, that may have influenced the path of the professional/parents relationship.

5 Analysis of the data

Data analysis will use an adaptive approach, using orienting concepts from relevant theory to frame the data initially (Layder 1998; Pawson and Tilley 1997). Data from the various sources will be compared and contrasted across time, across professionals and clients, and across the two client groups. Emerging patterns will be explored further using progressive focusing in subsequent observation, interview, and analysis of document texts. Through comparison and contrast, similarities and differences in the following domains will be identified: within the professional group, across professional and client groups, and across and within the client groups.

The referees' reports

At the ESRC seminar we discussed not only the research design but also the reasons for its rejection. Of the three referees who considered the proposal, two were positive. The third, whose view prevailed with the funding body, could not understand why it was called 'realist'. The research questions which emerged from using the orienting concepts to begin theory generation seemed to this referee to be illicit hypotheses, which had no place in the proposal unless they either had been or were about to be tested. In fact, Hart and Freeman – like realist researchers generally – began with patterns of concrete outcomes, i.e. at the level of the empirical. They brought in 'orienting concepts' as a first stage in 'translating' the empirical, beginning the preliminary model building which frames observations and enables research. In contrast, the referee's view of knowledge acquisition seemed to be one in which researchers chart patterns among recorded events, extrapolate from these to a larger population, possibly infer 'laws', and test hypotheses derived from these.

One of the referee's comments was that, to establish the causal influence of the interaction between health visitors and clients, it would be necessary to discover what the pattern of health inequalities would be in the absence of such interactions. This is a simplistic idea of causality which ignores the operation of countervailing mechanisms. Certainly in any research attempting to identify particular mechanisms contributing to the production and reproduction of health inequalities, it would be important to assess how far these inequalities are generated independent of the mechanisms under consideration. But the anonymous referee's comments seem to assume that causation can only be established on the basis of the 'method of difference', i.e. to establish a cause you have to demonstrate a difference between situations where the cause was present and where it was absent. However, doing this using a standard statistical design comparing a test group and a control group does not on its own establish what is the cause of any observed differences, for a different cause from the one hypothesised – perhaps one associated with it but not observable (a 'third variable') – might be responsible for the different outcomes. Or the mechanisms under consideration may work to increase the effects of other mechanisms, or otherwise to modify them. The various mechanisms which contribute to bring about particular states of affairs cannot be assumed to be additive. Social realists would argue that the contrast case is not only insufficient, but also unnecessary – though where it can be achieved, it may be reassuring. Sometimes there are no contrast cases. In the study of gender and organisations, for example, the lack of ungendered organisations for comparison does not prevent our being reasonably satisfied that gender has a significant influence on organisations. Whether or not such contrasting is possible, intensive research (such as proposed here) is still needed to find out what mechanisms are present and how and whether they generated the effect of interest (Sayer 2001).

Before such intensive research can be carried out, prior conceptual work is necessary to retroduce possible causal mechanisms from the patterns of outcomes. These do not speak for themselves (which is one of the points where realists part company with grounded theory) – active thought experimentation is needed before research even begins.

> The mode of inference in which events are explained by postulating (and identifying) mechanisms which are capable of producing them is called 'retroduction'. In many cases the mechanism so retroduced will already be familiar from other situations.
>
> (Sayer 1992:107)

The postulation of causal powers involves not induction but retroduction. If subsequent investigation of the nature and constitution of objects shows the retroduction to be successful ... we can claim to know the cause of some process.

(Danermark *et al*. 2002: 158)

It was because of their familiarity with the causal powers of institutionalised relationships in other settings that Hart and Freeman were able to retroduce such a mechanism partially to account for the reproduction of health inequalities. The research proposed not to test hypotheses, but to investigate 'the nature and constitution' of an 'object' (the professional/client relationships between health visitors and parents of young children) in order to discover how such relationships affected parents' actions, and thus the health status of their children.

Concluding comments

Health inequalities result from mechanisms at various levels, interacting in various ways – sometimes to increase, sometimes to inhibit or mask, the exercise and the effects of other mechanisms. Most of the relevant mechanisms were not within the scope of the research proposal. In Chapter 4 of this book Higgs, Jones and Scambler put forward the GBH – 'greedy bastards hypothesis' – as a central mechanism bringing about health inequalities. That mechanism involves people who own capital making adaptive decisions aiming to maintain and increase their own power and resources. Within capitalist social relations, such decisions inevitably reproduce social inequalities, including health inequalities. The present researchers did not propose to investigate mechanisms at this level. At another level, struggles over social policy are constantly taking place in which agents pressing for redistributive measures come up against the cultural, political and economic mechanisms holding capitalist social relations in place. The resultant policies are likely to be compromises between countervailing forces, but nonetheless have emergent properties of their own. One such is the policy of targeted health visiting.

At the level of culture (and discourse), professional constructions of different groups as advantaged or disadvantaged, deserving or undeserving, are also objects with generative powers (Archer 1995). They are drawn on to legitimise the practices involved in targeted health visiting, and are constitutive of the professional–client relationship. The research proposed to investigate both how the health visitors, as parties to that process, understood these ideas, and whether and how these ideas were changed during eighteen months of interaction with the parent-clients. This was a hermeneutic endeavour, so participant observation and interviews were appropriate methods. But the aim was not just to elicit and report on the health visitors' own accounts of the interaction, but also to compare them with those of the parent-clients. The design recognised that socio-cultural interaction may involve resistance by those whose interests are not served by dominant ideas (Archer 1995). A second researcher (with experience of having been a client of health visitors) was also to carry out participant-observation and interviews with parent-clients. For both parties to the relationship, the aim was to trace how the constructions of the other affected their interaction.

Social policy 'works' when the actors with the power to make the desired difference can be motivated to act in certain ways. The professionals' health intervention is designed to influence these other actors, the parent-clients. The relationship between them, set up and partially regulated by the targeting policy, brings together actors with different sources of power, different motives and intentions. The official aim of ameliorating inequalities in health outcomes depends on the two parties reconciling these differences, so that the parent-clients act in ways which (1) actually do improve their families' health outcomes and (2) are acceptable within the relationship. The researchers' informed guess was that the structural properties of the relationship made such outcomes unlikely. Their proposal to analyse the process of interaction, involving mutual interpretations, bargaining, actions and responses, over eighteen months is eminently realist, addressing as it does the interplay of structure and agency over time (Archer 1995).

Note

1   Of the three authors, Hart and Freeman are academic researchers but also professional practitioners working in the NHS. Hart is an adoptive parent as well as a researcher, and as such has also been a client of health visitors and other professionals. Freeman is a psychologist and an experienced health visitor. New was a discussant at the seminar where Hart and Freeman presented their design, and they invited her to collaborate in this chapter.

References

Acheson, D. (1998) *Independent Inquiry into Inequalities in Health Report*, London: Department of Health.

Aranda, S.K. and Street, A.F. (1999) 'Being authentic and being a chameleon: nurse/patient interaction revisited', *Nursing Enquiry* 6, 2: 75–82.

Archer, M. (1995) *Realist Social Theory: The Morphogenetic Approach*, London: Routledge.

Bartley, M., Blane, D. and Davey Smith, G. (eds) (1998) *The Sociology of Health Inequalities*, Oxford: Blackwell.

Benzeval, M., Judge, H. and Whitehead, M. (eds) (1995) *Tackling Inequalities in Health: An Agenda for Action*, London: King's Fund.

Bhaskar, R. (1989) *The Possibility of Naturalism*, Hemel Hempstead: Harvester.

Blaxter, M. (1990) *Health and Lifestyles*, London: Routledge.

Bloor, M. and Macintosh, J. (1990) 'Surveillance and concealment: a comparison of techniques of client resistance in therapeutic communities and health visiting', in S. Cunningham-Burley and N. McKeganey (eds) *Readings in Medical Sociology* London: Routledge.

Botes, S. (1998) 'The CPHVA view of health visiting and the new NHS', *Community Practitioner* 71, 6: 220–22.

Bowler, I. (1993) ' "They're not the same as us": midwives' stereotypes of South Asian descent patients', *Sociology of Health and Illness* 15, 157–78.

Chase Stovall, K. and Dozier, M. (1998) 'Infants in foster care: an attachment theory persepective', *Adoption Quarterly* 2, 1: 55–88.

Clark, J., Potter, D. and McKinlay, J. (1991) 'Bringing social structure back into clinical decision making', *Social Science and Medicine* 32, 853–66.

Cowley, C. (1999) 'From population to people: public health in practice', *Community Practitioner* 72, 4: 88–90.

Cunningham, P. and Hengeller, S. (1999) 'Engaging multiproblem families in treatment: lessons learned through the development of multisystemic therapy', *Family Process* 38, 3: 265–86.

Department of Health and Social Security (1980) *Inequalities in Health: Report of a Working Group*, London: HMSO.

Danermark, B., Ekström, M., Jakobsen, L. and Karlsson, J.C. (2002) *Explaining Society: Critical Realism in the Social Sciences*, London: Routledge.

Doyal, K. and Gough, I. (1991) *A Theory of Human Need*, Basingstoke: Macmillan.

Edwards, J. (1995) ' "Parenting skills": views of community health and social service providers about the needs of their clients', *Journal of Social Policy* 24, 2: 237–59.

Edwards, J. (1998) 'Screening out men: or "Has mum changed her washing powder recently?" ' in J. Popay, J. Hearn and J. Edwards (eds) *Men, Gender Divisions and Welfare*, London: Routledge.

Elkan, R., Blair, M. and Robinson, J. (2000) 'The effectiveness of domiciliary health visiting: a systematic review of international studies and a selective review of the British literature', *Health Technology Assessment* 4, 13.

Hart, A. and Freeman, M. (2004) 'Sometimes we make people worse not better: the effect of the professional ego on inequalities in health care provision', *Journal of Advanced Nursing*.

Hart, A., Lockey, R., Henwood, F., Pankhurst, F., Hall, V. and Sommerville, F. (2001) *Addressing Inequalities in Health: New Directions in Midwifery Education and Practice*, London: English National Board for Nursing, Midwifery and Health Visiting.

House, R. (2000) *Limits to Professionalised Therapy: Critical Deconstructions*, London: Free Association Books.

Illich, I. (1977) *Limits to Medicine: Medical Nemesis – The Expropriation of Health*, London: Penguin.

Kendall, S. (1993) 'Do health visitors promote client participation? An analysis of the health visitor/client interaction', *Journal of Clinical Nursing* 2, 103–9.

Layder, D. (1998) *Sociological Practice: Linking Theory and Social Research*, London: Sage.

Lupton, D. (1994) *Medicine as Culture*, London: Sage.

Macintosh, J. (1986) *A Consumer Perspective on the Health Visiting Service*, University of Glasgow: Social Paediatric and Obstetric Research Unit.

Menzies-Lyth, I. (1960) *The Functioning of Social Systems as a Defence against Anxiety: Report to the Centre for Applied Social Research*, London: Tavistock Institute of Human Relations.

Ministry of Health (1956) *An Inquiry into Health Visiting (Jamieson Report)*, London: HMSO.

Oakley, A. (1992) *Social Support and Motherhood*, Oxford: Blackwell.

Pawson, R. and Tilley, N. (1997) *Realistic Evaluation*, London: Sage.

Popay, J., Hearn, J. and Edwards, J. (1998b) *Men, Gender Divisions and Welfare*, London: Routledge.

Popay, J., Williams, G., Thomas, C. and Gatrell, A. (1998a) 'Theorising inequalities in health: the place of lay knowledge', in M. Bartley, D. Blane and G. Davey Smith (eds) *The Sociology of Health Inequalities*, Oxford: Blackwell.

Roberts, C. (1996) 'The proof of the pudding', *Health Services Journal* 106, 27.

Sayer, A. (1992) *Method in Social Science: A Realist Approach*, London: Routledge.

Sayer, A. (2001) Personal communication.

Siegler, M. and Osmond, H. (1974) *Models of Madness, Models of Medicine*, New York: Macmillan.

Stubbs, P. (1993) 'Ethnically sensitive or anti-racist? Models of health research and service delivery' in W.I.U. Ahmed (ed.) *'Race' and Health in Contemporary Britain*, Buckingham: Open University Press.

Svanberg, P. (1998) 'Attachment, resilience and prevention', *Journal of Mental Health* 7, 6: 543–78.

Tajfel, H. (1981) *Human Groups and Social Categories*, Cambridge: Cambridge University Press.

Titmuss, R. (1968) *Commitment to Welfare*, London: Allen Unwin.

Tudor-Hart, J. (1971) 'The inverse care law', *Lancet* 1, 405–12.

Turner, T. (1998/9) 'The family way', *Community Practitioner* 71, 12: 38–40.

Wilkinson, R. (1996) *Unhealthy Societies: The Afflictions of Inequality*, London: Routledge.

Wilkinson, R. (1997) 'Health inequalities relative to absolute material standards', *British Medical Journal* 13, 591–95.

8   Reflexivity and social science

A contradiction in terms?

Tim May

Introduction

The aim of this chapter is to explore ideas of reflexivity in terms of their relevance for the practice, aims and contexts of social scientific knowledge production. It is argued that there is a disjuncture between aspirations, contexts and consequences, such that the practices that are the targets of reflexive questioning remain intact. These interests are not simply reduced to those that lie 'outside' academia. Instead they are, by default, the result of 'internal' critiques that by-pass an understanding of the conditions and positions that enable such interventions in the first place, thereby exposing the limits to reflexive questioning. For this purpose, the chapter starts with an outline of approaches to reflexivity and then moves on to consider the issues, dynamics and conditions that inform the production of social scientific knowledge. It then concludes with an examination of epistemic gain and attainability within what is a pragmatic, realist defence of the role and purpose of social science in society.

Calling reflexivity

The reflexive movement may be defined as a stance from which ideas on ideas can be achieved through a distance from social practices. We can trace this in various forms. In one we find the exercise of reason as the guarantor against false beliefs constituted via experience. Free from the constraints of the external world, an overview from the privileged vantage point of the knower (subject) can take place in an expression of triumph over the distorting effects of the known (object). We also find acts of reflection providing the possibility of a heightened state of self-consciousness in the service of self-transformation (Fichte 1994). It has also been argued that a concern with the realm of ideas, separate from the operation of empirical interests, can enable the production of knowledge in the service of reflection (Hegel 1991). Finally, the act of reflexivity within language has provided the means through which mind, self and society are linked (Mead 1964).

To the above may be added the socially transformative dimensions of reflexivity. Derrida's focus on textual construction is employed in the service of exposing the paradoxes of Western metaphysics by deconstructing the self-evident (Lawson 1986). In the tradition of Critical Theory, critique holds open the possibility of transforming existing relations via an appeal to ideals implicit in practices that underpin social arrangements (Horkheimer 1972). This holds open the possibility, if not of transformation, then at least of the recognition of difference as a source of knowledge, rather than as an impediment to its achievement (see Calhoun 1995; Smith 1999).

In everyday life we also find such periods brought about by sudden interruptions in routine: for example, questions over mortality when faced with the reasons and consequences for major operations accompanied by periods of hospitalisation, as well as the loss of those close to us. A questioning of priorities can then occur along with a re-evaluation of those things held sacred. A pre-reflexive commitment constituted in practice thereby becomes open to scrutiny. In this process we find habitual actions being interrupted and this may become a cause for concern as existential ease becomes ambivalence and that may turn to uncertainty about our place in the world. This exists alongside the view that our habitual actions are nothing more than temporary capitulations to forces that can be shattered through acts of defiance and resistance. Actions are thus the product of continual modes of self-determination separate from the contexts in which we find ourselves. Reflexivity in everyday life therefore oscillates in the space between the logics of routinisation and transgression (Unger 1987: 205).

Given these different meanings and potentials, my principal concern in this section will be to explore ideas of reflexivity and their implications for social scientific research. The next section then moves on to consider how this relates to the issues that inform knowledge production. This is part of a more general project that seeks to add clarity to the interactions between social scientific knowledge and social life and the implications of such knowledge for social action (see May 1998a; 1998b; 1999; 2000a; 2000b; 2001).

Reflexive calls and their implications for social science

Reflexivity has been widely discussed in the history of the social sciences. In these discussions we see different senses of the term being deployed. In one sense we find a celebration of the reflexivity that is born and deployed within everyday life by lay actors who are regarded as skilled and accomplished in their performances. As a result, any account of social reality is taken as constitutive of that reality and so sense and reference are brought together within an over-arching methodology. As Howard Garfinkel puts it in relation to ethnomethodology:

> The central recommendation is that the activities whereby members produce and manage settings of organized everyday affairs are identical

with members' procedures for making those settings 'account-able'. The 'reflexive' or 'incarnate' character of accounting practices and accounts makes up the crux of that recommendation'.

(Garfinkel 1967: 1)

Reflexivity thereby contributes to social order via situated activities that are open to ethnomethodological description.

We also find a self-referential component in discussions on reflexivity. The production of knowledge about social life is, at the same time, part of that life and so constitutive of it. However, once we admit of this situation it is of little interest. Why, after all, having made the observation is it necessary to dwell upon it and for what purpose? Yet in terms of its implications for the study of social life this can leave the complacencies of scholastic reasoning intact, as if they were hermetically sealed off from the world of which they are a part. The interactions and implications of social scientific knowledge for social life no longer become a topic of interest. If, on the other hand, we examine this relationship, the result can be ever descending circles in which reflexivity induces paralysis within a vortex of relativism (see Ashmore 1989; Woolgar 1988).

There are also textual approaches to reflexivity that turn their attention to the authority of the knower to pronounce upon the known. As James Clifford writes of ethnography: 'The writer's "voice" pervades and situates the analysis, and objective distancing rhetoric is renounced' (1986: 12). To overcome this situation what is then required is a striving for 'a multiplicity of approaches' (Fontana 1994: 220), in which researchers need to constantly consider how language constitutes reality in the particularity of world views. In the meantime continual acts of textual dissemination may undermine all attempts to know the social world: 'The infinite substitutability of terms and of texts makes conclusions undecidable. Because infinite substitution cannot be a self-confirming process, the expanse that it opens up also seems to be bottomless' (Platt 1989: 649).

Jacques Derrida's aim to expose subject-centred reason as the 'disingenuous dream' (Boyne 1990) of Western thinking has added to the roller coaster of reflexive writings. A whole new publishing industry for textual reflections on the futility of past attempts to grasp something called 'social reality' has now appeared. Whilst allusions to 'voices' in the research process are said to open up the research text to 'multiple readings', the effect can be to render representation so incoherent that any form of illumination becomes difficult, if not impossible, with these accounts appearing as 'strangely self-contained, sealing themselves off from comment and criticism' (Law 1994: 190). The initial act of repudiating the authority of the author ends up reproducing the very targets of Derrida's critique: textual closure and the centrality of the researcher in the production of the research account.

Rather than assuming a one-way relation between reflexivity in social life and its analysis within social scientific texts, reflexive scrutiny can operate at two levels. First, the practices of the social sciences are forms of life that have to be learnt by their practitioners. This requires not only an understanding of the inculcation of forms of knowledge, but also the reasons and expectations that people bring to their studies and their positions within its hierarchies. Second, the relationship between lay and technical languages produces an interaction with consequences for everyday practice and social scientific knowledge production. A resulting 'double hermeneutic' then refers to the ways in which lay and professional concepts become implicated within a continual slippage between frames of meaning (Giddens 1984: 374).

In the process of reflecting upon the relationship between social science and social life, the generalised reflections on social life which are characteristic of the former are seen as separate from 'lay' reflexivity (Giddens 1990: 40–41). This can result in an overly drawn demarcation between expert and lay knowledge, with the hermeneutic dimension to scientific practice itself also being neglected. Amongst other issues, how the role of 'expert' is constructed in an encounter with the object of its attention remains unexamined (Wynne 1996). The social epistemology of knowledge reception is, as I shall argue, an important topic that relates directly to knowledge production.

These discussions centre upon three dimensions of knowledge production and reception: need, degree and consequence. When centring upon need, the question becomes:

> Who needs reflexivity and for what end? Is it to produce better science, to subvert science, or to alter the basis of its practice in some significant manner? In terms of degree, the question that informs any practice that seeks to be reflexive is 'How far do you go?'
>
> (Outhwaite 1999)

To understand the dynamics that inform questions of degree, we need to turn to the insider-outsider view. As Malcolm Ashmore puts it:

> In order not to be scientific, one must be outside science; but to study science or anything else from the outside is to be scientific. Therefore, in order to study science unscientifically one must abandon objectivity and study it from the inside. But to be inside science means to be scientific.
>
> (Ashmore 1989: 109)

The point is that one cannot consistently be either inside or outside. Indeed, much writing has been devoted to the impossibility of the move itself.

What this approach avoids is that reflexivity is not just a problem for social inquiry, but an inevitable part of the process itself. Authors can drive reflexivity into ever descending circles in their quest for satisfaction with paradoxical and self-defeating results. Whilst simple demarcations between literature, art, science, technology and social science might not be defensible, neither is the idea that they are all the same. Extremes such as these produce an inability to examine similarities and differences: for example, debates around the so-called Sokal affair, whilst having the potential to illuminate, have tended to generate more heat than light (Cooper 1999).

It is at this point that the third dynamic of reflexivity – consequence – requires consideration. Here we should ask not only about the social epistemology of different forms of knowledge reception and their relationships to practice, but also how these relate to the context of production. This is important for understanding the differences between forms of knowledge, and also for understanding the role, place and consequences of those forms of knowledge in society. After all 'in learning better how societies organize their sciences, we will gain resources better to understand how sciences organize societies' (Harding 1996: 506).

Approaches to reflexivity need to move beyond endogenous dimensions. Endogenous reflexivity refers to the ways in which the actions of members of a given community contribute to the constitution of social reality itself. Referential reflexivity, on the other hand, is not simply concerned with the manner in which the social sciences constitute their objects, but with the consequences of this for the study of the social world. It calls attention to a 'critical hermeneutic' (Thompson 1981) dimension in which the relations between power, language, knowledge, interpretation and practice are open to examination for the purposes of engagement.

To consider endogenous reflexivity alone does not allow an examination of the implications of what becomes, by default, a separation between social scientific knowledge and the context of its production and the consequences (if any) of what is produced. The effect, once again, is to separate social scientific research from social life. This is manifested, for instance, in ethnomethodological perspectives in which reflexivity *within* actions is given prominence over reflexivity about actions. The question then arises: 'if, and in what way, the "reflexivity" of actions implies the "reflexivity" of actors, or what kind of "reflective capabilities" are implied in the ethnomethodological perspective' (Czyzewski 1994: 166). Without this in place, actors within the lifeworld are denied the potential not only to reflect upon their actions, but also to change the conditions under which these actions take place.

The implications of calls for reflexivity depend upon the background of pre-reflexive assumptions. Ideas are developed from the continual scrutiny of these assumptions. At the same time, however, we need to recognise that a 'fixity' of assumptions is required on the part of the social researcher – without which one would collapse into infinite regress – in order to examine the social world in the first instance. The question is not whether this occurs, but with what implications for the practice of social science and our understanding of the social world?

With the above discussion in mind, I want to turn attention to some of the issues that inform social scientific knowledge production. Reflexivity will miss its mark without an understanding of the dynamics of context (which implies a context sensitivity that does not collapse into relativism or abstract objectivism).

The context of production: positioning, individualism and organisation

The context of social scientific knowledge production is core to the means of providing a distance from necessity upon which to analyse the constitution of social life. Here we have the occupation of a position that is apparently denied to those immersed in the business of everyday life. Therefore, a point of view on points of view, combined with a long-term exposure to a body of knowledge, turn the subject of research into an object of analysis. A combination of gaze and position, away from the pressures of everyday life, is said to allow for a movement away from reflexivity 'in' action to reflexivity 'upon' action.

Boundaries and relevance

Is there any controversy contained in the above claim? There cannot be. Any claim to scientific knowledge requires grounds upon which to validate its practices and this reaches a more mature state when the justification for such grounds becomes an object of its practitioner's considerations. Social scientific knowledge is associated by its practitioners, as well as by others, with identified persons with particular sets of educational experiences. When it comes to those whose knowledge is derived from elsewhere, its applicability to practice may be readily dismissed as irrelevant and the operation of this boundary closure is part of the claim to expertise. Clear differences in orientation are then constructed between those who lie within the boundaries of disciplines and share a common set of experiences and those who remain on the outside. A disciplinary orientation emerges which, in an organisational context, creates positions that stabilise practices sufficiently in order to turn subject into object.

Without these acts of reflection in place, accompanied by a clear defence of their role and value in society, justification can become the province of those who lie outside of the discipline. Not only can this undermine its distinctiveness, but it may also affect any defence of value freedom upon which its legitimacy might rest in the public realm. If anyone can practice its inner workings, it can no longer claim a privileged position for itself. If its positions are multiple and its forms of understanding generally accessible, where do the authority for its findings and the basis for its practices stand? The discipline is weakened and the positions that enabled knowledge production in the first place become more tenuous (not tenured!).

In practice we find that justification easily collapses into application with the result that calls to reflexivity fall somewhere between luxury and indulgence. Knowledge is 'what works' and that is conditioned by those with the power to determine the criteria of relevance for its evaluation. They will expect findings to confirm their prejudices. Whilst they may not be explicitly articulated, these prejudices can be activated when encountering a disconfirming instance. Yet to anticipate such prejudices would undermine the integrity of a discipline and its standing in the public realm where it is judged and ultimately legitimated.

Within this realm political demands for 'relevant' research increase and decrease in intensity at various points in time. As with all similar demands, they work within unexamined assumptions whose power resides in their supposed self-evidence. 'What do you mean by relevant?' The question cannot be asked because it betrays the very symptoms that are the object of attack by presuppositions so deeply held that they appear beyond question. Only those who do not understand this unarticulated self-evidence could possibly pose it in the first instance. In their asking, they betray a distance from necessity that should not be the object of reflexive problematisation, but of intervention for the purposes of finding the solution. Claims to expertise that do not take account of these relations can easily be identified as weaknesses manifested in indulgent and irrelevant questioning, accompanied by an evident failure to grasp what is taken to be important, immediate and necessary.

Knowledge is easily deemed irrelevant when failing to inform particular ends. We can see this in a culture of the clamour for 'deliverables'. The very term connotes the self-evident outcomes of practices that provide an 'objective' means to judge their effectiveness (for example, the Research Assessment Exercise). Allusions to the deliverable are shorthand demands by technicians framed within narrowly conceived administrative imperatives. They work by relieving people of the need to question. Questions of purpose, value and overall effect and place of a set of practices become seen as symptomatic of speculative indulgence. The power of these demands for deliverables works on their supposed self-evidence, and contingency appears to become necessity. In situations where there is more than one choice, only one way forward is deemed possible and social science becomes the slave of this one-dimensionality.

Faced with these environmental demands in situations where obtaining funding for research is everything, the *modus operandi* is to 'give them what they want'. There are benefits to this course of action. Research outcomes are validated and more funding may be forthcoming. Here we find the same attitude that drives the culture of deliverables. What then makes the sites from which knowledge production takes place so different?

To return to the relationship between position and reflexivity, this will vary. Those on temporary contracts will tend to have less latitude when reliant upon the next grant (which is not to assume compliance). Others, by default, may invoke their position as the guarantor of distance from these implications. However, there are evident limits to these claims when it comes to the practice of reflexivity. The assumption of mobility between 'inside' and 'outside' positions – thereby allowing a movement from immersion to critical reflection – frequently assumes a self that reproduces an authority at the level of assumed homogeneity and one that is not open to all. What is argued to be a critical, reflexive attitude ends up as nothing more than a process of 'normalisation' of assumptions that certain selves are mobile whilst others are not (Adkins 2002). The very process of production of social research, in relation to others, remains unexamined (Skeggs 2002). There is often a silence in relation to these issues from the calls to reflexivity. In other words, they focus upon particular issues to the exclusion of those that may lead to discomfort, particularly when coming too close to home.

For those who regard critical distance as a luxury in the face of apparent necessity, we can reserve the term 'doxosophers'. These are the 'technicians of opinion who think themselves wise' and who 'pose the problems of politics in the very same terms in which they are posed by businessmen, politicians and political journalists (in other words the very people who can afford to commission surveys)' (Bourdieu 1998a: 7). Doxosophers view those who refuse to grant self-evidence to existing states of affairs as guilty of naivety or bias in their 'refusal to grant the profoundly political submission implied in the unconscious acceptance of *commonplaces* … notions of theses *with* which people argue, but *over* which they do not argue' (Bourdieu 1998a: 8).

The doxosopher's view combines with the views of those who do not submit positionality and its implications for the production of social scientific knowledge to critical examination. In one case contingency becomes necessity by default as there is no challenge to existing states of affairs. In the other there may appear to be challenge, but not to the relations between position, social scientific knowledge production and its consequences for understanding social action. In both reflexivity is confined to the asking of uncomfortable questions as if that meant returning to the centrality of the subject, as opposed to relating the subject to a position within the processes of production. If the limits to reflexive thinking, despite textual pronouncements to the contrary, inhere in the absence of understanding this relationship and its consequences for understanding social science, how is it to be explained?

Fields, distinction and production

To illuminate the reasons for this state of affairs, we find a striving for distinction (Bourdieu 1986) informing the activities of those who contribute to social scientific knowledge production. Fields of production are constituted by distributions of capital that inform the struggles that take place within them and are exemplified by particular expressions of inclusion and exclusion: for example, references to 'junior' and 'senior' members of staff (a field being constituted by positions and relations among participants and characterised by the distributions of capital mobilised in the struggles that take [or have taken] place within them) (see Bourdieu 1993: 9). These terms exemplify the struggles for distinction that are part of the professional ethos in which a tacit knowledge of the mode of operation of the field, including its stakes and interests, is implied in its practices. Concern then focuses upon the conservation or subversion of the structure of the capital within the field, as opposed to the potential for its reconstitution and the consequences of that for knowledge production. People have a stake and a place within such relations and cannot but contribute to its reproduction at some level. However, to what degree and with what consequence?

Those who benefit from current arrangements will seek to defend orthodoxy when it speaks in their name. History, including their own biographical trajectories and positions in the field, may be displaced in a process in which forgetting becomes more important than memory. Yet if the resultant strategies and tactics fail to take account of the reconstitution of fields according to new forms of control and knowledge production, misrecognition will result from this presentist empiricism. Consequentially, this will serve to reproduce those distinctions that are indifferent to an explanation of the institutional conditions that enabled them in the first place. Any overall disjuncture, rather than being an object of reflection then taken forward in action, can be neutralised by the hierarchies and logics constituted by limited understandings of the changing conditions of knowledge production.

To return to an earlier point, those who castigate others for questioning the self-evident meet with those for whom the limits of critical questioning arise when it comes to an examination of the positions from which their pronouncements are made. As Pierre Bourdieu puts it:

> efforts to find, in the specifically linguistic logic of different forms of argumentation, rhetoric and style, the source of their symbolic efficacy are destined to fail as long as they do not establish the relationship between the properties of discourses, the properties of the person who pronounces them and the properties of the institution which authorizes him to pronounce them.
>
> (Bourdieu, 1992: 111)

A relational dimension thereby evaporates. The call for relevant knowledge appears without a concern for the context and consequences of what is produced. Social scientific hierarchies forged in networks of connections and accumulations then claim an epistemic superiority assumed to be beyond question. It then becomes self-referential and self-justifying, but not self-maintaining! Calls to reflexivity end up with boundary closure through closed systems, whilst starting out from an entirely different point.

Consequently, social science becomes vulnerable to de-skilling. There is a failure to understand what is produced in relation to the context of production and to the changes in that context. Social scientific pronouncements are not related to the institutional position in which people find themselves, nor are they submitted to critical investigation. This results in an inability to investigate the relations between the present and the past in terms of the constitution of the field of analysis. Historical critique, as the core element in reflexiveness, is then lost and with that the potential to 'free thought from the constraints exerted on it'. Instead, by default, we see a surrender 'to the routines of the automaton' and a treating of 'reified historical constructs as thing' (Bourdieu 2000: 182).

The revenge of individualism: exchange, accumulation and status

Reactions to this state of affairs are frequently expressed through tactics of individualisation. Here we witness general issues being reduced to the assumed peculiarities of persons, often accompanied by the assumption that anything else would be too political, idealistic or even unprofessional. Forms of lifeworld boundaries that are part of social life and provide for the conditions of production of knowledge about that life are not subject to comparative investigation in order to analyse their implications for understanding. Everyday life oscillates between being caught in the headlights of routine and our actions as individuals who seek to shape it and be afforded recognition (and redistribution) as a result. The sites from which social scientific work about the everyday world is produced are no different. The assumption is frequently made they afford difference in some way, but exactly how? Calls to reflexivity so often avoid this question.

Within the field of production, an apparent ability to rise above the particularity of established ways of seeing is a reason to be accorded higher status, reproducing the idea that individual characteristics are solely responsible for innovation (which is not to say they are not a component). The vantage point from which innovations are made is via a plethora of texts that seek to re-orientate by shattering habitual modes through which social reality is constituted. A willingness to consider and engage with ideas separates out those capable of epistemic insight from those left in the wake of new ways of seeing. Those pre-reflexive assumptions that were required to practise research in the first place (action could not include continual reflections as that would lead to a paralysis of actions) find themselves subjected to detailed scrutiny and then deconstructed in order to expose the fallacious reasoning informing the assumptions that enabled engagement in the first place.

Pierre Bourdieu noted how little respect he had for doxosophers: '"intellectuals" of the political-administrative establishment, polymorphous polygraphs who polish their annual essays between meetings of boards of directors, three publishers' parties and miscellaneous television appearances' (1998a: 9). He was equally critical of those who sought to demolish the work of critical intellectuals. Critique, after all, may be practised in a number of ways with different effects. It may be done in the service of clarification for the purposes of reconstruction, with the assumption that what exists requires reorientation and/or refinement. There are also those acts of deconstruction performed in the name of reconstruction whose overall results may be beneficial, but also contribute to destruction.

Critiques may derive from those 'outside' disciplinary practices, but also from 'insiders'. Yet in a culture where displays of knowledge set producers apart from each other, resultant texts add to the process of accumulation, which, in turn, relates to degrees of recognition afforded by those positioned as the judges of worthiness. In the process connections and capacities blur with the result that it is not what someone knows which is at stake, but who they know. Further, as ideas are imported from other fields and disconnected from those which have emerged within fields with their own histories, novelty can be claimed, adding to the process of accumulation and recognition for the individual scholar.

In the process of academic exchange and accumulation, individual thinkers are elevated to a particular status or pilloried and a currency of trading in ideas on ideas emerges. Such a trading should, of course, be part of the vibrancy of any discipline in order to appraise the efficacy of its practices. But does this trading result in clarification and illumination in the service of engagement with the social world, or in obfuscation and retreat within a whirlwind of self-referential discourses? How sensitive is this to the institutional conditions of knowledge production? Once again, calls to reflexivity are relatively silent on such issues.

In terms of this consideration we can see how many modes of thought coming into one particular discipline may claim novelty through an absence of any encounter with its past. With the search for new ways of seeing and constituting social reality as part of the uncertainty of the role and place of knowledge production and reception in society, the history of a discipline may easily be forgotten, condemned as misinformed or even as dubious and dangerous. Whilst we hope to learn from the past, mistakes can be easily replicated in such instances. A subsequent generation may be able to enjoy a distance from the immediacy of the current and thus more able to see error, but to do so without a sensitivity to context (which implies neither relativism nor excuse) is more likely to lead to the repetition of error.

Some disciplines appear to be characterised more by this practice than others. I would suggest that there is a relationship between these trends and the presuppositions of relevance accorded to different disciplines by their publics. Once again, without an understanding of this context, calls to reflexivity often assume a discipline has the political power to be more generally transformative when in fact its ability to question its presuppositions in the first place is an indicator of its political weakness! In contrast, whilst *laissez-faire* economic theories have long been challenged, they still appear intact to be regurgitated to new generations of students. As Joan Robinson wrote over thirty years ago:

the central teaching of academic economics has altered very little. The core of theory is still the exposition of the operation of a perfectly competitive market which ensures the optimum allocation of given resources between alternative uses. The vulgarised economic doctrines that enter into the stream of public opinion still proclaim the beneficient operation of the unimpeded play of the profit motive.

(Robinson 1970: 114)

What has changed?

Calls to reflexivity are then so far removed from the realities and constraints that inform disciplinary practices that they not only have no effect on practice, but also may even contribute to the demise of the potential for transformation. So much of what passes as reflexive thought can easily become nothing more than an addition to the enterprise of shooting oneself and/or (depending on position, career trajectory and overall material security) one's discipline in the foot.

Discussion: against (and for) reflexivity

The isolated subject, separate from context, might have been eradicated in reflexive texts, but in the practices, policies and politics that inform knowledge production, it enjoys a healthy life. There is a powerful pull to constitute subjectivity either as an apparent distance from necessity, or with reference to the unthought categories of scholastic reason that provide clarity through an absence of uncertainty, the latter being what Bourdieu (1998b) called the 'oxymoron of epistemic doxa'. Reflexive calls fail when they do not take account of the institutional conditions of knowledge production and in so doing replicate a false separation between production and reception. An examination of the connection between context, knowledge production, process and consequences gives way to an assumed homogeneity of the subject or a fatalism that turns contingency into necessity. This necessity is allowed to play out on those within the field in different ways according to the positions that they occupy and the pressures under which they find themselves.

The constitution of the social world through social science requires a conjunction of particular ways of seeing along with an attention to the constitution of fields of scientific practice. In the social sciences it is central to any reflexive programme to take account of this relationship in order to refine our understandings of social scientific knowledge and social life. These are not separate endeavours, but part of the same drive for understanding.

In those struggles within the fields of social scientific knowledge production, what is at stake is the capacity to produce true knowledge. The instruments of knowledge, when turned back against those conditions of production, endeavour to:

intensify awareness of the limits that thought owes to its social conditions of production and to destroy the illusion of the absence of limits or of freedom from all determinations ... Any advance in knowledge of the scientific field, with its power relations, its effects of domination, its tyrannies and its clienteles, also advances the theoretical and practical means of mastering the effects of the external constraints.

(Bourdieu 2000: 121)

There is thus a gap in what passes for reflexive thinking. As we have seen, this relates to the absence of an understanding of the social conditions of social scientific knowledge production and its relation to knowledge reception and context and thus its capacity for action. It is often accompanied by a dismissive attitude in relation to the empirical (often conflating it with empiricism), and by a claim to speak of how the world 'is'. Justification then becomes no more than a retreat to an unfounded belief in the right to speak from a position that has long since ceased to be a matter for contemplation – and this we call post positivism! Or, justification amounts to the claim that the author is but one voice among many others in a relativistic universe –even though it was their voice that was published! And this we call postmodernism!

Postmodernists, realists, feminists, social constructionists have all suggested the need to re-evaluate the role of science in society. Yet whilst numerous texts claim we are way beyond any such need in whatever age we now find ourselves, instrumental positivism still marches on despite these textual pronouncements. Hence the culture of the deliverable and the demands for relevant knowledge scripted for narrowly conceived ends. What appears is a disjuncture between aspirational pronouncements and the *realpolitik* of knowledge production.

We then witness increasing turns to those from different disciplinary trajectories who offer ways out of these dilemmas. In filling this gap there is a bypassing of the importance of the contexts of production and reception. This is not a defence of disciplinary homogeneity for there is an evident need for interdisciplinary work in the face of the changes that are informing knowledge production, but it is the latter and its implications for practice that require analysis and action. What are the medium-term implications, for example, of the argument that we have moved from a situation in which disciplinary control of knowledge content led to a focus upon endogenous reflexivity, to a more heterogeneous form of knowledge production in which referential reflexivity comes to the fore? Instead of considering this, the situation is evaded. In two studies on the changing modes of knowledge production (Gibbons *et al.* 1994; Nowotny *et al.* 2001), for example, the authors argue that there has been a transition from what they call Mode 1 to Mode 2 knowledge production. Mode 1 knowledge production takes place within a bounded environment in which scientists exert control through peer review. Mode 2 knowledge production, on the other hand, acknowledges that other professionals are now involved in this process and so accommodates a demand for more accountability and reflexivity, as well as a set of bureaucratic intermediaries to whom it is necessary to respond. The environment is one of increasing complexity and uncertainty.

To this we must add another ingredient: the expectations that people bring with them into the practices of the social sciences. As Agnes Heller notes in her discussion on truth and true knowledge:

> Weber clearly warned his students *not* to seek insight into the meaning of life in their pursuit of the social sciences: the search for true knowledge must be chosen as a vocation and not as a path leading to Truth. To offer insight into Truth through the pursuit of true knowledge is to make a false promise, one which the social sciences have not the authority to keep.
>
> (Heller 1989: 294)

In situations of Mode 2 we see an evident questioning of the idea that social scientists enjoy the authority to arbitrate in disputes over reality by appealing to past ideas of 'objective' knowledge to which they have a privileged and unmediated access (as if they ever did). Reflexive discussions therefore need recourse to something outside of the normal boundaries that are taken to inform knowledge production. If the significance of these results is given by the recognition that social research is a facilitator of communication between traditions and not a legislator (Bauman 1989), it does not follow that disciplinary rigour is abandoned, or that social science becomes a branch of literary criticism. Again, however, we see ambivalence played out in social scientific practice in different ways which miss the importance of the institutional conditions of knowledge production.

Summary: reflexivity, history and the *realpolitik* of reason

Instead of understanding that can be borne in practice, we find an oscillation between the revenge of positivism and the denial of position. Neither is capable of sustaining social scientific practice in contemporary times. In one we have the denunciation of doubt in the name of order and certainty and, in the other, the abandonment of understanding, leaving the terrain to those who are not so reserved when it comes to speaking in the name of organisational order. Both commit the fallacy of universal certainty but from totally different points of view. We should not seek the unattainable, nor deny the importance of what is attainable, but seek to understand the 'socio-historically variable degrees of attainable certainty' (Wagner 2001a: 30). Such a move enables not only a better understanding of the conditions that inform knowledge production and reception, but also of how the social sciences can achieve an improved understanding of social conditions.

It is not necessary to give up on 'epistemic gain' (Taylor 1992). Epistemic gain does not just derive from comparing the explanatory power of two theories and concluding that one explains more than another. Nor does it come from a refusal to engage, or through by-passing the history of explanation within a discipline. Gain comes in terms of how one explanation deals with another. Taking X as a previous position and Y as a new one, it may be expressed in the following terms:

It may be that from the standpoint of Y, not just the phenomena in dispute, but also the history of X and its particular pattern of anomalies, difficulties, makeshifts, and breakdown can be greatly illuminated. In adopting Y, we made better sense not just of the world, but of our history of trying to explain the world, part of which has been played out in terms of X.

(Taylor 1995: 43)

We can take from the above discussion that the social sciences are not just about falsification, which would be to misunderstand their role and place in society. Social scientific practices embody a process of interpretation–reinterpretation according to the conditions of the age. Moving away from the quest for timeless knowledge does not commit us to relativism. Instead, knowledge is produced according to particular contexts in which problems arise. This is not to commit knowledge to an instrumental view, for problems themselves arise from a process that is contested. The movements I have charted which appear to go in opposite directions, but end up in the same place, detract from the productive potential that comes with such engagement. Polarisations do little to aid this understanding. Whilst claiming to speak in the name of an unproblematic reality should be questioned, so too should the claim to speak of different realities mediated by alternative modes of representation. We see the same tendencies in both: legislation over the constitution of social reality and an absence of engagement with the social problems of the time.

If the social sciences are to remain vibrant and relevant to their day, they must attend to the dynamics that inform everyday lives and to the changing pressures, in terms of the past, that inform their current and potential form and character (Wagner 2001b). A sceptical attitude is a necessary condition for an engaged one. Necessary, but not sufficient. When it is assumed to be sufficient, consciously or by default, it undermines engagement and becomes, from a disciplinary point of view, the equivalent of speaking to oneself and believing that one is saying something of importance to others. It is not unreasonable to suggest that this impression might well be gained from examining many texts that call for greater reflexivity in practice. To contain such consequences and to provide a vibrant, challenging and productive practice, a sensitivity to the relations between the conditions of knowledge production and the social epistemology of knowledge reception is required.

I will end by paraphrasing Pierre Bourdieu. Reflexivity is not a tool to undermine science, but one that provides for a more realistic science through its contribution to a *realpolitik* of scholastic reasoning in the service of epistemic gain. The explanations that are required of the constitution of the conditions of knowledge production and reception are also a contribution to how the science of the probable can contribute to making the possible come into being.

References

Adkins, L. (2002) 'Reflexivity and the politics of qualitative research', in T. May (ed.) *Qualitative Research in Action,* London: Sage.

Ashmore, M. (1989) *The Reflexive Thesis: Writing the Sociology of Scientific Knowledge,* Chicago: University of Chicago Press.

Bauman, Z. (1989) *Legislators and Interpreters: On Modernity, Post-Modernity and Intellectuals,* Cambridge: Polity.

Bourdieu, P. (1986) *Distinction: A Social Critique of the Judgement of Taste,* London: Routledge.

Bourdieu, P. (1992) *Language and Symbolic Power,* Cambridge: Polity.

Bourdieu, P. (1993) *Sociology in Question,* London: Sage.

Bourdieu, P. (1998a) *Acts of Resistance: Against the New Myths of Our Time,* Cambridge: Polity.

Bourdieu, P. (1998b) *Practical Reason: On the Theory of Action,* Cambridge: Polity.

Bourdieu, P. (2000) *Pascalian Meditations,* Cambridge: Polity.

Boyne, R. (1990) *Foucault and Derrida: The Other Side of Reason,* London: Unwin Hyman.

Calhoun, C. (1995) *Critical Social Theory: Culture, History and the Challenge of Difference,* Oxford: Blackwell.

Clifford, J. (1986) 'Introduction: partial truths', in J. Clifford and G. Marcus (eds) *Writing Culture: The Poetics and Politics of Ethnography,* Berkeley: University of California Press.

Cooper, G. (1999) 'The fear of unreason: science wars and sociology', *Sociological Research Online,* 4, 3, http://www.socresonline.org.uk/socresonline/4/3/cooper.html.

Czyzewski, M. (1994) 'Reflexivity of actors versus reflexivity of accounts', *Theory, Culture and Society,* 11, 4: 161–8.

Fichte, J.G. (1994) *Introductions to the Wissenschaftslehre and Other Writings (1797–1800),* edited and translated by D. Breazeale, Indianapolis/Cambridge: Hackett Publishing.

Fontana, A. (1994) 'Ethnographic trends in the postmodern era', in D.R. Dickens and A. Fontana (eds) *Postmodernism and Social Inquiry,* London: University College of London Press.

Garfinkel, H. (1967) *Studies in Ethnomethodology,* Englewood Cliffs, New Jersey: Prentice-Hall.

Gibbons, M., Limoges, C., Nowotny, H., Schwartaman, S., Scott, P. and Trow, M. (1994) *The New Production of Knowledge: The Dynamics of Science and Research in Contemporary Societies*, London: Sage.

Giddens, A. (1984) *The Constitution of Society: Outline of the Theory of Structuration*, Cambridge: Polity.

Giddens, A. (1990) *The Consequences of Modernity*, Cambridge: Polity.

Harding, S. (1996) 'European expansion and the organization of modern science: isolated or linked historical processes?', *Organization*, 3, 4: 497–509.

Hegel, G.W.F. (1991) *The Philosophy of History*, Buffalo, New York: Prometheus.

Heller, A. (1989) 'From hermeneutics in social science toward a hermeneutics of social science', *Theory and Society*, 18: 291–322.

Horkheimer, M. (1972) *Critical Theory: Selected Essays*, New York: Herder and Herder.

Law, J. (1994) *Organizing Modernity*, Oxford: Basil Blackwell.

Lawson, H. (1986) *Reflexivity: The Postmodern Predicament*, London: Hutchinson.

May, T. (1998a) 'Reflexivity in the age of reconstructive social science', *International Journal of Methodology: Theory and Practice*, 1, 1: 7–24.

May, T. (1998b) 'Reflections and reflexivity', in T. May and M. Williams (eds) *Knowing the Social World*, Buckingham: Open University Press.

May, T. (1999). 'Reflexivity and sociological practice', *Sociological Research Online*, Special Section on 'The Future of Sociology', 4, 3, http://www.socresonline.org. uk/socresonline/4/3/may.html.

May, T. (2000a) 'The future of critique: positioning, belonging and reflexivity'. *European Journal of Social Theory*, 3, 2: 157–173.

May, T. (2000b) 'Reflexivity in social life and sociological practice – a reply to Roger Slack', *Sociological Research Online*, 5, 1, http://www.socresonline.org.uk/ 5/1/may.html.

May, T. (2001) 'Power, knowledge and organizational transformation: administration as depoliticization', *Social Epistemology*, 15, 3: 171–86.

May, T. (ed.) (2002) *Qualitative Research in Action*, London: Sage.

May, T. and Williams, M. (eds) (1998) *Knowing the Social World*, Buckingham: Open University Press.

Mead, G.H. (1964) *Selected Writings: George Herbert Mead*, edited by A.J. Reck, Chicago: University of Chicago Press.

Nowotny, H., Scott, P. and Gibbons, M. (2001) *Re-thinking Science: Knowledge and the Public in an Age of Uncertainty*, Cambridge: Polity.

Outhwaite, W. (1999) 'The myth of modernist method', *European Journal of Social Theory*, 2, 1: 5–25.

Platt, R. (1989) 'Reflexivity, recursion and social life: elements for a postmodern sociology', *Sociological Review*, 37, 4: 636–67.

Robinson, J. (1970) *Freedom and Necessity*, London: George Allen and Unwin.

Skeggs, B. (2002) 'Techniques for telling the reflexive self', in T. May (ed.) *Qualitative Research in Action*, London: Sage.

Smith, D.E. (1999) *Writing the Social: Critique, Theory and Investigations*, Toronto. Toronto University Press.

Taylor, C. (1992) *Sources of the Self: The Making of the Modern Identity*, Cambridge: Cambridge University Press.

Taylor, C. (1995) *Philosophical Arguments*, Cambridge, Mass.: Harvard University Press.

Thompson, J.B. (1981) *Critical Hermeneutics: A Study in the Thought of Paul Ricoeur and Jürgen Habermas*, Cambridge: Cambridge University Press.

Unger, R.M. (1987) *Social Theory – Its Situation and Its Tasks: A Critical Introduction to Politics, a Work in Constructive Social Theory*, Cambridge: Cambridge University Press.

Wagner, P. (2001a) *Theorizing Modernity: Inescapability and Attainability in Social Theory*, London: Sage.

Wagner, P. (2001b) *A History and Theory of the Social Sciences*, London: Sage.

Woolgar, S. (ed.) (1988) *Knowledge and Reflexivity: New Frontiers in the Sociology of Knowledge*, London: Sage.

Wynne, B. (1996) 'May the sheep safely graze? A reflexive view of the expert–lay knowledge divide', in S. Lash, B. Szerszynski and B. Wynne (eds) *Risk, Environment and Modernity: Towards a New Ecology*, London: Sage.

Index